THE MANAGEMENT OF SALES TRAINING

BY THE NATIONAL SOCIETY OF
SALES TRAINING EXECUTIVES

Edited by Jared F. Harrison
General Electric Company
Marketing Consultant and
Past President of The National Society
of Sales Training Executives
Assistant Editor Robert Whyte
Director, Eastern Region, Systema Corp.

ADDISON-WESLEY PUBLISHING COMPANY
Reading, Massachusetts • Menlo Park, California
London • Amsterdam • Don Mills, Ontario • Sydney

ISBN 0-201-05298-9
ABCDEFGHIJ-MA-7987

PREFACE

In 1975, William McGrath, Vice President Education and Training, UARCO, Inc., who was then President of the National Society of Sales Training Executives, formed a small task force to develop a new Handbook of Sales Training to replace the now out-of-print text. The task force, of which I was chairman, recommended the publication of two books, each to serve a specific need. One book was to be directed to the sales manager, focusing on the sales manager's role as trainer. The second book was to be developed specifically for persons who have been appointed as sales training managers for their companies.

The Board of Directors approved of this approach, and this book is the result of their action. It represents the work of 25 authors who are dedicated members of the National Society of Sales Training Executives.

NSSTE was founded in Cleveland, Ohio, in November 1940. Its purpose is to concentrate in depth in the field of sales training and thereby create a medium for better training results from training efforts and budgets. Membership in the Society is limited to 131 active members, all of whom must manage a function which has the authority and responsibility for training sales and marketing personnel. It is a working society in which each member must submit an Editorial Contribution to the entire membership each year, belong to an official committee, and attend at least one semiannual meeting every year just to retain membership.

Editing a book of this type has been a challenge in that each chapter author is, in his own right, an authority in the sales-training field. Thus, whenever there were needs to add, delete, or edit copy I have attempted to preserve the author's style, thoughts, and identity. The credit for the success of this book belongs rightfully with the professional trainers who contributed their ideas and thoughts and the forward-thinking Board of Directors of NSSTE who approved its publication.

Thanks also goes to *SM/Successful Meetings Magazine,* a publication of Bill Communications, Inc., for permission to reprint portions of articles by NSSTE members which were previously published by *SM Magazine.*

Bridgeport, Connecticut   JARED F. HARRISON
October 1976   *Editor*

CONTENTS

INTRODUCTION

You are the person responsible for sales training within your company. You may have acquired this position as a result of a successful sales record, or in recognition of superior performance as a "people developer" when serving as a sales manager, or in any of a variety of positions calling for the ability to educate and communicate.

Now as a member of the company staff, your performance will be evaluated according to your ability to produce effective sales-training programs which will maximize the performance of the entire sales force. You have a serious responsibility; one which will challenge your ability to create, innovate, and administer valid programs. Although you will be able to call on other staff members for help, your position is unique in that it involves securing total cooperation from all field sales personnel and total backing from company management. Also, you are the only one in your company performing sales training, and thus have no one to consult with on matters of training methodology, content, resources, or ideas. Your real peers are the practicing sales-training executives in other successful companies spread across the country.

This book has been written by your peers with the specific purpose of providing you with their experience, knowledge, and creative ideas on how to manage a sales-training function. It offers you the experience of 25 of the country's leading sales-training executives. Each chapter is aimed at a vital segment of your job, and describes how it is being accomplished by a recognized training professional.

For your convenience and ready reference, the book has been divided into five sections:

Section I   Identifying Training Needs
Section II   Planning for Training
Section III   Directing and Coordinating Training
Section IV   Measuring and Evaluating Training
Section V   Continuous Self-Development of the Trainer

Recognizing that each of these sections could be a book in itself, the subject matter has been chosen with a view toward what is critical for you to know and apply, rather than what is nice to know. Where additional information could be beneficial, the authors have included bibliographies to help guide your further study.

Section I, Identifying Training Needs, encompasses the work of six training professionals. It focuses on the vital task of properly determining what the real training needs are and how to respond to them in the most appropriate manner.

John N. Spain, Manager of Sales Training for the Tire Division of Uniroyal, Inc., discusses the concept that identifying real training needs is really problem solving. He stresses the importance of identifying the real problem and describes a system of help you zero in on what may be causing a sales-performance deficiency.

R. Anthony Dowson, Sales Director of Burroughs Wellcome, Ltd., focuses his chapter on diagnostic techniques and methods for measuring training needs. He discusses the What, Why, When, Where, Who, and How of analysis, covering such techniques as climate surveys, field visits, questionnaires, and team approaches to needs analysis.

Melvin Lamster, Manager, Management Development and Training for Philip Morris, U.S.A., focuses on the unique needs of the new salesperson. He discusses the use of written surveys, oral surveys, and interviews, giving you actual examples of sales-training questionnaires used by his company to identify training needs.

Roger V. Lippincott, Corporate Director of Training and Management Development, Lehn & Fink Products Company, provides expert guidance for the training manager who must help train distributors and retail salesclerks. This is a field in itself, since the role of the training manager is to help make it easier for noncompany personnel to sell to the eventual end user.

Charles H. Singler, General Sales Manager of the Burroughs Wellcome Company, shares his expertise in assessing the specific training needs of the senior, experienced sales representatives. He also discusses how you can help field sales managers, and provides specific advice on the training of female and minority sales representatives.

Gustav W. Hengel, Director, Sales and Operations, Delicious Orchards, discusses the pros and cons of using external resources to help identify training needs and present training programs. This chapter is of particular value to training managers who have limited staff and must get help from others outside of their department.

Section II, Planning for Training, provides you with expert advice on how to plan your department, perform the budgeting activity, select personnel, and design training facilities. Six accomplished training directors have contributed their knowledge to this section to bring you their best ideas.

John A. Foley, Corporate Manager of Sales and Marketing Training for the Miller Brewing Company, starts off Section II with a discussion of how to plan your department's staff, scope, and structure. He ties this into the important subject of setting the initial objectives for a new training department so that staff and objectives will be in proportion.

Frank G. Mitchell, Education and Training Manager of the Marketing Division of Cessna Aircraft Company, concentrates his chapter on selecting your staff. He stresses the critical importance of establishing position profiles and identifying the characteristics of a successful trainer. He also gives advice on how and where to locate potential staff members.

Charles M. Field, Director of Sales Training for Sterling Precision Corporation, covers in detail one of the most important aspects of managing an effective department; the administrative aspects of sales training. He suggests guidelines for staff effectiveness and provides actual examples of filing systems, forms, and control records. A sample company policy statement is also included for your reference.

James N. Henderson, Manager, Sales Training, The Goodyear Tire & Rubber Company, advises you on putting together your first training budget. In this compactly written chapter he describes what you will need to consider to develop programs, teach them, and select facilities to hold them in; and provides a sample of a format used to keep track of training expenses.

George J. Lumsden, Manager, Sales Training, Chrysler Motors Corporation, discusses in further depth the importance of the training budget and illustrates how he budgets at Chrysler, showing how to submit, justify, and cut, when necessary.

John R. Perry, Supervisor of Sales Training for Proctor & Gamble Company, completes Section II with specific advice on how to locate, design, and equip an ideal training facility. This is a most valuable chapter, covering the multitude of considerations which must go into the selection of a facility. He even provides charts, showing suggested seating arrangements for various types of meetings.

Section III, Directing and Coordinating Training, gets to the real heart of your important job by providing you with ideas on content for training, techniques, evaluation of trainees, and the need for establishing good relationships with other departments.

Robert P. Dies, Manager of Training and Communications for the B. F. Goodrich Tire Company, opens this section with a discussion of training techniques you can use. With charts, examples, and descriptions he leads you through Job Instruction Training, participation techniques, nonparticipative techniques, lecture method, audiovisual presentations, and a myriad of other proven approaches for accomplishing your training objectives.

William J. Bryan, Manager, Education and Training for the Glidden-Durkee Division, SCM Corporation, gives you his best advice on the subject of developing training programs. This chapter, complete with sample agendas, covers whom you should train first, subjects which can be covered, and how to accomplish the training.

Joseph F. Bova, Senior Sales Trainer, Smith Kline & French Laboratories, describes the value of pretraining home-study programs for preparing new employees for formal training programs. This valuable idea can greatly improve the impact of formal training conducted at centralized locations.

Donald W. Frischmann, CLU, Vice President, Agency for the State Farm Insurance Companies, provides a step-by-step approach for training a new sales trainer. This is part of your management job, and results in your getting work done through others. Included in this chapter is a valuable list of references you can use to help develop your trainers.

C. Robert Appel, Director of Sales Training, Ortho Diagnostics, Inc., focuses on an often overlooked aspect of your job; the care and feeding of sales trainees. He illustrates why it is important to provide a good reception for trainees, and makes specific suggestions on ways to make sure your class participants are well taken care of during their training.

Richard H. Schoenlank, Director of Sales Training, Vick Chemical Company, stresses the importance of follow-up training for participants once they return to the field. He gives actual examples of field follow-up visits, shows how to make use of experienced salespeople to assist you in the follow-up, and illustrates ways to use both audio and video tape recordings to reinforce a training session.

J. Donald Staunton, Director, Manpower Resources Development for National Starch & Chemical Corporation, covers the critical subject of evaluating the performance of sales trainees. Illustrating with charts and examples, he shows you what should be evaluated and how to accomplish it effectively.

Thomas R. Currie, General Director, Human Resource Development for the Reynolds Metals Company, completes this section with a graphic description of the need for coordination of activities with other company programs and departments. He shows you how to do it and suggests ways to improve cooperation.

Section IV, Measuring and Evaluating Training, provides you with the tools to do an effective job of assessing and measuring your training results. This is a highly important part of the training cycle which, if not done properly, can literally spell the doom of a training department. Fortunately, three leading training directors have documented their approach toward evaluation and assessment in a way which, if followed, will enable you to prove the value of your work.

James F. Evered, Manager of Marketing Education and Development for Redman Industries, leads off this section with an explicit set of measurements you can use to assess and measure your training effectiveness. He illustrates the importance of proving to management that you are accomplishing your training goals and shows you exactly how to build your proof.

Ian E. McLaughlin, Chairman of the Board of Training and Educational Consultants, Inc., and formerly Director of Training for Del Monte Corporation, discusses the pros and cons of using the training department as a stepping stone or a career position. This is a problem all companies and training managers face, and realistic advice is given toward solving it.

Antonio J. Perez, Manager of Sales and Service Training for the Airtemp Division of the Chrysler Corporation, gives you guidance in assessing training-staff performance and self-assessment. Included in this chapter are actual forms used for evaluation plus a bibliography of publications which offer additional ideas on assessing training performance.

Section V, Continuous Self-Development of the Trainer, provides a fitting conclusion for this book by emphasizing the fact that your own learning must never cease. Two respected training executives contributed their experience to this section.

Keyte L. Hanson, CLU, Superintendent of Education and Field Training of the Agency Department of the Northwestern Mutual Life Insurance Company, describes a philosophy for sales-training managers. He emphasizes the importance and the inevitability of change, and counsels you on how to develop your own philosophy.

James Rapp, former Director of Education for Berol Corporation, and President of Outlook Associates, a consulting firm, provides a fitting conclusion for this book by describing the educational career path for professional trainers. He looks to the future and describes specific emerging trends in training which must become part of your training repertoire.

All of this is what you can expect from this text written especially for you as a manager of sales training. Every idea and program described has been proven in the real training environment. By providing you with this chance to consult with your peers, it is the hope of the National Society of Sales Training Executives that you will develop to your full potential.

Section I

IDENTIFYING TRAINING NEEDS

CHAPTER 1

WHO SAYS IT'S A TRAINING PROBLEM?

JOHN N. SPAIN

John N. Spain is a salesman, field manager, and trainer of many years experience who has directed and conducted sales training for many divisions of Uniroyal, Inc., including chemical, textile, tire, and international. He handled all the initial sales training for his company's new operations in Turkey and Australia. Mr. Spain has written numerous self-instructional materials that have been broadly used in business management and personnel development. Author of an award-winning NSSTE editorial, Mr. Spain's articles on training have been published in numerous trade magazines. He was a panel member for the "Listening Post" series of instructional tapes. Mr. Spain has carried his training activities into Boy Scouting, and was a recipient of their highest honor, the Silver Beaver.

A problem is to the trainer what an order is to the salesperson: it's an opportunity to play a part in forging a critical link in the chain that will mean success to the company. As a training manager, your reaction to properly identified "training problems" should be and probably has been one of elation, "I've got the order!" It's important to your success that you retain that inner sense of elation when problems arise that challenge your ability to contribute. Every order a salesperson is offered is a chance to contribute to the company's profit. But not every training order you will be offered can or should be accepted at face value. This chapter focuses on how the trainer can be most effective in analyzing problems and determining the proper solutions to the many so-called "training problems."

PROBLEMS—PROBLEMS

It's important to think first about why people are likely to bring problems to you, the training manager. One of the special roles the trainer should play is that of father confessor and confidant to other company managers. This role places you in a unique position to receive early-warning information on problems that may call for training solutions. A certain amount of "inside" information may prove immensely helpful in the process of analyzing "training problems." This isn't meant to imply that you should go nosing around for "inside" information; that would be poor practice at best. What is being suggested is that your dealings with all people should be on a basis which encourages frank and open discussion of all types of problems.

Dr. Thomas A. Harris, in his book *I'm O.K.—You're O.K.*, talks about what makes people want to change. Although his remarks are applied to individuals, they seem equally appropriate for the manager who desires changes in his or her people. Harris says:

> Three things make people want to change. One is that they hurt sufficiently. They have beat their heads against the same wall so long that they decide they have had enough.
>
> Another thing that makes people want to change is a slow type of despair called ennui, or boredom.
>
> The third thing that makes people want to change is the sudden discovery that they can.*

When any of these circumstances occur within your management group, will your relations with staff and line people be such that they will want to discuss them with you? Hopefully, they will.

What's a "problem"?

A problem is a deviation between what is happening and what should be happening. The gap between these two positions is the actual problem. The way to define a problem is to describe carefully all the elements of what is happening which differ from what should be happening. In many instances, training will not solve the problem and should not be considered as a potential solution.

As a trainer you will be asked to help solve many different types of problems which involve the performance of people. Often the problem is only in the eyes of the supervisor who complains that a per-

---

* Thomas A. Harris, *I'm O.K.—You're O.K.* (New York: Avon, 1973), p. 85.

formance deviates from the way it should be accomplished. In this case, you must carefully look at the end result and determine if it matches expectations. If so, how the task is accomplished is only a problem in the eyes of the manager.

A common and particularly troublesome situation involving problems is when the problem presented is really a combination of many problems. These multiple problem situations have many causes, and training solutions can only be effective when all of the causes involved are clearly identified.

Assume, for example, that the marketing manager presents you with a problem. Because the salespeople are not pushing line X as they are other lines, "they need a special training program." Before you can talk intelligently about possible solutions, you first need to determine the cause or causes. An investigation might disclose the following:

- Line X is currently priced out of the market.
- The lowest commissions are given on this line.
- Product quality in this line has slipped.
- Most salespeople don't really know the features and benefits of this line as well as they should.

It is evident the marketing manager has several problems, only the last of which can be solved by training.

Other typical multiple-cause problems might be:

- The salespeople aren't making good use of their time.
- The salespeople aren't handling new account-opening orders properly.
- The field sales managers are not hiring the right kind of people.
- The dealers are not selling the right product mix.

Each of these problems may require separation into a series of causes which contributed to the problem. Each cause can then be attacked effectively on its own.

Keeping the pulse on problems and likely causes

If you are to become efficient at identifying performance problems and establishing likely causes, you are going to have to develop a network of information sources and cooperative people.

Some ways of accomplishing this are:

- Wherever possible, be a part of management planning meetings.
- Keep up and expand your field contacts.
- Get to know and work with a broad range of staff people.
- Keep an open-door policy for people at all levels.
- Make field trips to contact customers and company people as often as you can.
- Use your training sessions as a listening post for what is or is not happening.

Dispensing the training pill

A major problem facing every training manager is that many regard training as a cure-all for personnel ills ranging from poor attendance to shoddy workmanship. Line managers turn to the training department to dispense the "training pill," and countless dollars are spent on elaborate programs attempting to solve all problems with training. Success or failure in responding to these appeals depends upon how well the problem is initially diagnosed.

In his book *Formula For Success,* Lawrence Appley, Chairman of the Board of the American Management Association, writes that,

> Formal training is more important than it ever was. It is based, however, on the needs for such training as indicated by careful, personal analysis.
>
> Having decided the functions of each job, having decided the results that will be secured if the job is well done, and having discovered how well each employee is performing as compared with the standards, an executive or supervisor has the required information to determine what each person under his direction requires for individual improvement. That seems to be the intelligent and commonsense basis for a training program.*

More often than not, the training manager will be presented with the "training problem" and the "training solution" in the same breath: "We have this problem and we want you to conduct a training program to correct it."

---

* Lawrence Appley, *Formula For Success* (New York: American Management, 1974), p. 88.

QUESTIONS—QUESTIONS—QUESTIONS

A key role you must play as a trainer is that of a diagnostician. This is simply a matter of asking the right questions (of the right people) and getting honest answers. Once you get the hang of it, you may find you are the only person in your organization really capable of defining what are and what are not training problems.

First a word about how to get open, unguarded answers to your diagnostic questions. You could refer to this as the training manager's "bedside manner." A physician has to ask a lot of diagnostic questions of patients. A good physician will seldom argue with the patient about the answers the patient gives. It becomes a matter of probing to draw out the answers which will indicate the real cause of the complaint.

Where to begin questioning

First, you may be obliged to determine all the things contributing to a complex problem. If you need to separate the various causes, it will become evident early in the questioning process. Be on the lookout for multiple likely causes. Also, listen for the mention of any deviations from what should be happening which are included in the statement of the problem. For example, such responses as "Some salespeople are selling too much of it, some not enough," or "Some clerks can't make out the forms, others won't make them out" indicate clearly that the manager believes that something that should be happening is not happening. Once you've broken down the problems, you have to deal with them one at a time.

Robert Mager and Peter Pipe, in their book *Analyzing Performance Problems; or, You Really Oughta Wanna* describe some basic questioning processes. Properly applied, they guide the trainer to a correct analysis of the problem. As a rule, the discrepancy will be revealed through the answers to the following questions:

- Why do I think there is a training problem?
- What is the difference between what is being done and what is supposed to be done?
- What is the event that causes me to say that things aren't right?
- Why am I dissatisfied?*

* Robert Mager and Peter Pipe, *Analyzing Performance Problems; or, You Really Oughta Wanna* (Palo Alto, Calif.: Fearon, 1970), p. 9.

SO WHAT IS A TRAINING PROBLEM?

The cause of a performance deficiency on the part of an employee is often a combination of factors which require multiple solutions. In practice, training by itself can only effectively cure about 15 percent of the problems you will face.

A true training problem is identified by determining if a real deficiency of knowledge or a lack of skill exists. If a person does not know anything about a given subject, there is obviously an educational need. If a skill is lacking, coaching and practice are necessary to produce acceptable performance. To help you quickly identify true training problems, use the handy checklist shown below.

PROBLEM DISCRIMINATOR CHECKLIST

Check if answer is "Yes"

Knowledge/Skill Deficiency (Solutions involve training of some type). I can conclude that I have a deficiency in Knowledge/Skill if any of the following exist:

- ☐ 1. This work has never been done before by the level/function in question.
- ☐ 2. This work is seldom done and no practice is given.
- ☐ 3. This level/function does not know what constitutes good performance in this area.
- ☐ 4. This level/function could not do this if their lives depended upon it.
- ☐ 5. This level/function used to do it, but may have forgotten how.
- ☐ 6. This level/function does not know the "new way" to accomplish this responsibility.
- ☐ 7. No training has ever been given on the right way to do it.
- ☐ 8. This level has developed bad performance habits in this area.

By asking yourself these questions and then investigating to determine the correct answers, you will be able to isolate pure training problems.

All of this means that you as a trainer have to develop a talent for problem analysis before attempting solutions. This in turn means that you have to educate all those who turn to you for help to the fact that no training-program assignment will be undertaken until the problem-analysis stage has been completed. Some people get very offended at the suggestion that their stated problem and training solution may not be the answer. They *know* that more training is what's needed, so "let's get on with it." Here's where tact (and your boss' solid support) are needed. Your clients will soon learn that the time spent on analyzing the problem is the best investment they can make.

CHAPTER 2

DIAGNOSTIC TECHNIQUES AND MEASUREMENT METHODS
R. ANTHONY DOWSON

RAnthony Dowson is Sales Director of Burroughs Wellcome, Ltd., responsible for overall sales management and sales training of four operating divisions within the Canadian company. He joined Burroughs Wellcome, Ltd., in 1957 as a sales representative, has held positions as District Sales Manager, Sales Promotion and Sales Training Manager, Marketing Manager, as well as a two-year assignment as Marketing Director of Burroughs Wellcome, Ltd., in Pakistan.

Mr. Dowson graduated with a B. Comm., majoring in Economics and Business, and has taken post-graduate MBA courses. He was born in England, has lived in Canada since 1952, and is now a Canadian citizen.

Congratulations! So you have just been promoted, and now you are a manager of training! Now it is up to you to make the most of this opportunity by showing what a great job you can do in the important area of training. Where to start? That's the problem!

All companies differ in regard to their products or services, organizational structure, and sales/marketing philosophy; their training needs will also vary greatly. Therefore, I must necessarily deal in generalizations. These are offered to you as alternatives in developing a successful training program. You must decide which procedures or methods will fit best in your organization and will work with your personnel, budgets, and corporate objectives.

At this point in identifying program needs, you may want to get started by using a "cafeteria approach" in the selection of the appropriate diagnostic techniques available. From the following list you can select those approaches which most appeal to you, or those which you are able to afford either in terms of budgets, staffing restrictions, or the practical limitation of your own training experience to date.

NEEDS ANALYSIS

The most important task and the one with the highest priority is a "needs analysis." This involves looking at the total requirements of the training department, always keeping in mind the needs of the people to be trained, the corporate objectives, and the organizational needs.

A proper needs analysis produces answers to questions starting with: What? Why? When? Where? Who? How? Some of the most common questions you may want to include in the needs analysis for your company are as follows:

1. *What must the trainee know in order to sell or service our company's products?*

This question is perhaps the most crucial, and the answer will never be short and simple. A great deal of in-depth surveying will be needed to establish the criteria. Keep in mind that it is the trainer's responsibility to determine this need. Do not let new trainees determine the need!

2. *What skills and knowledge do the trainees possess right now that are relevant to the analysis resulting from Question 1?*

This can be assessed as related job experiences, present performance evaluation, or by means of tests and quizzes.

3. *What particular knowledge and skills must be imparted to the trainees to insure that they can satisfactorily meet the performance standards being developed?*

The setting of performance standards has been covered elsewhere in this book. The answer to the question of *"What must be taught?"* is measured as the difference between the answers to Questions 1 and 2.

4. *What training methods would best suit our purpose and resources?*

In answering this question, you must determine what methods are available to you in terms of physical facilities—as well as equipment available, and personnel. This leads to a further series of questions.

5. *What physical training facilities are required?*

In most cases, you have to live with what is already available in your company. The answer will also be related to the number of people to be trained at any one time. If no in-house training facilities currently exist, you should consider the use of outside facilities—preferably nearby. They can often be rented at reasonable cost, and many come equipped with a variety of audiovisual equipment.

6. *What types of audiovisual equipment will you require?*

This can run the whole gamut from a simple chalkboard or a flip chart to more sophisticated audiovisual items such as:

- closed-circuit television
- overhead projectors
- 35mm slide projectors
- tape recorders
- movie projectors

The selection of equipment will be determined by the types of training programs now available or in preparation. If one looks back on the history of sales training in most companies, it is safe to say that most of us started out with a chalkboard and over time progressed to the more sophisticated electronic equipment. Usually we stop buying audiovisual equipment when we no longer understand how to operate it!

7. *What kind of training staff will you need?*

This will depend on who is available. The important thing is to remember that the training department need not be limited to those individuals selected as "training staff." It is in fact most beneficial for you to use the services and resources of all the personnel in your corporate headquarters. After all, you cannot be an expert in all departments; and therefore you should call upon the experts to explain to trainees their particular job functions and responsibilities and/or products. Besides providing expertise, the use of other staff members provides the trainees with a welcome change of instructors.

8. *How much time should be allocated to a training program?*

How long should anyone's legs be? This is a tough one. For example, how much time can we actually allocate to training? How long should each training session be? Some believe that the total training program should be given at one time, even though it may last 12 weeks.

Others feel that training should be split into progressive programs of no more than 2 or 3 weeks duration, with in-field practical training experience between sessions. (I favor this approach myself).

Flexibility should be the key word in determining total training time. At this point, consider doing a "difficulty analysis" of the duties and knowledge required for specific products. At the same time, take into account the fact that the trainees' learning curves are also variable —some people just learn faster than others.

9. *What are the Corporate objectives?*

Too often training departments become so totally engrossed in analyzing training needs that they fail to relate them realistically to overall company objectives. Most corporate objectives are clearly stated and are available to those who ask for them. If by chance your organization does not have clearly stated objectives, then perhaps your first training task should be to help establish the need for such objectives!

10. *What are your priorities for training?*

A careful review of corporate objectives should enable you to establish realistic priorities in the design of your training programs.

11. *When will you do the training?*

The answer to this depends upon whether your business is cyclical or seasonal, and whether the trainees are beginners or experienced salespeople who require additional training. This will also have to tie in with the availability of other personnel in your organization whose help will be needed in training. Arrangements for these services generally have to be made well in advance of actual training dates.

12. *What training materials are required for each program?*

Before scheduling any training program, all the written material must be prepared and produced beforehand. In some cases this preparation can take considerable time. To undertake a training program before this task is completed is to court disaster. Experience has shown that written material, particularly of a technical nature (including product knowledge), should be made available to trainees both before and after formal training, and as a reference source.

Summary

In conclusion, the needs analysis which addresses itself to the topics listed above should result in a blueprint or charter upon which you can build a meaningful training program. Finally, one should never forget that objectives must be clearly stated and that the training program must always be designated with the trainee in mind.

JOB DESCRIPTION

I want to emphasize the absolute necessity of a job description for each trainee's job function, assuming they are different. If all trainees are salespeople, then one job description may cover them all.

INTERVIEWS

In identifying training needs you should include interviews. You should leave your office and ask your fellow employees in other departments within your division what they perceive to be the needs of a sales-training program.

Discussions with your colleagues will bring to the surface some of the attitudes you will have to contend with in setting up your training program. These will range all the way from "Who the hell needs it?" to "It's about time." The majority viewpoint will probably lie somewhere between these extremes. By this method you will soon be able to identify those people who will gladly help as well as those who may need to be persuaded to help.

Why do I say you need help? Because there is no way you can administer a successful training program without the cooperation and support of many people within the organization. The benefits of training need to be explained to everyone. Presumably, senior management already feels this way, which is why you've got the job. Nevertheless, make sure you keep others informed of your plans and the benefits they can look for from your training programs.

Some companies have developed a great deal of expertise in using formal attitude surveys to help identify what attitudes exist in the field toward training, how it should be conducted, when, where, etc. An attitude survey usually refers to the personal one-to-one relationships of an employee to his or her subordinates or superiors within a particular division and therefore reflects *personal viewpoints* which you may have to contend with in the implementation of any training program. If you find, for example, that morale is terrible because the sales force feels it is vastly underpaid, you need to do everything you can to remedy this (presuming the gripe is valid) before you undertake a formal training activity. Sullen mutinous trainees are poor learners!

ORGANIZATIONAL CLIMATE

Expanding on attitude surveys can lead to a useful analysis of people and practices. This is known as an organizational-climate survey. It isn't much good going ahead and designing a training program based on a thorough needs analysis without considering the "culture" and philosophy of the organization itself.

There is some confusion between attitude surveys and organizational climate analysis. They are, however, two distinct tools. Organizational climate considers the collective view of the employees in defining the type of place or company in which they work. It incorporates both the formal and informal structures within any organization. It is more than a question of morale. It can be in fact a measurement of productivity; namely, high performance or low performance results.

Examples of the kind of questions used in measuring organizational climate are outlined in Attachment 1. Only the first page of a five-page questionnaire is shown. The following are some questions commonly asked about climate surveys, and their answers.

Attachment 1

CLIMATE SURVEY QUESTIONNAIRE

Instructions: Circle the appropriate number beside each statement which most accurately describes the degree of your agreement or disagreement with the statement.

Number Key

(1) Strongly Agree   (2) Agree   (3) Tend to Agree

(4) Tend to Disagree   (5) Disagree   (6) Strongly Disagree

Example:

1. There is nothing I enjoy doing more than filling out questionnaires.   1 2 3 4 5 ⑥

---

1. The jobs in this organization are clearly defined and logically structured.   1 2 3 4 5 6

2. In this organization it is sometimes unclear who has the formal authority to make a decision.   1 2 3 4 5 6

3. The policies and organization structure of the organization have been clearly explained.   1 2 3 4 5 6

4. Red-tape is kept to a minimum in this organization.   1 2 3 4 5 6

5. Excessive rules, administrative details, and red-tape make it difficult for new and original ideas to receive consideration.   1 2 3 4 5 6

6. Our productivity sometimes suffers from lack of organization and planning.   1 2 3 4 5 6

7. In some of the situations I've been in, I haven't been sure exactly who my boss was.   1 2 3 4 5 6

1. *What is a climate survey?*

Answer: A climate survey attempts to develop a profile of how people view the organization they are part of in terms of: structure, degree of individual responsibility, reward, risk, support, standards, conflict, identity, and communications. These categories have proven to be the key dimensions of high performing organizations. It is *not* an attitude survey and does *not* deal with individual boss/subordinate relationships or degree of happiness on the job.

2. *What is the value of a climate survey?*

Answer: By analyzing how the majority of participants respond to each question, it is possible to identify areas where the climate can be changed or improved, if so desired by management through such means as: training programs, improved communications, management systems, or management action.

3. *Is there any norm or right and wrong responses?*
Answer: No. The survey only shows how a given group of participants view the organizational climate. Since each organization is different and has different objectives, there is no one correct profile. The responses to the survey do, however, allow management to decide if the climate in existence is the one best suited to achieve the organization's objectives in line with management's expectations. If management decides such a change is in order, then selective and specific actions can be taken to change the climate.

4. *Will individual responses be identified?*
Answer: NO. Since there will be a large number of responses from each, they will become a part of aggregate data which will be shown to management. The individual replies will be sent directly to the person conducting the survey and no one else will have access to them. No names will be required on the survey form. The *only* identification will be by job title and location. This is a common procedure to eliminate any feeling of threat and because the data is only useful on an aggregate basis.

5. *How long does it take to complete?*
Answer: The total survey consists of about 50 questions. All that a participant need do is read each question and then check a box indicating that he/she strongly agrees, agrees, tends to agree, tends to disagree, disagrees, or strongly disagrees. The total survey should take only about 25 minutes.

FIELD TRIPS—FEEDBACK

If you are primarily concerned with the design of training programs for sales personnel, then it is essential for you to get a first-hand look at where the training is going to be used and how it is going to be used. Talk to as many salespeople as you can to get their perceptions as to what they feel they need.

Field visitations will give you positive feedback. This feedback should start with your customers. Find out what they expect of your company's representatives. Determine what your customers see as the strong and weak points of the company representatives who presently call on them. Ask the customers what kinds of information or services they would most like to have which they are not presently receiving.

As a rule, sales representatives will be open and frank in discussing with you the weaknesses that they have felt in their own training and development. They must, however, first be assured that you are seeking this information in order to improve your company's past performance in training—and not to evaluate them! Two or three days spent with representatives on the job should give you sufficient time to talk with customers and the representatives and observe what goes on in the real world.

Do not overlook the recommendations of field sales management!

Obviously, different field sales managers will perceive different training needs for their sales representatives. For this reason, a composite survey must be made. If possible, all field sales managers should be visited, and their opinions and suggestions synthesized into practical specifics.

There is no doubt that field visitations can result in different responses than you would get if the same field sales managers visited you in the head office. The answers you get on the territories are usually far more valid and valuable than those obtained in a formal structured office setting. You must also bear in mind that follow-up training and on-the-job training are the responsibility of field sales managers. After all, you will only have the trainee for a fraction of the time which will be spent out in the field. In effect, field sales managers will become your second line of trainers and will reinforce and support your training programs—if they are properly briefed, trained, and committed.

VENTILATION SESSIONS AND QUESTIONNAIRES

As an adjunct to field visitations, and not to be used instead of them, you can compile questionnaires for circulation to field personnel and head-office staff. These questionnaires should be designed in such a way that they encourage frank and open comments on training needs. Examples are shown in Attachment 2.

In a similar way, "ventilation sessions" represent an opportunity to ask the same questions in an informal, nonthreatening way. This is done by breaking the group up into teams (of four to six) and sending them off to "break-out" rooms to develop a list of what they collectively agree to be their major needs. Since the needs are reported back as a consensus, individuals are willing to be more candid and realistic. If each team organizes its list according to some order of priority, it can be an extraordinarily valuable resource to the trainer.

THE TEAM APPROACH

In some organizations it is possible to establish training needs through a team approach. This calls for selection of representatives from various departments to sit on a "training committee." They are asked to consider and suggest training needs as they relate to their particular department and the organization as a whole. The trainer's job is to pull together the various opinions and suggestions to help formulate a training program acceptable to all and incorporating the common characteristics.

Attachment 2

TRAINING NEEDS

In your view, please check the degree of importance of the following training topics.

	DEGREE OF IMPORTANCE		
	High	*Average*	*Low*
Practical sales skills			
Product knowledge			
Work habits			
Attitudes			
Motivation			
Time and territory management			
Policies and procedures			
Competition			
Pricing			
Product distribution			
Sales budgets			
Expenses			
Call reports			
On-the-job training			
Tests and quizzes			

The term "diagonal slice" has been used to describe a process of selecting team members from the various departments within the company, who are at different organizational levels, and who do not report to each other. Such a group might include a marketing vice-president, a field sales manager, a production supervisor, a financial manager, an advertising executive, and an experienced salesperson. By covering a wide spectrum of company activities, responsibilities, skills, levels, and viewpoints, there is more likelihood that the resulting training design will be a realistic reflection of total organizational needs.

The second approach, which is to form a team that acts as a *training task force,* may or may not include people reporting to each other and need not necessarily represent all of the divisional functions in an organization. For example, a task force to establish training needs for sales representatives may consist of a selected group from marketing and field sales management, together with the training manager.

OUTSIDE PERSONNEL

The use of outside consultants in developing training programs is becoming more and more popular. You should not regard the use of outside consultants as something to be considered *if all else fails.* Rather, outside consultants should be considered right at the outset as the best way of providing an unbiased analysis of your training needs without the problem of the subjective or politically motivated biases common to all organizations. The use of outside personnel has a further advantage in that such people usually keep abreast of the latest techniques in training. They can offer the training department a variety of ways to fulfill your commitment, providing they have been given a clear picture of your financial and personnel restrictions.

In addition to outside consultants and companies who specialize in training, there are a multitude of "off-the-shelf" training programs available in a variety of packaged presentations. These range from film to video tapes to audio cassettes. In a sense, such programs can be considered as a *source of outside personnel.*

The suitability of using such material depends on you. Only you can determine if the material available is appropriate to your organizational and training needs. That means reviewing it carefully—and personally—beforehand. Don't take anyone else's word for it! Don't, of course, overlook the value of the written word and the worth of training texts such as the one which you are now reading!

PRODUCTIVITY ANALYSIS

The ultimate test of any training program is whether it produces the results projected for it. Oftentimes managers want training programs to solve problems which do not have training solutions. It is important for you to be able to differentiate between a problem that has a training solution and one that does not.

For example, in your field visitations or needs-analysis surveys you may be presented with problems which need to be solved and for which people will ask you to develop a training program. Such problems are often categorized as performance problems. Before you can do anything, it is important for you to distinguish between the performance deficiency which is simply due to lack of implementation and the performance deficiency which is due to lack of knowledge. These can be summarized as performance deficiencies involving:

1. don't know,
2. can't do,
3. don't care.

The first one is a performance deficiency in knowledge, and is amenable to a training solution. The second one may or may not be a training problem. If it is the result of a lack in a skill that can be taught, then you can look to training to solve it. If it turns out to call for a skill than an individual cannot realistically master, then there is no training solution. The third one is obviously a motivational problem, and is better handled by supervisory or management personnel in a performance-appraisal or counseling session. Training isn't going to solve it.

Attachment 3

POSTCALL EVALUATION—CHECK LIST

	POOR	FAIR	AVERAGE	GOOD	EXCEL-LENT
	1	2	3	4	5
1. Did I know my customer needs?					
2. Was my product knowledge adequate?					
3. Did we have a "dialogue"?					
4. Did I *listen?*					
5. Did I anticipate objections before they were raised?					
6. Did I overcome objections which were raised?					
7. Did I use product features and benefits (together)?					
8. Was my presentation structured, i.e., opening—middle—close?					
9. Did I use "colorful language"?					
10. Did I demonstrate the product adequately?					
11. Did I appeal to the senses?					
12. Did I offer proof to convince?					
13. Did I *close* well?					
14. Did I *ask* for the order?					
15. Did I get the business?					
POINTS TOTAL:					

RATING: 45 is average only.

15 to 44—low
45 to 60—above average
61 to 75—excellent

Periodic performance-counseling sessions provide a good opportunity to assess training needs and performance difficulties which may be overcome by training. Be sure to get training information from these sessions whenever possible. In analyzing productivity it is also helpful for each trainee to be able to get instant feedback on the job as to his or her own performance. There are many ways of doing this. A sample checklist of "postcall evaluation criteria" is often sufficient to guide trainees in analyzing their own productivity and in improving their success rate. If the training department helps develop this guide as a continuous training aid, then the productivity of the training department consequently increases. An example of a postcall evaluation checklist is shown as Attachment 3.

SUMMARY

In summary, identifying training needs is not a simple task, but it is one of the most important tasks that you have. Let me leave you with a short list of some of the biggest mistakes made by sales trainers. Be aware of them. Avoid them at all costs!

1. *Putting too much emphasis on methods and not results.*
   Don't be carried away by electronic gadgets or by your academic aspirations. The final results of your training will be in face-to-face selling. Success should be your goal.

2. *Trying to do everything yourself.*
   Remember: you are the training manager, not the whole organization. Keep in mind there are many valuable people in your corporation. Use your inside experts as much as possible and outside consultants when necessary. You can't be all things to all people.

3. *Ignoring field managers.*
   Continuing training is in the hands of field management. Involve them in training at every opportunity—in the formation of the program, in the implementation of the program, and in the continuation of the program.

4. *Staying in the office.*
   You may love your brand-new office, but if you don't get out in the real world and find out what it is your trainees have to do every day, then you will never really know the best way to teach them how to do it.

5. *Over-emphasizing product knowledge and neglecting sales skills.*
   All the product knowledge in the world will not help close a sale if

selling techniques have not been mastered. Incorporate both into your training program.

6. *Becoming a behavioral scientist.*
   Lapsing into jargon is a common mistake. Behavioral science is a fascinating subject best reserved for the university and not a selling situation. By all means use the principles; incorporate them into your program. But don't *teach* the subject.

CHAPTER 3

ASSESSING TRAINING NEEDS OF NEW SALESPERSONS

MELVIN LAMSTER

Melvin Lamster, Manager, Management Development and Training, for Philip Morris, U.S.A., is directly responsible for the design, development, and implementation of sales-training, management-skills, and organization-development programs for Philip Morris's marketing and sales organization. He is also a consultant to the various Philip Morris subsidiary companies on all manpower development needs. A former Manager of Training at Air Reduction Company and Administrator of Engineering Placement and Training at Curtiss Wright Corporation, his skills range from the teaching of specific job skills and personnel evaluation to meeting leadership, human-relations training, and organization development.

Mr. Lamster received his B.A. in psychology from City University of New York and furthered his education, also at City University, with coursework in industrial psychology. An active member of the Organization Development Network, Management Development Forum, and NSSTE, where he is Chairman of the New York Chapter, Mr. Lamster has also served as lecturer and conference leader at various seminars and workshops.

Where do you start? How do you find out what is needed? How do you develop a training curriculum that meets the needs of your organization, gains acceptance from top management, has the support of the people taking the programs, and, most importantly, produces results?

The answer to these questions depends on your ability as a training manager to assess the needs of your organization. As you know from your field exposure, every group in your organization has a different idea of what is needed in a training curriculum. Your home office has a set of ideas; your field management has another set; and the sales representative has yet a third set of ideas.

What does this tell you about assessing training needs? It is clear that the first step in assessing the needs is to survey all the groups. By surveying all groups, you:

1. gain support and therefore reinforcement of your program;
2. make sure that the group that is being trained will have a "stake" in the program, which will set your program well on the road to success.

In developing your needs assessment, the best and most commonly used method is the survey technique. There are two basic forms of the survey technique:

1. the written survey in the form of a questionnaire and
2. the oral survey, which takes the form of an interview.

Let's take a look at both techniques, and see under what circumstances you might use each.

THE WRITTEN SURVEY-QUESTIONNAIRE

Again, I want to emphasize the importance of surveying all groups that would affect the training. The first obvious advantage of the questionnaire is that you can reach a great number of people in a short period of time. This insures that everyone is heard. A questionnaire can be designed so that tabulating or compiling replies can be done easily. Responses to questionnaires can be anonymous, insuring more "honest" answers, particularly in sensitive areas. A shortcoming of this method is that clarification of responses or in-depth answers are impossible to get.

When designing the questionnaire, several things should be kept in mind. As you are building your training department, you presently do not have a training curriculum for new sales representatives nor one for the continued training of experienced sales representatives. Your management has made this the number-one priority and has some definite ideas as to what is needed. You also know that field sales management has some ideas and that the field sales representatives have felt the need for training in certain areas. Additionally, you also realize that to build a program overemphasizing the needs of one group is to lose the support and interest of the other group. This is where the survey questionnaire becomes your means of solving the dilemma—getting the inputs of a large group of people with different ideas to develop a program requiring the support of all.

The first step in the design of your questionnaire is to determine specifically what you wish to learn. In the case of our example for a training curriculum, we would want to find out:

1. the elements of the sales representative's position,
2. the comparative value of each responsibility—what is most important and what is least important,
3. the comparative value of the difficulty of doing each task in the sales representative's job, and
4. the comparative value from "not important" to "highly critical" that the sales representative would assign to the skills for each responsibility.

The answers to these four questions apply to the development of all training programs.

Now, we recognize that the three groups having a direct stake in this could respond differently to the questions. It is the responsibility of the questionnaire to help you determine where there is agreement, where there is disagreement, and the degree of each. Again, an objective in any training program is to have those in the program and those reinforcing the program feel they have ownership in the program.

After listing questions to be answered, you then develop all the elements of the sales representative's job and place a weight on them. This is accomplished through a question requiring each group to identify or weigh a series of tasks as being: "major responsibility," "minor responsibility," or "no responsibility at all."

Once having identified the responsibilities, you would then need to gather additional information on how critical each responsibility is to the job. Here you would use a question requiring a response of ranking responsibilities from "most important" to "least important."

Your third basic requirement in developing the data for designing your training program is to deal with those things that are considered as presenting difficulty on the job. This question deals directly with establishing ownership of the training by those being trained. Therefore, that question should seek to identify those items that cause the greatest amount of difficulty on the job.

Now that you have identified the major responsibilities, how critically each is viewed, and the degree of difficulty they have caused on the job, the next step would be to identify and rate the individual's assessment of the skills required to do the job. This can be accomplished by developing a scale on every skill which would rate each one from "not important" to "highly critical."

The final question, tying it all together, would direct the respondents to list those things they would most like to see emphasized in a training program. This question serves as a means with which to gauge if the respondents place any relationship between their evaluation of their training needs, what they feel causes difficulty—and what is critical to their jobs. (See Attachment 1, Sales Representative's Questionnaire.)

You have now completed the questionnaire for the sales representatives. The other major group to survey is the management group. What changes do you have to make in your questionnaire in order to insure that management responds meaningfully to the job of the sales representative from their own perspective? Their responses, you recog-

Attachment 1
SALES TRAINING QUESTIONNAIRE
FOR RETAIL SALESPEOPLE

Name _____

Division _____

Date _____

I. Identify your responsibilities. Check all items which pertain to those responsibilities.

	A major responsibility	A minor responsibility	Have no responsibility
a. Switch selling	_____	_____	_____
b. Sampling	_____	_____	_____
c. Store sales	_____	_____	_____
d. Secure and maintain product distribution	_____	_____	_____
e. Collect competitive information	_____	_____	_____
f. Merchandising of product	_____	_____	_____
g. Service customer problems	_____	_____	_____
h. Erection of counter and floor displays	_____	_____	_____
i. Reports and paperwork	_____	_____	_____

II. Of those that you have checked as being a responsibility, rank them in order of most critical to least critical. Use letter designation of above items.

Most   Least
important _____ _____ _____ _____ _____ _____ _____ _____ _____ important

III. Of those items which you have ranked, list at least three which you feel have caused you the greatest amount of difficulty on your job.

1. _____
2. _____
3. _____
4. _____
5. _____

IV. The following is a list of skills commonly required by salespeople. Please indicate the degree of importance to you of each in selling your products.

Place an X on each scale below to indicate how critical you feel each item is (1 not important to 7 highly critical).

	Not important	Highly critical
1. Planning and developing sales strategy for individual accounts. (Ex. Displays—How to obtain maximum distribution, etc.)	1__2__3__4__5__6__7__	
2. Planning and controlling time (frequency of sales calls and paperwork)	1__2__3__4__5__6__7__	
3. Writing effective reports	1__2__3__4__5__6__7__	
4. Determining territorial distribution potential	1__2__3__4__5__6__7__	
5. Giving effective oral presentations	1__2__3__4__5__6__7__	
6. Understanding customer needs	1__2__3__4__5__6__7__	
7. Utilizing sales tools (ad reprints, reports, displays)	1__2__3__4__5__6__7__	
8. Basic selling-skills preparation, approach, presentation, handling objections, and closing	1__2__3__4__5__6__7__	
9. Company sales policy	1__2__3__4__5__6__7__	
10. Evaluating and using competitive information	1__2__3__4__5__6__7__	
11. The proper use of questions	1__2__3__4__5__6__7__	
12. Setting individual call objectives and evaluating results.	1__2__3__4__5__6__7__	

V. From the list of skills and knowledge you have checked as pertaining to your job, list below the items you have received training in.

Training received in	When last received date	Who did training? (div. mgr.) (section mgr.) (region mgr.)
1.		
2.		
3.		
4.		
5.		
6.		
7.		
8.		
9.		
10.		

I have not received training in any of the above items _____ check

VI. Do you feel it would assist you on your job if there was a continuous program of sales training?

_____ Yes   _____ No

VII. What would you like to see emphasized in such a sales-training program?

1. _____
2. _____
3. _____
4. _____
5. _____
6. _____

nize, constitute the criteria and priorities of the sales representative's position with which they are concerned.

The first question on your questionnaire for sales management is the same as that for the sales representative. This question enables you to see where both groups agree or disagree on what are major and minor responsibilities associated with the sales representative's job. It aids you in establishing training priorities, as well as giving you some insight into the communications between these two groups.

The second question is designed to test which of the responsibilities they view as being "most critical" to "least critical" to the success of the sales representative. Comparative analysis of responses to this question is essential in developing your training priorities.

The third question in determining which and what you emphasize in program development compares those areas of the sales representative's job the sales representative views as most difficult with those areas of the job that sales management views as being performed least effectively. This type of question helps to identify areas of performance deficiency as seen by sales management and compares those with the areas the sales representatives indicate give them the most difficulty.

The fourth question for sales management requires them to evaluate skills needed by the sales representative to do the job effectively. As with the sales representative, managers are asked to rate each skill on a scale of "not important" to "highly critical." You can compare their responses to this question in two ways—the first, directly with the sales representative; and the second, with those responsibilities that were evaluated as being most critical for success on the job. Remember, in training new sales representatives the amount of time and the position in the program of each element often determines the importance of that element to the person being trained. As an example, if in your training you treat administrative matters first, it is most likely that the person will leave feeling that part of the job is the most important. Experiences such as this make it evident that in our training programs we communicate not only verbally but also by implications, by where we position the elements and how much time we allocate to each. (See Attachment 2, Sales Management Questionnaire).

Attachment 2
SALES TRAINING QUESTIONNAIRE
FOR SALES MANAGEMENT

Name _____

Region or
Division _____

Date _____

I. Identify the role of the retail salesperson. Check all items with degree of responsibility which pertain to that role.

	Major responsibility	Minor responsibility	Have no responsibility
a. Switch selling	_____	_____	_____
b. Sampling	_____	_____	_____

c. Store sales _____   _____   _____

d. Secure and maintain
   product distribution _____   _____   _____

e. Collect market intelligence _____   _____   _____

f. Merchandising of product _____   _____   _____

g. Service customer problems,
   i.e., shortages _____   _____   _____

h. Erection of counter and
   floor displays _____   _____   _____

i. Determine pricing within
   guidelines _____   _____   _____

j. Reports and paperwork _____   _____   _____

II. Of those items which you have checked, rank them in order of most critical for success to least critical for success in the role of the salesperson. Use letter designation of items on previous question.

Most   Least
critical ___ ___ ___ ___ ___ ___ ___ ___ ___ ___ critical

III. Of those items which you ranked, list at least three which you feel are generally performed *least effectively* by your sales force.

1. _____
2. _____
3. _____
4. _____
5. _____

IV. The following is a list of skills commonly required by salespeople. Please indicate the degree of importance of each in order to sell our products.

Place an X on each scale below to indicate how critical you feel each item is. (1 not important to 7 highly critical)

	Not important	Highly critical
1. Planning and developing sales strategy for individual accounts	1__2__3__4__5__6__7__
2. Planning and controlling time (frequency of sales calls and paperwork)	1__2__3__4__5__6__7__
3. Writing effective reports	1__2__3__4__5__6__7__
4. Determining territorial sales potential	1__2__3__4__5__6__7__
5. Budgeting and forecasting for territory	1__2__3__4__5__6__7__

6. Giving effective oral presentations   1__2__3__4__5__6__7__

7. Understanding customer needs   1__2__3__4__5__6__7__

8. Controlling sales expense   1__2__3__4__5__6__7__

9. Utilizing sales tools (ad reprints, reports, displays)   1__2__3__4__5__6__7__

10. Basic selling skills preparation, approach, presentation, handling objections, and closing   1__2__3__4__5__6__7__

11. Company sales policy   1__2__3__4__5__6__7__

12. Evaluating and using market intelligence   1__2__3__4__5__6__7__

13. The proper use of questions   1__2__3__4__5__6__7__

14. Setting individual call objectives and evaluating results   1__2__3__4__5__6__7__

V. From the list of skills and knowledge you have checked, please indicate how your present salespeople are trained.

Training received in	Type of training (On-the-job, in-office sales meetings, etc.)	Frequency of training (how often, by month)
_____	_____	_____
_____	_____	_____
_____	_____	_____
_____	_____	_____
_____	_____	_____
_____	_____	_____
_____	_____	_____
_____	_____	_____
_____	_____	_____
_____	_____	_____

VI. Of the sales-training approaches you have checked, please indicate what percentages of each you utilize in training your retail salespeople.

Example: On-the-job   Office sales meetings   Home-study program
               30%   60%   10%

VII. Is the training for new experienced and inexperienced salespeople different from the training of present salespeople?

New experienced   New inexperienced
(Previous sales experience)   No selling experience

_____ Yes   _____ No   _____ Yes   _____ No

VIII. Please describe briefly the training for each:

A. New experienced

B. New inexperienced

If you use specific sales-training tools, please list these. (Example: home-study courses, outside seminars, film presentations, etc.)

By comparing all the responses from sales management and sales representatives, you now can build your program to meet the needs as identified by each, assist the management group in resolving areas of difference, bring to their attention those things they are not communicating, help them establish priorities, and, most importantly, start defining areas of performance deficiency.

THE ORAL SURVEY-INTERVIEW

The second basic form of survey technique is the oral survey, which takes the form of an interview. The major advantage of this type of survey is that you can get in-depth information. Answers can be followed up with questions. Unclear responses can be clarified, and incomplete information can be readily updated. The disadvantage of this method of assessing training needs is that it takes a great amount of time and only small numbers of people can be surveyed.

As with the questionnaire, extensive planning should go into developing your oral-survey interview. The planning starts with identifying the kinds of information you need to know. Once you have done this, then start writing specific questions needed to get answers. Your questions should be open-ended, not "yes or no" questions. Open-ended questions will enable you to get in-depth, qualitative responses. List as many questions as you can think of at first. Then, go down your list, carefully eliminating and combining questions. In this way, you will work down to your final list of questions.

Now that you have your list of questions, there are several steps to follow in the interview:

1. *Set the stage.* Explain what you are doing, why you are doing it, and what will happen with the information. It's best to read directly from the list of questions. Explain that you will be doing this before the interview. Make it plain you are not there to evaluate the individual or report to anyone your opinion of his or her performance or attitude.

If trust is not developed, the responses will include only what the sales representative thinks you want to hear.

2. *Be relaxed.* Don't let your gestures evaluate responses. An approving or disapproving look or nod can cause the individual to edit future responses.

3. *Take notes.* Taking notes is important. If not handled correctly, however, note taking can inhibit the interview. If you write down only negative responses, all responses will soon become guarded. You might have an occasion to use a tape recorder in some of your interviews. If time permits, play it back so that the interviewee can hear it.

4. *Be positive.* Follow up responses with positive statements such as "That's good," "I understand," "I can appreciate that." Remember, you're on their side! You are a recorder, not an evaluator.

5. *Get specific responses.* Probe general responses for specific answers with such statements as, "Could you expand on that?" "What prompts you to feel that way?" "That's interesting, tell me more," and "How did that come about?"

The methods described are basic to assessing training needs for large groups. Once you have built your major programs, there are other methods available for determining the training requirements by identifying performance deficiencies. One of the main skills you have in doing this is your own experience as a sales professional. You know the proper methods to doing the job. Observation of how others do that job is a direct means of assessing specific training needs.

The training professional must be aware of one major pitfall in assessing training needs. You are doing just that—assessing the needs of the organization that can be fulfilled through training. Training and training programs are designed to correct deficiencies in *knowledge and skill;* they are unable to do anything else. The training director will soon realize that *performance* deficiencies often have other causes such as supervision, peer pressures, lack of tools, inappropriate information systems, lack of feedback on performance, and inappropriate consequences.

These causes of performance deficiencies cannot be solved through the development of a training program, in spite of what sales managers think. It requires a great deal of strength to say to your management, "No, this cannot be overcome by training, but by changing some of the ways you are operating the sales force."

Identifying true training needs is not an easy task, but your ability to do it effectively will form the basis for any future success you may have as a trainer.

CHAPTER 4

TRAINING NEEDS OF DISTRIBUTOR SALESPERSONS, RETAIL CLERKS, AND CUSTOMERS

ROGER V. LIPPINCOTT

Roger V. Lippincott is Corporate Director of Training and Management Development, Lehn & Fink Products Company, Division of Sterling Drug, Inc., Montvale, New Jersey. He received his B.A. in speech science from Ohio State University and attended graduate school at Bowling Green State University. Prior to joining Lehn & Fink, Mr. Lippincott was a public-school teacher, speech therapist, and department manager with J. C. Penny Company. He began his association with Lehn & Fink in 1965 as a staff instructor in sales education and was appointed manager of the department in 1966. In 1970, he was promoted to head up the newly created company-wide manpower development function. In his present position, Mr. Lippincott is responsible for the development and implementation of all training and development programs for over 2,000 employees.

Salesperson: John, as sales manager of one of our largest distributors, I'm sure you're interested in increasing your volume on our line. In order to help you do this, we're introducing a whole new line of Widgets next month. I'd like to get with your sales force, at your convenience, and give them a complete rundown on how to sell it, who the customers are, and so on.

John:
(Distributor
Sales
Manager)
Gee, Hank, that really sounds great. We're all excited about the new Widget line. Le me look at our schedule ...let's see... Oh here's a good slot... We can give you ten minutes and slip you in between Acme and Gramit on Friday at 6:10. How's that?

Hank: Well?

John: Good, I'm glad you agree. And don't worry, we'll really
                 go out there and push those new Widgets. Sounds like a
                 real winner.

This episode has probably been repeated too many times. Salesperson after salesperson gets stuck with a time slot between Acme and Gramit in which to make a big impression. This situation is probably the prime example of somebody somewhere at the Widget Company not fully understanding the problems faced by the salesperson or the distributor. This chapter is designed to help that person back home do a better job of uncovering the needs of not only the distributors, but of the customers and retail clerks as well.

DIFFERENT STROKES FOR DIFFERENT FOLKS

This is not intended to be a lesson in Transactional Analysis. The "different folks" referred to are the three audiences we're concerned with in this chapter. Each differs in its set of values, demands on the training manager, ways of doing business, and needs. Before venturing into any type of needs analysis, the first and most important rule is to understand your audience.

Equally important to the audiences you're dealing with is the role you'll play in designing the "strokes." Finally, you should always keep in mind the intent of your "strokes" from your company's point of view. What follows then is a short analysis of each audience along with your role and your company's objectives.

Customers. Most customer-training programs fall into the service area. They probably have already bought your product or services and need to be trained on its use. Some companies include training programs as part of the purchase deal. Others come in later and offer (or sell) it as a means of more efficient use. Either way, your training program will probably be designed to increase the use (consumption) of the product or create customer goodwill. In spite of the differences of this audience from the others, your assessment process will take many of the same forms.

Distributors and retail clerks. By definition, these two audiences can be grouped into the same category; they are responsible for the sale of your products to the end user. The main difference within this grouping has more to do with whether or not they are your employees. You have certain advantages in working with your own employees and certain problems with distributors not employed by your firm. You should be aware of these basic differences before attempting to satisfy their training needs. Here are five basic assumptions you can make in dealing with distributors and retail clerks that are not your own employees.

1. There will be less training time available than with your own people.
2. They may decide the when, who, where, and even if of training.
3. Their salespeople are less motivated to sell your products than your own people are.
4. You can't always count on support from their management.
5. It is almost impossible to make them as technically competent as your own people.

Your role. One of the biggest mistakes training managers make is telling an organization what they need before finding out what their problems and situations are. It might be important for you to remember that your role is that of a consultant. Let them give you their input so that by the time you implement the program, they'll feel it's theirs, not yours. In developing programs in this manner, you will gain the credibility needed for implementation. Several companies have successfully carried this concept to the point where they insist on your training programs. This permits your complete control; you may even find yourself in a position of establishing training standards that an organization must meet in order to maintain a business relationship.

Your company's objectives. Check with your own company to uncover problems, opportunities, and directions. Gain greater insight into what your company wants. Evaluate these objectives carefully to determine exactly how they fit into your objectives and those of the distributors, customers, or retail clerks. Hopefully, all of your objectives are pointed in the same direction. If not, you may have to reconcile the differences and negotiate for more common goals, or try to accommodate both.

Check with many different departments to see the company's goals from the different perspectives. Each will have its own point of view. By putting them together you'll be better equipped to draw some overall conclusions. To help you uncover some areas of need within your own company, here are some typical needs of various departments:

Sales and marketing
- New products
- Market penetration
- Product emphasis
- Product diversification
- Addition of new distributors
- Greater emphasis on slow-moving items

Sales promotion and advertising
- Incentive programs
- Special deals
- Product brochures
- Advertising schedule

Credit
- Economic trends
- Discounts
- Collection problems

Customer service
- Order and billing problems
- Order flow

Traffic and distribution
- Familiarity of shipping rates
- Effect of rate on profit

METHODS OF ASSESSING NEEDS

Below are listed some of the time-proven methods of finding out what your distributor, retail salesclerks, or customers need in the way of training. Each method can provide valuable data, but using only one will certainly limit your scope of input. Therefore, it is recommended that a combination of methods be used in order to test the validity of each. One may show a great need for technical expertise while another may say that too much technical expertise can be dangerous. At the end of gathering data using these methods, you'll probably be in a good position to judge how far you want to incorporate technical knowledge in your program.

Don't limit your fact-finding research to only successful dealers, retail clerks, or customers. Go to your unproductive sources as well. Only through a cross section of groupings will you get a cross section of opinion. An unsuccessful source may give you some ideas as to what to avoid. They won't be able to tell you what's wrong with them, but their input, when compared to the successful group, will tell you what problems can occur to create failure. Then again, they may very well give you good ideas.

Surveys. In the context of this writing, surveys are intended to mean some sort of structured questionnaire either mailed to members of your audience, asked of them over the phone, or used in a formal interview situation. It is not our intent to evaluate the means by which a questionnaire is used, but rather to give you some ideas on how to structure survey questions which give you a maximum amount of information.

One good clue to the successful return of mailed questionnaires is to include a self-addressed, stamped envelope. It will increase your response percentage two-fold.

Open-ended questionnaire. The responses to an open-ended questionnaire are usually unlimited in scope. The advantage of this type of questionnaire is that it gives the respondent an opportunity to say whatever he or she feels. The disadvantage is that you'll have to sift through all the verbiage to find out what is really being said and how it relates to training, and then tally this information in some objective way.

Open-ended questions should be worded to overcome the problem of giving the respondent *too* much scope in the answer. *Don't* ask questions like:

- What problems do you have handling our products?
- What do you need in a training program?
- What did you think of our last program?

It is far better to structure questions which zero in on specific topics, like:

- What problems do you have selling with Widget X?
- List below those subjects you feel would be of value in a training

program. (Examples: sales skills of Widget model D, company policy on discounts, product knowledge of Widget X.)

- In our last program we emphasized Widget X theory. In what ways could we improve our approach to this subject?

Closed-end questionnaire. The responses to a closed-end questionnaire are usually limited to the types of responses you intended. The advantages are that you can isolate specifics, more people will respond, and the results are easy to tally. The disadvantage is that because the respondent is restricted an important area might be overlooked.

Most closed-end questions are the typical "yes-no", "true-false," checklist or multiple-choice variety. Probably one of the more unusual and efficient varieties is based on a principle that comes from Desired Learning Outcomes (DLO).

DLO is generally used to explain levels of learning and is used as a guide to determine at what level your audience should be at the end of training. Several trainers have found that they could adapt this principle to determine at what level an audience is *before* training begins. As you might guess, this approach works especially well in the area of product knowledge, but it could work just as well with other subject matter.

Here is an example of the DLO principle in action. First, each respondent is told the definition of the levels of familiarity and a code letter for each level, as follows:

CODE	DEFINITION
A	*Awareness*—The individual is aware that you have such a product or service, but does not know the specifications, capacities, etc., of the product.
K	*Knowledge*—The individual has knowledge of the product, can quote models, specifications, features, and prices in general terms. Does not have an understanding of *why* a product may do what it does.
U	*Understanding*—The individual is beyond the A and K level, and understands how the product functions and why it functions the way it does. When a person "understands," he or she is able to explain the "how's" and "why's" of a concept as well as its implications. Cause-and-effect relationships, as well as advantages and disadvantages, are a part of understanding.
S	*Skill*—The ability to perform, such as in the operation or demonstration of the product.

A typical questionnaire using the DLO approach might look like the diagram in Attachment 1.

Attachment 1

CO. NAME

FAMILIARITY SURVEY

Name _____

Code:

 Y—Yes, the product is marketable in my area
 N—No, the product is not marketed in my area—go on to the next product
 A—Awareness that there is such a product
 K—Knowledge about models, specification, and price
 U—Understanding of how it functions, its features and benefits
 S—Skill in operation sufficient to demonstrate

Y	N	PRODUCT	A	K	U	S
		Widget X				
		Tinker Tram				
		Fram 2				
		Snar Bagger				
		Bling Energizer				
		Widget CC				

Interviews

Face-to-face. Occasionally, the face-to-face survey will provide for more thorough investigation. It certainly provides an opportunity to probe further into the problems, opportunities, and attitudes. Probably the biggest drawback to the face-to-face interview is expense of time and possibly travel. You may have to pull people from their work station, or you may have to travel to various locations, resulting in expensive travel and living. A somewhat less satisfactory form of interviewing is by means of the telephone.

Telephone. Telephone surveys will certainly give you an opportunity for two-way communication. You can probe, uncover areas of concern, and get a feel about attitude. It's a lot cheaper than face-to-face interviews, and it may save you the time of traveling from location to location. It has two main drawbacks, however. One, people don't generally like to expose themselves on the phone—therefore, information you receive will tend to be more restricted than face-to-face. Two, you won't be able to see the subtle expressions and gestures of the respondent. These body-language clues can be beneficial in determining genuine areas of concern.

Interviewing methods. You must be as well prepared for an interview as you are for a mailed survey. Plan what information you want to receive through some type of structured or unstructured outline. A programed or structured interview is simply asking open-ended questions that are prepared ahead of time. As in the written, open-ended questionnaire, leave the interviewee plenty of room to answer. Questions beginning with "what," "how," "when," and "where" usually give the interviewee an opportunity to express more complete thoughts than questions that begin with "is," "would," "are," or "do." These types of questions will usually elicit a simple "yes" or "no" response.

"Work-with" programs

Spending time out in the field working with the salespeople or management will pay off in big dividends in determining training needs. You'll be able to observe what is actually going on at the firing line. This observation will not only be a good learning experience for you, but you'll also be able to observe some of the problems and situations they face on a day-by-day basis. This type of observation will go a long way toward making your training programs more pragmatic.

Sales-contact observation. Obtain permission to work with some of the salespeople (good and bad) as an observer of the sales call. Don't go as a coach but more as a scout. Watch the salespeople at work and keep track of how they conduct their business. Be observant and ask questions related to administrative work, precall analysis, sales techniques used, sales effectiveness, activities during the sales contact, and use of visuals. You might find it helpful to jot down your impressions of this type of information in a systematic way. Doing so will help you compile data that can be easily compared at a later date. The points you might want to consider for observing a sales call could include:

1. Type of call

2. Methods of buying
   a. Direct
   b. Warehouse
   c. Chain
   d. Indirect

3. Your position with the customer
   a. Better than competition
   b. Equal to competition
   c. Less than competition

4. Activities (time in minutes)
   a. Waiting
   b. General conversation
   c. Training
   d. Checking inventory
   e. Arranging stock
   f. Selling products
   g. Service

5. Selling effectiveness
   a. Precall planning
   b. Sales objectives
   c. Opening statements
   d. Suggested orders
   e. Use of benefits/features
   f. Use of visuals
   g. Success stories
   h. Handling objections
   i. Closing
   j. Postcall analysis

Attending meetings or conventions. Another "work-with" approach is to attend Trade Association meetings or conventions. Find out what's going on in your customer's business and what their main areas of concern are. If you can, get a few minutes on the agenda in order to find out what they require from you in the way of training. Go to their conventions and get in one of those small-group rap sessions at a cocktail party. When appropriate, rent a booth at the convention and share the cost with the sales department. You'll find many customers and distributors much more receptive to your queries when conducted on their home ground.

Analysis of current data. Look at information you can gather from home base, and you'll probably find some very meaningful data that will assist you in making training recommendations. Here are a few considerations.

• *Company statistics*—Most companies keep records of sales statistics which will give you insight into your analysis. Products are broken down by size, territory, customer, states, and so on. Profit and loss statements will help you determine priorities. Personnel statistics will give you information related to the manpower situation. These and dozens of other sources, within your own company, can be used to assess your situation.

• *Student feedback*—If you already have ongoing training programs for your distributors, customers, or salesclerks, ask the students attending your sessions not only to critique your existing programs but to give you input regarding additional training requirements. Find out what they feel may be wrong with your existing programs which will help you decide what to do about the future. Posttraining surveys with students who have attended your sessions will help you determine what might be lacking. This type of survey can be in writing, conducted by your department or by your own line managers.

• *Customer attitudes*—Analysis of your users' needs, objections, reasons, and problems can reveal many areas of concern for your distributors and retail clerks. These attitudes can be determined while conducting your "work-with" programs through surveys, questionnaires, or interviews. If you're lucky enough to have a market-research department, either in-house or as a consultant, ask them. They'll be able to give you good raw data concerning customer attitudes.

• *Your sales force feedback*—If your sales force comes into direct contact with your dealers, retail clerks, or customers, ask them their feelings on the subject. Sales meetings, questionnaires, surveys, interviews, and "work-with" programs are good vehicles to uncover this information.

Distributor advisory boards. Many large companies maintain a council of representatives from their dealer management ranks. This council is made up of any number (usually 6 to 12) of members who meet several times a year at the company's expense. The purpose of the group is to provide counsel for the company on many subjects, including pricing, marketing policy, ethics, products, billing terms, and training. This can be an invaluable source that you can tap concerning assessing distributor needs. If you do not have such a source, it might be wise to consider establishing one. But the subject should be approached by looking carefully at both the advantages and disadvantages.

ANALYZING THE DATA AND MAKING RECOMMENDATIONS

Once you have gathered all of your data, it is time to begin your analysis and recommendations. While you were collecting the data, you probably began to develop your own conclusions. Be careful not to discount data simply because you "feel" such and such is needed. Also, don't be tempted to solve the situation too early with ideas or programs with which you are comfortable. Making these early judgments can produce results that are way off the mark. If you feel entirely uncomfortable with your early conclusions, keep gathering data until you begin to see the "real problems" rather than the symptoms.

For a purely objective approach to analyzing your data, consider using a straight quantitative approach. One such approach might be to set company priorities, measure your data (surveys, interviews, questionnaires) by percent and numbers of response to certain problems, then give weight values to training criteria to determine your ultimate priorities. Someone from your statistics department may be able to assist you with this method.

Many times it is a good idea to draw up your conclusions via a formal proposal. These documents serve as a communication and approval tool to top management. An entire chapter could be devoted to writing training proposals. For the sake of simplicity, the following outline usually will encompass all of the information contained in a formal written proposal.

Title Page

Preface

Table of Contents

I. *Objective.* (Describe in a sentence or two your charge or mission concerning the proposal.)

   A. Primary Objective—(Your greatest concern and/or goal usually beginning with the word "to")

   B. Secondary objective(s)—(Other concerns which affect the primary objective)

II. *Situation Analysis.* (A series of brief statements concerning where your company, distributors, retail-clerks, or customers stand now. These statements could be devoted to such subjects as share of market, size of sales force(s), size of training department, restrictions, past trends, company objectives, etc.)

III. *Research.* (An explanation of the research you conducted during your needs analysis, along with any pertinent raw data.)

IV. *Problems and Opportunities.* (The conclusions concerning the problems and opportunities discovered during your needs analysis.)

V. *Recommendations.* (Simply stated action plans of programs you are proposing. During training, managers will also include dates and persons responsible for the development and implementation.)

VI. *Costs.* (Include an estimate of materials, travel, time, capital expenses, etc. If possible, always try to include sales, cost savings, or time efficiency you expect to gain from the investment. Including this type of return will help "pay the way" and most assuredly "sell" your proposal to top management.)

CHAPTER 5

ASSESSING SPECIFIC TRAINING NEEDS

CHARLES H. SINGLER

Charles H. Singler is General Sales Manager of the Burroughs Wellcome Company of Research Triangle Park, North Carolina. He joined the Company in 1941. He had previously held positions as Sales Promotion Manager, Assistant Sales Manager, Assistant Advertising Manager, District Sales Manager, and Sales Representative.

Mr. Singler is a graduate of the Cincinnati College of Pharmacy with a B.S. degree in pharmacy and is registered as a pharmacist in the states of California and Ohio. He is a member of the Sales Executives Club of New York and serves on the Board of Advisors of the Research Institute of America. He is also a member of the Board of Directors of NSSTE and in 1967, 1968, and 1975 received Silver Awards for his editorial contributions. In 1973 he was awarded a Gold Medal for his editorial entitled "Potential Problem Areas with Minority and Female Sales Representatives."

THE SENIOR OR EXPERIENCED SALES REPRESENTATIVE

Assessing the sales-training needs of an internal or external (field) sales organization is a process of identifying the kind and caliber of performance that will produce the desired sales results and expose variance from desired performance. As such, it applies equally to all sales personnel: new trainees, senior or experienced sales representatives, female or minority sales representatives, and even field sales managers. In fact, this single standard of performance makes possible the fairest and most appropriate training of females and minorities.

It is essential to recognize the kind and caliber of performance that will produce the desired sales results. Then, having produced and implemented the sales-training program to achieve the "desired sales results," a second assessment of sales-training needs is required. This is when you measure, evaluate, weigh, determine, and judge the differences between the kind of performance you want and the kind of performance you are getting, and then reduce or eliminate the difference.

In other words, the objective of the first process of needs assessment deals with the initial and ongoing sales training for *new* representatives, and as such is related to the differences between the level of performance you want and the qualifications of those you hire. Quite obviously, the sales-training needs of your initial-entry sales personnel will vary considerably, depending on the type of product or service you sell, the education and expertise of the customers to whom you sell, and the level of education and amount of experience you require of those you hire.

The second process of needs assessment deals with identifying the variation between the actual and desired levels of sales performance of existing sales personnel, determining the cause, and then developing the training program to fulfill the need.

WHERE TO START?

While "Assessing Training Needs of New Salespersons" is covered in another chapter, it is important to review the process for assessing these needs in order to recognize the differences between the first and second processes.

In oversimplified form, the process for *assessing the sales-training needs of new sales personnel* might start with:

- Identification of results to be achieved or accomplished
- Tasks or performance required to achieve the desired results
- Standards by which those tasks or performance will be evaluated
- Measurement of trainees' level of qualifications in areas of tasks or performance
- Means or strategies by which those tasks or performance will be taught and trainees' needs satisfied
- Testing to determine in restricted sample whether means do in fact enable the trainees to perform up to the standards
- Revision to correct program deficiencies

By contrast, the process for *assessing the sales-training needs of experienced sales representatives* might start with:

- Analysis of results achieved, above or below standards

- Are the desired results understood and agreed to by those responsible for achieving them?
- In what areas did the variations occur? Were they general or restricted to specific areas?
- Were the results above or below standard, to signal problems or opportunities?

↓
- Analysis of performance to identify variations
  - Are the tasks consistent with the results to be achieved?
  - Were performance variations general or specific? Did they reflect knowledge or skills? Did they represent deficiencies or opportunities for growth and development?

↓
- Review of standards against which performance is measured
  - Are standards current, complete, adequate, achievable? (Your field sales manager should be pleased to provide these and review them with you.)

↓
- Review of appraisal system by which standards are applied
  - Is system being applied correctly, fairly, objectively? (Your field sales manager and sales supervisors can provide evidence of this program and its implementation.)

↓
- Identification of variations from standards which can be identified as training problems or opportunities
  - Does the deficiency signal a condition of "don't know how," "know how but can't," or "don't wanna?"

↓
- Means or strategies by which the performance-deficiency variations can be corrected and experienced representatives' needs satisfied

↓
- Testing to determine in restricted sample whether means (or strategies) do in fact enable the experienced salesperson to again perform up to standards

↓
- Revisions to correct program deficiencies

Initially, without giving the process sufficient advance thought or researching your new responsibilities as sales-training manager, you may "get the cart before the horse" in your efforts to do something. Why? Perhaps because of a reluctance to ask for assistance, information, or guidelines; for fear of appearing uninformed; or of not knowing where to start. Too many of us in sales training have belatedly discovered, after years in the job, that we were designing sales-training solutions (programs) for problems we hadn't properly identified, for jobs we hadn't critically analyzed.

THE SPECIAL ROLE OF SALES TRAINING IN ASSESSING NEEDS

Getting the sales representative to implement the strategies and achieve the objectives of the marketing plan is a multi-departmental function and responsibility, and performance problems with sales representatives have been variously categorized as "don't know how," "know how, but can't," and "don't wanna."

The *"don't know how"* problem is basically a lack of knowledge and/or skills. This is the traditional and undisputed domain of training. Examples are the new sales representatives whose initial-entry knowledge or skills are not up to the required level; or the sales representative who was "tuned-out," ill, or absent during a phase of initial or subsequent training, but whose deficiency wasn't noticed until he or she was faced with performing up to standard on the job.

The *"know how, but can't"* performance deficiency is related to demands beyond the control of the salesperson; namely, such factors as conflicting demands on the representatives' time, conflicting priorities, and lack of resources with which to implement the task. The cause may be within the company, competitive or customer area, and it is usually considered the responsibility of the field supervisor or sales-training group to at least report, if not correct it. Care and tact should be exercised in the handling of these problems, since the ultimate solution frequently involves the activities of other departments.

The *"don't wanna"* problem is one of lack of motivation. The salesperson knows how and faces no impediment to carrying out the task, but lacks motivation. This is a supervisory problem, not a training problem, at least initially. It may eventually become an attitudinal-training problem for the salesperson or a motivation-training problem for the field supervisor, but it is not initially a responsibility of the sales-training department.

The job or position description of the sales-training manager should spell out in detail the critical performance areas of his or her responsibilities to minimize or eliminate areas of overlap or "no-man's land" with others in sales or marketing administration or field sales supervision.

Resources for assessing sales-training needs

Although the foregoing *process for assessing the sales-training needs of experienced sales representatives* provides a set of guidelines to follow in identifying and correcting the problem areas, the question frequently arises, "Where do I look for answers to the problems I discover?"

The following resources will provide information to help you discover your answers.

1. *Company personnel* are probably the single greatest resource. You should tap the experiences, ideas, and expectations of the sales- or marketing-management personnel, the field sales supervision, and the sales representatives themselves.

- Can sales be *accurately measured* to reward the sales representatives' efforts equitably?
- What tasks or critical areas of performance do the *sales representatives* identify as essential components of their job description?
- What information do *they* identify that the salesperson "needs to know" as compared with information that is "nice to know"?
- What skills do *they* identify that the salesperson "needs to have" as compared with skills that are "nice to have"?
- How can *they* describe the depth of knowledge and skills in measurable or observable terms?

The single most useful way of tapping resources involves repeated direct conversations, consultations, and feedback sessions with the same sales- and marketing-management personnel, field sales supervisory personnel, and sales representatives to gain their active involvement, understanding, acceptance, agreement, and commitment at every stage of your assessment of the training needs of the sales staff. This can be accomplished by:

- *Direct observation in the field* of salespeople representing a cross section of types and degrees of success.
- *Telephone survey* of the same types of company personnel in other divisions, and among competitors and customers.
- *Written surveys* or questionnaires.
- *Private interviews.*

- *Workshop* or brainstorming sessions.
- *Quizzes* devised as diagnostic tools.
- *Search of company files* to identify allies (as well as opponents) and areas of need.

Having tapped the resources and established the sales-training needs, it becomes necessary in the real world to determine whether the company can afford to provide additional training sufficient to achieve the desired level of performance. Not infrequently it will be necessary to negotiate compromises because of limitations of budget, personnel, time, or existing performance standards or practices.

Special needs of the experienced sales representatives

Obviously, the experienced sales representative could have a deficiency in any one or several of the areas of performance we identified in our discussion of the process for assessing sales-training needs. Additionally, because of age, experience, ambitions, or personal limitations, the experienced salesperson has special needs requiring the trainer's attention.

Many training efforts directed to experienced sales representatives fail because they aren't aimed specifically at their needs. As a result, it is essential to the success of the training that needs assessment be focused on this group, and almost on specific individuals.

Listed below are environmental factors peculiar to experienced sales representatives that may or may not be within the province of the training department. Even if not, the sales-training manager can still help by identifying alternatives to training for sales management and field sales supervision.

1. *Equal treatment.* On one hand, the experienced representative and senior peers are the backbone of the successful sales organization, and the steadying influence among the new trainees.

On the other hand they are frequently the forgotten men (or women) in the field. The unequal attention necessarily given a trainee takes management time and attention away from the experienced sales force, to the detriment of their technical updating and psychological needs. In short, we frequently ignore "our gifted children!"

The training department must provide new technology and background information, and the field supervisors must maintain a fair balance of attention or awareness of the needs of these individuals.

2. *Declining performance.* Through the lack of effort/interest/self-discipline/attention/capabilities (choose one), the experienced sales representative sometimes reaches a plateau; doesn't rise to the level of management expectations; doesn't keep current with the knowledge, skills, and market; and becomes out of phase with customers.

The time to correct these situations is *before* they happen. Preventive therapy in the form of regular performance reviews, knowledge and skills evaluations, and training updates may either reverse early down-trends or identify them before they become serious casualties.

3. *Lack of challenge.* Because of familiarity with products, customers, skills, market, and competition, the job loses its challenge and the salespeople lose their motivation.

In order to enable experienced sales representatives to develop to their full potential, on-the-job application of the principles of motivation must be a primary objective of modern-day sales training and sales management. Job rotation, new assignments, and added responsibilities are essential to experienced sales personnel.

4. *Self-Doubts.* Because of their growing seniority and the increasing number of junior sales representatives (particularly those who are spectacularly successful and move ahead quickly), some experienced sales representatives experience self-doubts even though they may be performing at better-than-average levels.

These can frequently be resolved with explicit performance standards and objectives which enable the senior sales representatives (and the junior ones too) to monitor and evaluate their own effectiveness and compare their performance with others.

5. *Opportunities for growth.* Experienced sales personnel with qualifications for promotion are not infrequently disappointed with the lack of opportunities.

Although it is not usually the responsibility of the sales-training department, you can help identify activities or responsibilities that might be converted to interim promotional categories. In the meantime, career counseling is useful.

6. *Work interference.* On occasion, the performance of experienced sales representatives will be at variance with that of their less experienced peers because of work interference, conflicting tasks, or multiple responsibilities which have caused them to develop priorities which differ from those set by sales management. Because of local knowledge and experience they may see the needs differently.

Your role may be to help them change their position, or—through training—to help their peers (and sales supervision) change theirs. The latter is a difficult but necessary task if sales training is to fulfill its total responsibility.

ASSESSING THE SPECIAL TRAINING NEEDS OF THE FEMALE AND/OR MINORITY SALES REPRESENTATIVE

It is impossible to overemphasize the fact that the *primary* training needs of female and minority sales representatives are the same as the training needs of all male and nonminority sales representatives. They all have the same basic knowledge, skills, planning and organizing, and attitudinal training needs.

What those needs are, realistically, can only be determined by measuring the differences between the desired levels and the entry levels of knowledge, skills, planning and organizing abilities, and attitude in those you hire.

There are special needs that may exist, either in degree or in content, with female and minority sales trainees. Some are unanticipated organizational needs, and others are sales-training needs. The unanticipated organizational or environmental needs may or may not be the responsibility of the sales-training manager. If not, the sales-training manager should be alert to these needs and help identify alternative solutions, other than training, for sales management and field sales supervision.

What are these special training needs?

Single performance standard

It is absolutely essential that a single standard of performance be used for *all* sales personnel—minority, female, nonminority, and male—and that *all* sales personnel understand this. Strict adherence to this policy will forestall complaints about partiality, "double standards," tolerance of lowered productivity, and similar comments by nonminority and male sales personnel. At the same time, a single performance standard will convince minority and female sales personnel that their performance achievements are genuine and they are not "second-class performers"—nor are they being patronized because of their Affirmative Action Program status. In fact, it is this single standard of performance that produces the fairest and most valuable training program for females and minority sales personnel.

Positive reassurance

Although most trainees will evidence or at least feel some fear or apprehension of the training program, females and minorities may actually encounter an even greater incidence of this initial reaction. If it occurs, it may be related to a lack of previous experience or background in business, or previous competition with predominantly white or male associates.

Whatever the reason, a special effort must be made by the training personnel to put the female and minority trainees at ease by explaining the program in detail and getting them involved as quickly as possible. If this is not done, their attitudes could be misinterpreted as hostility or lack of desire or understanding, whereas it may simply be fear of apprehension of the training process. Minority and female trainees may require more encouragement because of the obstacles to success as they perceive them.

Peer acceptance

As with fear of the training program, female and minority representatives initially may be more ill at ease, hypersensitive, or defensive in a group of trainees who are predominantly male or nonminority. This situation is relieved if there are several females or minorities in the group, and is best resolved by helping all trainees learn as much as possible about one another and discover mutual points of interest or experience.

Realistic objectives

Either because of a true lack of understanding of the magnitude of the training assignment, a minimizing of the competition within the company, or a real or imagined promise of success, a number of females or minorities may have unrealistic objectives, or indicate expectations of "instant success." An early review of their immediate and long-range career objectives will help put this in perspective.

Sensitive issues

Whether or not to discuss social issues with female and minority sales representatives is an individual decision. Success in these discussions and the relationship that develops is closely related to the sincerity, sensitivity, and open-mindedness of those involved. Perhaps most important is how the principles of fairness and equal opportunity are practiced within the company.

Spouse's attitude

The wives of most sales representatives are considerably involved with their husband's jobs and know their major customers and products. To achieve that same degree of involvement with the wives of minority sales representatives, or the husbands of female representatives, special orientation by the company may be necessary.

Female or minority resentment

Although an effective, ongoing Affirmative Action Program presupposes sincere and enlightened management at all levels, particularly of the sales-training staff, and first-line supervisors who are sensitive to the feelings and problems of females and minorities, it is fair to say that some individual habits and unthinking actions may unintentionally provoke resentment in the female or minority trainee. As a result, flareups will occur. While the normal reaction would be to do whatever is possible to prevent a recurrence, it is important to confirm that whatever caused the problem was "unintentional" or "unthinking," and not a deliberate effort to scuttle the program.

Acceptance of performance appraisal

Closely related to peer acceptance discussed above, special care must frequently be exercised by the trainer when conducting a performance appraisal. Usually the female or minority trainee is so eager to learn and to excel that almost any suggestion for improvement or criticism provokes a hasty defense. On the other hand, it is essential that a single standard of acceptable performance be maintained.

Extra training

Women and minorities are relatively new to some types of field sales and certain industries, and the selling profession has not carried its story of its career potential to the female and minority populations. Often, minority and female sales trainees have a foggy view of business; the profit motive, how goods are manufactured, sold, and paid for, what happens to the profits—and what role the sales representative plays in all this. As a result, a good job of company orientation is necessary. Special pretraining or remedial training in business language and practices may also be needed to develop their full future potential.

Business time requirements

The minority or female trainee to whom you have explained the job responsibilities and the amount of effort required may react with some surprise and concern about the magnitude of the job requirements. This is particularly true in the amount of study, planning, call preparation, reporting, and other after-hours duties required. This phase of the job orientation may be shortchanged during your initial screening presentation, and thus may require greater emphasis during training.

Relocation

For reasons which may relate to personal feelings of insecurity, minority applicants may be less willing to relocate from where they were recruited. This is particularly true if the job opening is in a far distant part of the country. This could be a bigger problem with females and for reasons different from those of minorities: loneliness and the severing of ties with family and friends when traveling to their new location. In contrast to the male trainee who relocates, the female does not have available such organizations as the Jaycees or 20–30 which she can join to become quickly acquainted and establish new contacts in a community. The obvious solution is to recruit women from the area in which the vacancy exists. Failing that, it is important to determine as fully as possible during the screening process whether the applicant can survive relocation.

Driver training

If you require all applicants to have an effective driver's license, it is important to confirm their driving expertise in heavy traffic, repeated parking, and general familiarity with traffic laws. Perhaps a driver-education training program may be indicated for some of these individuals.

Whether their training needs be those basic to all sales trainees, or the special needs discussed above, well-trained female and minority sales representatives can add materially to the success of your sales force.

ASSESSING THE TRAINING NEEDS OF THE
DISTRICT SALES MANAGER

Before solving an assigned problem it is frequently necessary to resolve certain other problems, policies, or procedures. Such is the situation in assessing the training needs of the first-line field supervisor, or
district sales manager.

- Have the standards of selection been set by which qualified candidates for field supervision can be identified and minimum (or
maximum) training needs and objectives established?
- Have the critical areas of responsibility and performance, which
comprise the position or job description of the district sales manager, been identified and agreed upon?
- Have standards of performance been established by which the deficiencies and achievements of existing district sales managers can
be identified and measured, and thus the training and/or development needs determined?
- Has a performance-appraisal system between the district sales
manager and his or her superior been devised by which agreement
on deficiencies and corrective training measures can be achieved?

In a newly structured field supervisory staff or newly established
field sales organization an orderly progression from step one is possible. In the existing business world, one, several, or none of these
steps may have been taken. Whatever the existing situation, however,
an accurate assessment of the training needs of the district sales manager depends largely on the solid foundation of a coordinated selection
system, position (job) description, performance standards, and performance-appraisal system, designed to satisfy the needs of your particular sales organization.

Selection standards

One of the charges most frequently leveled against ongoing field supervisory selection systems is that they usually consist of the identification and promotion of the best salespeople. This often results in the
loss of a productive salesperson, and the selection of a mediocre field
sales manager.

Solutions to this problem have included:

- Hiring experienced field sales managers from another organization.

This can further complicate the training problem, because the established work patterns of the experienced field sales manager may be in direct conflict with those of your company.

- Setting up personal job specifications based on "working characteristics" which are largely personality and character traits; namely, judgment, sensitivity, communication skills, leadership qualities, maturity, integrity, aggressiveness, and friendliness.
- Developing specifications that are results oriented and thus related to the job requirements.

The preferred solution depends upon the urgency, magnitude, and specific nature of the needs of the organization, with perhaps a blend of the personal specifications and a critical analysis of the candidate's experience, whether the individual is promoted from within the organization or hired from the open market. Whatever the method, reasonably strict adherence to at least a set of minimum selection standards is desirable if a wide variation in training needs and performance is to be avoided.

JOB (POSITION) DESCRIPTION AND PERFORMANCE STANDARDS

Fundamental building blocks in assessing the training needs of the district sales manager are the job (position) description and performance standards. Only through the identification and definition of specific areas of responsibility and performance and the quantification of what constitutes satisfactory compliance of the district sales manager can deficiencies be recognized and training or development be structured. Obviously, an individual cannot be held accountable for tasks that have not been identified or defined. Neither can needs be assessed or training designed where these fundamentals are lacking or incomplete.

PERFORMANCE-APPRAISAL SYSTEM

Closely related to the success of any training or development effort is the understanding and agreement by the individual receiving the training of the need for that training. Out of understanding and agreement come support for the objectives of the training program. This sequence of events is directly related to the validity and application of the performance-appraisal system. Too frequently the needs assessment for training of all members of the field sales staff is based upon faulty application of the performance-appraisal system. This is often caused by improper identification of deficiencies, disagreement on the application of performance standards, or ineffective communications. Where this occurs the training program is doomed to mediocrity or ineffectiveness.

Having recognized and hopefully satisfied the foregoing specific requirements against which a DSM training-needs assessment can be made, the process becomes one of:

1. Relating and comparing the duties and responsibilities of the district sales manager of your sales organization to the well-recognized planning, organizing, leading, and controlling functions common to every manager.
2. Adding the specific operating responsibilities assigned to the first-line field supervisor within your company's method of management.
3. Orienting the district sales manager to his or her revised responsibilities.

In actual practice, consideration of the activities and subdivisions that make up the management responsibilities of planning, organizing, leading (directing), and controlling should best be made at the time the position or job description is developed. In order to assess the training needs of your district sales manager accurately, we suggest the following checklist. Those management activities which it includes should be reviewed in greater depth through seminars and business publications on topics of specific interest. By asking the following questions, and probing for answers, you should be well on your way toward identifying areas of potential training for district sales managers.

- *Planning.* If planning is defined as the management of time to achieve an intended or predetermined result, with what responsibilities have your district sales managers been charged in the area of planning?

    - *Forecasting.* Is the DSM required to predict sales, customer growth, personnel needs, equipment, or capital requirements for this district? Do you have a formal means for reporting these estimates? What program do you have for training the DSM to fulfill that responsibility?

    - *Setting objectives.* How are objectives set for the district? Are the areas for objective setting clearly identified? Are they realistic? Measurable? Does the DSM participate (actually) in setting them? Does the DSM know how?

• *Performance standards.* Have standards been set for the DSM's performance? For that of his or her salespeople? Does the DSM understand and accept the standards? Can he or she distinguish between satisfactory and unsatisfactory performance? Does the DSM know how to set standards of acceptable performance?

• *Policies.* Does the DSM understand and accept the company policies and know how to apply them? Are they available for easy reference?

• *Procedures.* Is the DSM familiar with existing procedures related to his or her new responsibilities and does he or she understand the reason(s) for their existence? Is the DSM required to establish or revise procedures? Does he or she know how?

• *Programs.* Does the DSM understand the process of writing programs, and the methods of scheduling? Is the DSM familiar with existing programs? Are they available for ready reference?

• *Time management.* Is the DSM aware of the time requirements of the multiple job responsibilities and their relative importance as indicated by company management practices? Is the DSM knowledgeable about the importance of and methods for recording, managing, and consolidating time and thereby setting up priorities for activities?

• *Budgeting.* Is the DSM responsible for budgeting, finances, personnel, resources, and/or time? Does he or she know how? Do guidelines or standards exist for proper guidance?

• *Organizing.* If organizing is the process of relating or coordinating resources so that company objectives can be achieved most effectively, what responsibilities do your DSM's have in the area of organizing?

• *Formal structure.* Does the DSM understand the concepts and types of formal organization structure that exist in the business world? Does the DSM understand the basis for your present organization structure and the procedure for reviewing and changing the present structure? Does he or she understand the limits of authority for changing the organization structure? Does the DSM understand your existing line-staff relationships?

• *Informal structure.* Is the DSM aware of the informal organization structure within his or her district, division, or region? Does he or she understand the workings of the informal structure?

• *Leading (directing).* If leading is the guiding or directing of people to attain the intended results or objectives, how extensive are the

DSM's responsibilities and authority, and how knowledgeable and skillful is the DSM in meeting those responsibilities?

• *Management communications.* Does the DSM understand the importance of the communication process? Are certain types of communications scheduled and formalized within your organization, and are examples available for ready reference?

• *Problem solving and decision making.* Does the DSM understand and have the ability to use a logical thinking process?

• *Motivation.* Does the DSM understand and agree with the philosophy that he or she is less a manager of sales than a manager of *people* who manage sales? Is the DSM familiar with his or her role in motivating the field sales staff toward achieving the sales objective? Does the DSM understand and apply the principles of the human (psychological) needs as well as the biological needs? Does the DSM understand his or her role within your organization's salary administration?

• *Selection.* Is the DSM responsible for selection? Are there selection standards and a screening and hiring procedure, and is the DSM able to apply them? Does the DSM have responsibilities which he or she understands and is able to apply for maintaining a field sales staff? Does the DSM understand responsibilities relative to the company's obligations under EEOC, Fair Employment Practices Act, and other federal and state regulations?

• *Training.* Does the DSM understand his or her role in home office, field, and/or follow-up training of sales representatives? Does he or she have ready reference to the procedure for and evaluation of field sales training? Is the DSM familiar with the principles of and techniques for sales training?

• *Development.* Does the DSM understand the importance of and methods for personnel development, and the company plan for career planning and development?

• *Delegating.* Does the DSM understand the difference between operating and management work and the uses of delegation in personnel development? Does the DSM understand and apply the concepts of delegation of authority, responsibility, and accountability, and the limits of delegation within your company?

• *Controlling.* If controlling is defined as the assessment, measurement, and regulation of performance and resources in use to achieve the company's objectives, does the DSM understand the responsibilities in the areas within his or her control, and is he or she willing to fulfill them?

• *Performance appraisal.* Is the DSM qualified to conduct a performance appraisal of sales representatives against agreed-upon performance standards? Is the DSM qualified to conduct a counseling session, measuring and reporting results, rewarding achievements, and following through with an action plan? Is he or she qualified to conduct a "curbstone counseling session" on the job?

• *Expense control.* Is the DSM familiar with methods for auditing and controlling expenses?

• *Counseling session follow-through.* Does the DSM understand the limits of authority in recommending or acting on the findings and results of his or her performance appraisal and counseling session? Does the DSM understand the company probation procedure? Does the DSM understand the limits of his or her authority in terminating a sales representative? Can he or she follow through correctly and legally when doing so? Does the DSM understand his or her responsibilities in recommending or authorizing in-house or outside follow-through training or development programs?

The above provides a basic outline of most of the *management* activities of the district sales manager or first-line field supervisor, which should be weighed in assessing the training needs of this individual.

Additionally, there may be very specific field sales *operating* responsibilities within your company's method of management which are assigned to this first-line supervisor. Obviously, the DSM's training needs must include these.

Finally, the district sales manager must be carefully and thoroughly oriented to his or her new responsibilities to ascertain that he or she knows them, or knows where they are stated; understands them to the limits of his or her comprehension at that point in time; and agrees with them.

It is repeatedly stated in the literature, and experience certainly confirms, that the transition from salesperson to field sales supervisor or district sales manager is the single most difficult transition in the sales career ladder. The difficulty is primarily based on the transition in duties from managing sales to managing salespeople who manage sales, and all its attendant problems. A good orientation and early and frequent reviews by the next level of field sales supervision will help the DSM complete the transition successfully.

CHAPTER 6

THE USE OF "EXTERNAL" RESOURCES TO ASSESS TRAINING NEEDS

GUSTAV W. HENGEL

Gustav W. Hengel is Director of Sales & Operations for a large farm-based retail food business, Delicious Orchards, Colts Neck, New Jersey. Formerly he was a Management Consultant, an Internal Consultant in Organization Development for the STP Corporation, Corporate Director of Management Development & Training, International Paper Company, New York City; Corporate Training Manager, Schering Corporation, Bloomfield, New Jersey; Sales Training & Development Manager, Merck Company, Rahway, New Jersey. He also has extensive field sales and line management experience in consumer and industrial product oriented industries.

Mr. Hengel has served as a training and manpower development consultant for the New Jersey Departments of Institutions & Agencies, Civil Service and Agriculture as well as a variety of corporations. For over eight years he served on the faculty of Rutgers University in the Management and Extension Divisions and the Center for Continuing Education designing and conducting programs in General Management, Organization Behavior, Appraisal Systems, Interpersonal Communications, Team Building, Leadership Process, and Performance Analysis and Improvement. He has published articles on sales training, performance analysis, and management by objectives.

Mr. Hengel is a graduate of Upsala College (1952) and has attended the University of Richmond Professional Institutes, specializing in business management and marketing programs.

Whenever anyone suggests to a sales trainer that "External Resources" be considered to help achieve some objective or conduct a program, the normal tendency is to think only in terms of an "outside" organization, product, or service. While there are many occasions when we should be going "outside" for help, we should first take a good look at the potential resources within the total organization. In other words, the term "external resources" should be thought of as any form of assistance outside of the training department itself.

While there is a definite place for the consultant firm, there are also many individuals and departments within the company that can be of immeasurable help to the training department. The challenge is finding out who they are and what they can do to help meet the company's training goals. So, when we speak of using "external resources" we should be thinking in the broadest possible terms.

As indicated above, everyone "external" but within the organization is potentially a training resource. To fail to involve them in the assessment of training (or organizational) needs (since they are often the very ones closest to the problem) makes little sense.

Let's stand back and reassess our role in organization life:

- Are we a staff/service organization created to help and serve the needs of others?
- Should we be seen by others as doing our "own thing"?
- Can we be sure of doing the right thing without involving others?
- Can we afford not to become knowledgeable in our "customer's" business and operational needs?

What better way for the training and development function to earn its stripes than to be seen out there beating the bushes—analyzing problems and coming up with alternative solutions. Working in isolation has another risk—the risk of survival. Think about it: in tough times isn't it difficult to secure corporate funds for "unknowns"? "Satisfied customers are our best advertisement."

"CUSTOMERS" AND THE TRAINING FUNCTION (OR HOW TO GET IN BUSINESS)

Why not view every department in your company as a "customer," especially if your mandate happens to extend beyond basic sales training. If a salesperson solves customer problems and helps satisfy needs, can't we? But first, we've got to get into business. Here are a variety of possibilities, and ideally all might be happening concurrently:

- The training function has an organization charter or mandate from top management which states to the rest of the organization its mission in organization life. If you don't have one—write one—present it—modify it—sell it—but above all, get one.

- Find out what dollars are being invested in the training function. And, since several other departments in the organization are undoubtedly paying their share of your overhead, find out what they want for their money. Like the salesperson, start knocking on doors.
- Find out early in the game who are your supporters and who are not. Find out why not. What can be done to change their views?
- Since the training and development function should be dedicated to helping improve individual and organization performance, survey your "potential" customers on what kinds of performance problems exist. (Note: Tact and diplomacy are important here—don't come on in such a way as to make your "customer" feel incompetent or negligent.)
- Does your management receive any incentives/compensation based on human-resource development goals achieved? Ask your vice president of personnel to identify which managers are committed to what kind of human-resource development actions. Get his or her help in "opening doors."
- Write yourself a "business development plan" and find a way to present it at a senior staff meeting as a basis for requesting a "contract" to do a study or analysis within a given area or department.
- Design a survey. Survey at least 100 people at all levels. Ask them how they feel your function can best contribute to the organization.

A situational example—using internal resources

This is an actual situation.

A sales trainer joined an organization with approximately 100 retail account salespeople. Turnover ranged up to 20 percent annually; the cost in sales and impact on customers was significant. Related administrative costs were also high, and training new people was a constant, ongoing round of programs. It was constantly said, "We need a better training program." How should the sales trainer respond? By writing a better manual? Or by attempting to learn the underlying reasons for high turnover? Here, in brief, is the approach taken.

1. An entry strategy was designed (how to get invited to solve the problem).

- An invitation to a senior staff meeting was requested. The trainer asked for an opportunity to assess training program effectiveness *as well as* to research:
  - the type of individuals involved (were the right people hired?)
  - the kinds of problems field sales managers have
  - whether this is "normal" for the industry

  These are fairly neutral questions, generally producing positive responses. A three-month contract evolved; "Report back to us on . . . ."

2. The following interviews took place.
  - 20 *former* salespeople were asked about:
    - quality of training (what kind? how much?)
    - quality of field supervision
    - effectiveness of compensation and how it supported desired performance
    - job satisfaction
    - their experience, background, etc.
    - what turned them "off" or "on" in the job

  - 20 *currently* employed salespeople were asked:
    - the same questions

  - 12 regional and district sales managers were asked:
    - all the above questions
    - what demands were made on their time
    - what their background, skills, and experience were
    - what their specifications and procedures for selecting and hiring salespeople were

  - A general sales manager was asked:
    - all of the above questions

  - 20 distributor customers were asked to describe:
    - general sales strengths and weaknesses
    - in what areas the company could do more and less

  - Company personnel staff were asked:
    - their views on all of the above

- 3 employment agencies were asked:
  - if there was any consistency in screening selection
- General research included:
  - analysis of 60 terminations in terms of education, appraisal histories, age, marital status, industry experience, etc.
  - corresponding analysis of 20 "high performers"
  - study of the performance-appraisal system (did it support/report on desired results?)
  - study of sales-performance standards (what kind and how developed?)
- The following general questions were asked:
  - was there a formal marketing plan?
  - what was the salesperson's job and the direction of effort?
  - what did field managers expect of salespeople?
  - what did the company expect of salespeople?
  - what was the salesperson's view of the job?

Only through these resources could it be demonstrated that:

- Formal sales training was only *one* facet of the problem. Consistent company-wide policies and programs had to be implemented for:
  - standards of performance and job measurement
  - a more relevant and supportive compensation system
  - development of field-manager training skills, as well as the time to perform this role
  - a redefinition of the salesperson's job (when and where does the salesperson direct effort, how often?)
  - information sharing, performance reports, competitive data, etc.
  - new hiring specifications
  - revised field reporting systems
  - realistic workloads by type market, territory—as well as an improved "home-office" training program.

In summary, if you don't use internal resources first, here is what you risk:

- limited functional identity ("what do they do?")
- vulnerability in hard times
- the difference in being committed to *their* as opposed to *your* program
- less insight into your organization, how it operates, its problems, its people, and what makes it tick
- loss of an opportunity to influence the organization with relevant solutions to major problems and enhancing the growth and development of the internal training function
- curtailment of your own professional development; fencing yourself in
- a great loss of valuable time

USING OUTSIDE CONSULTANTS

There is a real place for them—but their use (or misuse) can be influenced by many things. Like an attending "consulting physician," consultants can play a valuable role to the organization when:

- there is a limited budget (or when there is plenty of money!)
- there is a limited staff expertise in specific disciplines
- sensitive situations exist, and a consultant can be seen as coming from a neutral corner
- an urgent problem demands an immediate solution

Just be sure your consultant has *demonstrated* analytical problem-solving expertise. And watch out for the character with a "bag of tricks!" The individual who sells ready-made programs rather than tailor-made solutions may well compound the difficulty. A good consultant can help out with any or all potential "trainer" roles and problems. Just be certain he or she is a creditable emissary who will reflect favorably on your department.

An occurrence which is sometimes a problem is when top management initiates unilateral action involving a consultant—and not you. We may not like it, but it has happened and must be recognized and accepted as a management prerogative. It may or may not be a reflection on the training department—what it can or can't do—and what it should or should not be involved in. You must decide:

- whether or not to *attempt* a union of resources;
- whether to let it be and develop priorities and projects elsewhere in the organization. Often this is the only realistic alternative!

EXTERNAL TRAINING RESOURCES

What kinds of external training resources are available to us? Where should we go for help? The following list (which, to be candid, only scratches the surface) gives some insight into the wealth of people, services, media, texts, and packages available to the sales trainer.

Kinds of available resources

- Software packages on most any subject from dozens of reliable sources.
- The Federal Government—the U.S. Government Printing Office will provide a catalog listing scores of available programs. The General Services Administration also publishes a catalog on U.S. Government films.
- College and university seminars and courses. Don't overlook the Division of Continuing Education at your local college or university.
- Industry associations—excellent sources frequently overlooked.
- Sales and Marketing Executives International (seminars, film guides, etc.).
- Federal, state and local agencies.
- Armed Forces—excellent programs on leadership, etc.
- Your company's suppliers. Find out what's available through their training departments.
- Correspondence programs.
- Business service organizations, such as the Bureau of National Affairs, the Conference Board, etc.
- The American Management Association.
- Commercial industry giants (for example, Dupont, Xerox, General Electric, 3M) frequently make some of their programs commercially available.
- Professional associations, such as the NSSTE, ASTD, etc.
- Consultants—specializing in a wide range of general and highly specific training and development specialties.

There is no shortage of available training resources; there is only a shortage of skill, expertise, and discretion in their use.

Thousands of medications available to physicians can be likened to the many training resources available to us. The physician, however, is a disciplined professional who, when confronted by a health problem:

- collects general and, then, highly specific data;
- weighs the data (what is happening versus what should be happening);
- *then* prescribes solution (his or her "program");
- then calls for a period of evaluation and feedback, and again retests "vital signs."

A physician's use of medication is carried out strategically, and deliberately. All too often, however, in human-resource development we are "program responsive"; that is, we write the prescription before we make the diagnosis. Consequently there is an incredible waste of resources, time, money, and opportunities.

Why are we "program responsive"?

Frequently there is a deficiency in analytical skills in dealing with the many intangibles of behavior. Another reason is lack of awareness of the many conditions within the organizational environment that influence performance behavior. Other reasons are:

- The pressure of time. Sometimes it is seemingly the best solution.
- Pressure from higher up. Frequently top management writes the prescription for you: "Send the salespeople to . . . ."
- The organization as a whole has a narrow perception of training. If an organization has always been "program responsive," it's the easiest pattern to perpetuate. After all, "What can be wrong with training?"
- We are frequently enchanted by our own program measurements— the kinds of measurements that ask the program participants how they "rate the program," or the "speaker's effectiveness," etc. These kinds of measurements tend to be "happiness indices," and not indicators of genuine performance/behavior change.
- Trainers (and management in general) are usually action-oriented. When we see something called a problem, we seek fast action, a

ready solution. The only problem is that human beings do not change as precisely, as positively, and as rapidly as we would like.

Analytical steps worth taking—before the "program"—and before deciding on the need for "external resources"

Any job (or performance) can be analyzed and described in terms of:

- essential *skills* needed to perform the task/job
- essential things about the product or service that must be *known*
- a comparison of the conditions that will actually exist after desirable performance (in relation to actual existing conditions)
- the controls, measurements, feedback, or incentive systems required to insure that desired performance actually happens
- tools, equipment, or resources that must be available so that the job can be performed

If any performance problem is dissected in this manner, frequently one finds that solutions are readily available *within* the organization. The automatic tendency to seek outside help should be avoided. A comprehensive program or seminar may or may not be the answer. Similarly, a packaged program of a general nature might not address your "missing links"—but, then again, it may!

Other considerations

- How many times do we send someone to a "program" because it seemingly offers a quick cure—and then leave the entire process of change up to the individual? This might be likened to sowing seeds without first cultivating the soil.
- Make certain your program is highly participative and that it incorporates mechanisms to involve participants intellectually if not physically.
- One tremendous benefit from an external program is that participants have the opportunity to practice new skills or behavior in a nonthreatening environment.

This is not an indictment of the quality of outside training resources, but rather a criticism of how they've been used—or misused. There are hundreds of valuable programs, films, management games, and software packages available. The right one only becomes truly meaningful when:

- Specific learning objectives (problems to solve) are known—and met.
- The training is directly related to the job.
- The new knowledge or skills learned can be realistically applied *on the job.*

There is, however, value in attending programs for the sake of general exposure to a subject. Such experiences create new insight, perspective, or scope to a particular job or function. Be certain, however, that program-attendance objectives are clear.

Attending an "outside" program may also provide other valuable experiences; namely, "talking shop" and exchanging experiences with others. Again, the opportunity to experiment with new concepts for behavior should not be overlooked.

The use of consultants

What are some characteristics of the ideal consultant? Your consultant should be:

- an objective analytical resource, highly skilled in asking questions and correlating and generating data;
- an individual from whom you can acquire new insights, skills, etc;
- one who generates trust, confidence, and respect within the organization;
- ethical and of high integrity;
- able to provide objectivity, experience, and perspective not now available within the organization;
- one who is expert in "training" but also has expertise in organization psychology, dynamics, systems, and structure—as well as having good business sense;
- one who can relate to all management levels avoiding trade jargon, buzz words, and behavioral terminology;
- one who has a proven track record (subject to confirmation by at least three other clients).

A consultant resource will only be as good as:

- your selection standards;
- the definition of the assignment parameters;
- your performance requirements and expectations and how well they are understood;
- any limitations imposed on him or her as to what can be done, where, and with whom.

Consultants *can* provide inestimable value to a "needing" organization when those in the organization really understand what they need and why.

SECTION II

PLANNING FOR TRAINING

CHAPTER 1

PLANNING THE DEPARTMENT'S
STAFF, SCOPE, AND STRUCTURE
JOHN A. FOLEY

John A. Foley is the Corporate Manager of Sales and Marketing Training for the Miller Brewing Company. Prior to joining Miller, he held similar positions with the ITT North America Telecommunications Group and the Continental Can Company. Mr. Foley graduated from Georgetown University. Following postgraduate work at Columbia and N.Y.U., he joined Continental as a salesman. After a variety of territory assignments in Los Angeles and Boston, he was appointed a Division Manager of Sales Training in 1968 and, the following year, Corporate Manager. His outside activities include contributions as a member of NSSTE, occasional articles in training magazines, and serving as a guest instructor for industrial seminars conducted by the Universities of Southern California and Wisconsin.

Being a sales trainer will provide you with more than a fair share of satisfaction—and frustration. To earn a living by devoting your efforts to the development of others offers multiple rewards. The variety of the work, the privileged lines of communication within the organization, the freedom from strong controls on your activities, even the travel to exotic places like Corinth, Mississippi, make the job desirable. To choose to make a living in this way also sets you somewhat apart: to have sought the job and been selected indicates your strong sense of idealism and conviction that there is one right way of doing things. This will be both your strength and your weakness. To survive for any length of time in sales training you will have to sacrifice some of the "right" for the "possible," but not so much that you become jaded or cynical about human nature. People have an image of a sales trainer as a knowledgeable person who will battle for a belief, gracefully settle for something less, and return to battle, and probably settle the next time; a person who is essentially an idealist, and sometimes a conscience. The mold is flexible, but it is a mold, and you are expected to grow into it.

The fitting process will probably begin when you are escorted to your new office. If it does not have a window, your first objective will be to get a window! Who, after all, is going to be influenced by someone without a window? Other mundane details such as office size, carpeting, secretarial help, the distance from the boss's office, and, in fact, just where your boss is in the hierarchy are clues to management's actual commitment to sales training. These clues do not always provide an accurate reflection of management's attitude, but they are worth keeping in mind.

These thoughts can be overwhelming if you ponder the desired end result, a complex mosaic of continuing programs for all levels of the sales force. You will be much more comfortable in this new position if you forget about creating one grandiose plan for leading the division out of the darkness. Management is not looking for salvation; they are looking for a little honest advantage. The best of training programs are perceived by management as providing what they want, not what someone else wants them to have. Understanding this is perhaps tempering to your ambitions, but also calming to your nerves. Furthermore, the best training programs do not hatch, they evolve in response to ever-changing needs. Therefore, as you begin, consider the virtues and benefits of thinking small, of planning ahead only so far as you have to, of compromise, of full retreat—of getting out of this high-risk endeavor altogether.

If you have not accepted this last option, your first task will be to plan an initial course of action. The businesslike procedure is to advise your boss of this decision and to agree on a tentative (for the first two years lead off everything with "tentative" or "proposed") date for presentation of your initial objectives and plans to achieve those objectives. This deadline should not be set haphazardly. Timing can be more important than content. This may seem an exaggeration, but in fact there is one long-time sales trainer who attributes his considerable success to timing and a total dedication to bar charts for management presentations. He claims that as the sense of sight is alerted by primary colors, the sense of hearing is dulled. (The same principle used in pickpocketing.) In any case, before making this commitment consider:

1. how much you know about the organization;
2. how well the organization knows you;

3. how sure you are of immediate training needs and of ways to satisfy those needs; and

4. how well you understand what the key functional manager wants.

How much do you know about the organization? If you have been around the division for a while it is tempting to think there is not much purpose in covering old ground. The danger of neglecting a new look at the old organization is that all previous information was received and filtered from a different angle. Your present working assumptions are based on a different and probably narrower perception of the operation. A restudy of the organization is really for the purpose of testing and adjusting these assumptions. For instance, a regional sales manager in a northeastern state knows that the ratio of package sales is 70 percent bottles, 30 percent cans. When forecasting sales for the next year in this region he can safely assume the ratio will remain about the same. If he relied on that same assumption to forecast national sales, his presentation would take on the proportions of a bad accident. Nationally, the ratio is approximately reversed.

A restudy requires careful listening to hear what you previously tuned out and careful reading to see what you previously skipped across. Get a copy of the five-year business plan. This is the statement of objectives and planned action by general management. It synthesizes the operating premises, problems, opportunities, strategies, and programs of all departments in the division. In this plan the separate statements by all departments will show a convergence on the main thrust of the business operation. Your sales-training plan must be keyed to the marketing department's statement of planned action. You will find it practically impossible to function if your plan does not demonstrate your understanding and desire to be in the mainstream. Certainly it is the job of the trainer to create change, but you don't have to get way out in front of the parade.

How well does the organization know you? Assuming you have been with the corporate family for some time, you are probably well-acquainted with some and have a nodding acquaintance with most. But when positions change relationships change. For example, as district manager you may have attended meetings at which you exchanged ideas with your contemporaries on the need for training. If so, there was probably mutual agreement on needs and solutions. However, it could prove very disillusioning if you assume this same group will express the same needs and solutions to you now as the sales trainer. You are no longer one of the group. You belong to another group, per-

haps antagonistic to your previous peers. If you try to cling to old relationships, you are likely to have the respect of neither. It's one of the
minor curses of upward mobility. Again, you should allow yourself
enough time to test your personal power base in this new role before
making a commitment to action.

How sure are you of immediate training needs and of ways to satisfy those needs? If you feel an urge to experience ritualistic suicide,
you might at the outset make an issue of the idea that a training program should begin at the top and proceed downward. Conceptually this
may be the "right" approach but from your present power base it will
sound pompous and needling. The next thing you will wonder is where
everybody went. The better initial strategy is the highly acceptable
"first-things-first" approach. The idea that every sales-training department should have a basic sales-training program is not very fancy, but
it does make some sense.

Unless you have received a direct order to the contrary, you should
propose to build your program from the foundation of basic sales
training. You will feel much more comfortable on this familiar ground,
and will be able to do something that is visible to management more
quickly. This is important. Don't take seriously the friendly advice about
taking your time, getting comfortable, or being in no big hurry. Aside
from the conducting of seminars, what sales trainers do is something of
a mystery to most people in the organization. They become nervous
when a lot of time elapses without a training session they can see and
hear.

The shape of a basic sales-training program can vary greatly depending on many factors, such as the size of the sales force, the product, the market, whether the company and industry are expanding or
losing market share, previous training, facilities, and budget. The proper
shape for one program might be a two-week seminar in which many
managers participate as instructors; or the same two weeks might be
devoted to heavy role playing of presentation skills. Another might require that the trainer travel in the field for several weeks with trainees.
These are visible activities. But if, for instance, the proper way to satisfy the immediate need is the arduous task of developing a series of
manuals which will require months of work, you should probably plan
to do something of a stop-gap nature during the development period to
gain some exposure.

Proper timing will not often coincide with an understanding of immediate needs and ways to satisfy those needs. When the time for action arrives, you should do something even if you feel it is less than

right. Sales trainers are forever fixing, patching, and looking for the lost, perfect chord.

How long does the key functional manager think it should take to implement a course of action? As a matter of fact, you should be deeply interested in this person's ideas and attitudes on just about everything. The key functional manager for the sales trainer is usually the division marketing manager or division manager of sales, depending on specific delegation of responsibilities and the personal power structures within the division. Whatever the title and whether or not you report on a direct line, this is the person you most want to be in accord with in the initial phase of training development—and beyond.

From the beginning, you should cultivate a candid, harmonious relationship with the key decision maker. This may require considerable persistence and tact on your part. Being action-oriented, this person gravitates toward what's happening now. At this point, sales training is just an idea and therefore not very high on the list of priorities. It is well worth the effort to secure your ground. This manager probably knows all the people and most of the skeletons, has accurate insights to individual strengths and weaknesses, and has earned more respect than anyone else among the sales force. In addition to considerable managerial clout, this manager enjoys the privilege of leadership. The key manager must feel you are a reliable and valuable assistant. With this person as an ally, things will not only get done, they will get done with enthusiasm.

The key functional manager probably rose to this preeminent position in large part because of an impeccable sense of timing. You should hitch on to this finely tuned instinct. More than by words communicated, you will know you are getting in step when your contacts become more comfortable and your discussions more free-flowing. Any actual training activities on your part prior to establishment of this relationship should have a built-in capability for self-destructing.

When you have settled the matter of timing for the presentation of your plan, you will want to conduct a needs analysis. Consider for a moment before xeroxing an old dog-eared survey form and ordering a string of airplane tickets. The plan should be developed something like a legal brief. Whatever position you take will have to be supported by evidence. The document should be heavy with relevant and, if possible, quantifiable facts that will lead, without stilted rationalizations, to a natural conclusion. Facts are something that you can see or hear. Regardless of whether you decide to use a survey form or some other probing technique for your analysis, the questions you ask should be designed as a control against cluttering up your plan with the irrelevant and unsupportable.

Begin the creation of a fact-gathering design by asking yourself a very basic question, "Is this department being developed strictly to train new hires?" This is possible, but not probable. After all, new hires were somehow learning to do the job before you came on the scene. This is not to say the training of new hires is not important, only that management was motivated to act because they perceived or anticipated unacceptable performance problems at other levels in the sales force.

The first step in a needs analysis is to find out why management is feeling uneasy. What you are pursuing here are standards of performance. You want to develop a list of criteria for each level of responsibility which the key functional manager will accept as satisfactory performance. To accomplish this first step you might think it would be enough to collect all the job descriptions and arrange for an interview to review them with the key person. It is not quite that easy.

Developing a set of standards is a never-ending labor. Establishing your initial objectives is only the beginning of the process; but it is the right place to start. Job descriptions usually are broad statements of responsibilities, and as such they are not adequate for appraising an individual's performance. Appraisals deal with results. Standards are statements of desired results. For example, one item in a job description might say, in essence, ". . . provide satisfactory coverage in X territory." What does "satisfactory coverage" mean? One manager might say, ". . . call on five prospects per day and make two complete presentations per week." This is one person's desired end result. Another sales manager in the same division and in a roughly similar situation might say, ". . . be able to show me complete fact sheets on every prospect and account in the territory."

The diversity of desired end results, or standards, is the reason why it is not enough to interview only the key functional manager. Although you do want to limit the decision making with regard to your plan to as few people as possible, preferably to this one person, in establishing your standards you should acquire a quantity of information that forms a consensus of the feelings and attitudes across all levels of the sales force. Your role is to be the key functional manager's eyes and ears, not vice versa.

At the same time you are developing evidence of division standards of performance for each job level, you should be probing, observing, and recording existing performance. Again, limit your analysis to the facts. One structure you might use would be to draw four columns on a piece of paper and write in the headings, (1) Responsibility,

(2) Desired Performances (End Results), (3) Observed Performances, (4) Analysis of Training Needs (Discrepancy, quantified if possible, between item 2 and item 3). Under Responsibility write in the first responsibility listed in the job description. Use a separate page for each responsibility. Considering the number of responsibilities enumerated in all the sales-force job descriptions for your division, you may think this approach is going to squander a lot of paper. You have not heard the half of it, for it would probably be best to use a separate set of forms for each interview.

Let's consider an example. Assume one level of performance to be analyzed is that of regional sales manager. The immediate superior for this level of sales management is the regional manager. To determine a general set of performance standards for regional sales managers you arrange for interviews with five regional managers. At each of these interviews you would ask the regional manager to consider one by one each responsibility listed in the job description for a regional sales manager and to tell you exactly what is expected from subordinates having that responsibility. On an average, there should be four or five end results listed for each responsibility.

You can expect considerable resistance to this unfamiliar line of thinking, but with fortitude and about five interviews on the same level you should have a fair list of desired end results. With this list as a basis of comparison, you then schedule a series of "work withs" (visits to observe and learn how a manager functions) with five regional sales managers. Do not attempt to guide their actions for the purpose of matching actual performance against desired performance. Simply record the actions you see and hear in the third column. Record observations editorially; who, what, where, when, and how ("why" is not pertinent). You now will have information with which to describe a performance discrepancy.

Your first analysis of desired versus actual performance can lead down many blind paths that will need rechecking. An expressed desired end result may appear to have no relationship to what actually happens, or some items of actual performance may not appear in the list of desired performances. Check out and resolve apparent contradictions. Compare and codify all your notes for this one position into one list. Strive to quantify. The last step in this analysis of needs is to sort out those discrepancies for which a lack of training seems to be a problem from those for which some other management solution would appear to be more appropriate.

With this type of analysis, continued for as long as proper timing will allow, you should obtain a fair initial grasp of the training needs for this position. Concurrent with this analysis you would, of course, be conducting similar analyses of needs for all other levels of the sales force.

To satisfy determined training needs you must devise ways to close the gaps that appear between desired and actual performance. The gaps provide you with an agenda of training subjects for each level, or for selected individuals on each level. Any training subject that does not pertain to a discrepancy exposed by your analysis is superfluous filler in your initial statement of objectives and course of action. You may, for instance, attend a lecture on motivation and think the information you hear is the greatest discovery since the seven-ounce bottle, but if it does not attack a specific need, you are better off filing it for future reference. Of course you have more leeway with "shotgun" subjects when creating agendas for basic sales training or basic sales-management training than you do with "advanced" or "experienced" levels of training, where specific performance problems must be addressed. Even so, evaluations by participants in "basic" programs and seminars prove time and again that unnecessary information is quickly discerned and definitely unappreciated.

With knowledge of specific discrepancies (needs) and specific subjects to improve performance in areas of discrepancy (training objective), you are ready to consider how you are going to do it (course of action). The way you propose to solve each problem will be determined by the scope of each problem. Your initial proposal for structuring and staffing your department will be determined by the scope of those problems you intend to handle initially.

SCOPE

What is the cumulative impact of your analysis of needs? How many people need some form of training? How much? How quickly? How often? Which discrepancies are most severe? Which have the greatest impact on contribution to profit? For which are you qualified to be the trainer? For which do you need outside material and/or instructor assistance? Should the training be conducted in the field or at the divisional offices? Such speculative questions are endless. The key question probably is whether the scope is such that you should consider it your primary function to be an administrator or a stand-up trainer. All other decisions regarding structure and staffing will stem from this decision.

In your statement of objectives you should demonstrate awareness of the complete scope of needs but try to limit the scope of your proposed initial action to training that you can do. Again, you want to make a visible impact in a relatively short period of time, and you want to do it without including a towering budget request. Your long-range training program, not to say your survival, will rest on your ability, now or in the not distant future, to obtain a separate sales-training budget. You have a much better chance of achieving this important objective if your initial request for funds is modest while your regard for your own ability as a trainer is immodest.

If the scope of sales training extends beyond the division sales force (for instance, to distributors or retailers), you will have an extensive building program. You should then, by all means, plan to build outwards and upwards. Control the situation by showing a logical development. Start with a program for the immediate sales force working upward from basic sales training.

When the critical levels of this program are firmly established, move outward to distributor training, again moving from sales to sales-management levels. Repeat the process at retail level if necessary. Maintain control. Use outside resources for assistance and learn to do what they are doing or can do for you before adding to your training staff. Adjust your primary function from trainer to administrator reluctantly. Enjoy watching yourself and your budget grow gracefully.

STRUCTURE

If you have done as suggested up to this point, the initial structure of your training department will be a description of your secretary. But, assuming you have opted for an empire, the structure you devise should evolve naturally from the increasing scope of your training activities. The process, however, should be reversed. As scope moves outward and upward, structure should move inward and downward. Consider downward. What would be the fun in structuring if the structure did not expand downward from your position? By inward it is meant that with each addition to the staff the responsibilities of a position in the structure are split so that the structure proceeds downward from generalist to specialist. Furthermore, as the structure expands the need for centralized coordination, communication, and control increases.

The more training that is going on, the greater the potential for duplication and contradiction. Training should strive for uniformity of language and thinking processes to improve communication across the organization. For this, centralized control of training is a constant necessity—whatever the scope.

Training departments themselves can become ludicrous examples of communication breakdown. Some training specialists need translators to speak to other training specialists. The structure, therefore, should be built to group specialists by specialty rather than by geographic location, or training "teams," or classification of training.

The ultimate structure of your sales-training department will not necessarily relate directly to the size of your division. Some factors which should influence your structuring plan are: (1) the nature of your business and the markets you serve, (2) the number of division sales locations and number of salespeople at each location, (3) the degree of complexity of product knowledge, (4) the education and experience level of your sales force, (5) the attitude of your organization toward training, and (6) most important, the design should reinforce the policies and procedures you establish for effective administration and control of the department. You might benefit from the experience of others by researching the structures in other organizations with situations similar to your own.

STAFFING

At the same time that you are preparing an initial course of action, you should be preparing your own position description. This document should clearly delineate the functions and activities for which you are responsible. When approved by your immediate superior and the key functional manager, this position description serves not only as your ticket to assume a place in various organizational activities and to initiate your own activities but, perhaps more important, it prevents your being imposed upon to perform miscellaneous marketing tasks.

You want to avoid becoming the marketing department "go-fer." The rationale for creating initial training-staff positions should stem from your initial position description. Proper delegation of responsibility dictates that staff-position descriptions branch from one or more of the functions and activities described in your own position description. It would show good form, therefore, to write out a position description, complete with duties, knowledge, and skills to be applied, normal qualifications, and accountabilities for whatever training-staff position you contemplate. The basic justification for any staff position is either that you cannot perform the needed function or activity or that you do not have the time to perform it.

As mentioned earlier, if the need is not urgent, try to delay training you cannot personally accomplish. Establish a foundation with which you feel comfortable. If the need is urgent, first investigate the possibility of getting yourself prepared to perform the task. If this is not feasible, consider employing an outside training resource. Search the division's management for subject specialists to be part-time trainers. Weigh the expense of all possible options against hiring a full-time staff member. Count the actual number of hours per week of work you would have for an addition to the department. Unless you can come close to 40 hours, some other alternative would probably be more economical. From management's point of view a more understandable reason for you to want to create a staff initially is that you do not have sufficient time to do the job alone.

The first criterion in selection of a staff member is that the person will be able to perform a major function or activity immediately. The nature of the immediate task will probably determine whether your best prospects for the position are within the division or outside.

For example, if the immediate need is the development of manuals containing specialized divisional information, your best prospects are probably within the company. If the immediate need is for an experienced instructor, you will probably find your best prospect outside. Whatever the need for which you are recruiting, you should make an effort to select from within the organization first. Many positions in an organization are pass-through slots for fast-track individuals. The sales-training department can gain considerable influence by creating one or more of these desirable slots.

Your initial staff should have the capability to interchange functions and activities and the readiness to accept any task, be it collating, running audiovisual equipment, instructing, or hosting a reception for the president. Prospects should have the potential to be creative and aggressive in the performance of a myriad of demanding or unfamiliar tasks. A few such individuals can eliminate the need for many specialists.

Every staff member, including specialists, should clearly perceive that you expect them to grow and, with personal development, to move up in the department or elsewhere in the organization. The training department should be recognized as the advocate and best example of growth and development. You cannot afford stagnation, much less the label of retirement home for organizational retainers.

Ready or not, the time will arrive to present your sales-training plan to management. A certain style of presentation that top management feels most comfortable with has probably developed in your division. Find out what this style is and use it. Utilize any advantage you can find. You are selling your plan and will be expected to demonstrate your capacity to sell. The first rule of selling is to sell results. The rule is no less applicable in this situation. Whatever the format, the emphasis in your statement should be on quantifiable results in areas of great-est profit potential.

Begin the presentation of your plan at the lowest level of sales-force training needs, probably basic sales training. State the problem, the causes, several possible solutions, the solution you have decided to implement, your plan of action, and the means by which management will be able to evaluate your progress toward implementation and the effectiveness of your solution. Invite probing of your plan. Determine to gain acceptance and approval to proceed with this part of your plan before proceeding to the next part. Remember, the more people in-volved in the decision making, the more difficult it is to get a clear-cut decision. Don't complicate the process by trying for a blanket approval of the plan. Expect to negotiate. Be firm with those parts that will uti-lize your personal strengths. Calculate which parts are dispensable and which parts, if lost, would undermine the initial training effort.

Management always probes to uncover potential profit versus risk of expenditures. Money is only one kind of expenditure. Consider these types of management probes, and be ready with the answers:

What? Is this an idea that fits within the business objectives, stra-tegic plans, and physical limitations of this organization?

Who? Who would be involved and what are the implications, if any, with regard to personal power structure or structures?

Why? Does it promise to add value in terms of a quantifiable profit?

How much? What are the total cost and the time/cost effectiveness of recommendation?

What else? What other options have been considered that can be used as a basis for comparison with this idea?

What next? Is there a look into the future to anticipate the conse-quences in terms of the worst and best that can happen? If the worst should occur, how fast can we pull out? If the best should occur, how can we obtain the maximum ad-vantage?

You should expect management approval to proceed with at least the key elements of your plan. You should not expect total commit-ment. Planning is an introverted exercise. On paper, you have demon-strated that sales training might contribute to the achievement of the division's goals. To implement your plan successfully, you will have to deal with people successfully. Just as every new position on your staff separates responsibility from another existing position, so new departments are perceived as threats to the jurisdictions and budgets of existing departments. Who in your division is going to feel this kind of pressure? You must seek out these people and turn aside their protective predisposition to thwart your efforts. Convince them that you desire your activities to contribute to the achievement of their personal goals. Freely involve other people in your initial successes. Protect them from your failures. This consideration will be returned in good time.

CHAPTER 2

SELECTING THE TRAINING DEPARTMENT STAFF

FRANK G. MITCHELL

Frank G. Mitchell, as Education and Training Manager of the Marketing Division of Cessna Aircraft Company in Wichita, Kansas, is responsible for all sales, product, franchise, and management development programs. He joined Cessna in 1964 as an educational specialist and is currently active in the Aviation/Space Writers Association, the American Society for Training and Development, and NSSTE.

Before you hire your first staff member, it's important that you spend some time analyzing the structure of your new sales-training department. An easy and practical way to do this is to write a job description for each of the positions on your miniature organization chart.

Assuming that you're working within a limited budget, you will probably start small and grow. The organization chart and job descriptions will help you define what kind of people you need in the beginning. Just as important, they will force you to think of how you want the department to develop in the future and how the duties of your people will change with growth. If you know what your goals are, you will know how to start.

If you're not experienced in writing job descriptions, the personnel department can help you. As a matter of fact, you should work closely with personnel. The more completely they understand your specific needs, the more valuable their assistance can be. Since they screen all applications, they can help you get exactly the right combination of talent and experience.

In the new department one individual might fill several job functions. While the number of people might increase, the basic functions won't change very much. So start with your functions, distribute them among the number of people your budget allows, and write the job descriptions so they accurately describe reasonable expectations.

The basic training structure includes a manager of training, so put your own name in that slot. Then (if you are more than a solo operation) consider administrators, training supervisors, trainers, writers, program developers, and clerical/secretarial help. Some departments even include artists, photographers, and all sorts of technical people who produce training materials. For our purposes, let us assume that actual production will not be a function of your department.

The most difficult jobs to fill will be those requiring skills that are unique to your department. Who is a trainer? Where do you find one? How do you recognize a trainer when you see one? Should your trainers do program development and writing? Do speaking ability and writing ability necessarily go together? These are questions that plague every training manager.

Obviously, the people involved in training, development, and writing will have some unusual talents. They must be able to research material, adapt the material to modern training methods, organize a lesson plan, work with your client departments in developing objectives, and develop methods of measuring results to see whether the objectives are being met in the training sessions. Then, of course, the trainer must have the ability to make an organized, interesting presentation, handle questions, and manage the discussions to keep the program on schedule and on track. If a trainer does not have the necessary conference leadership skills at the start, then he or she must soon develop them.

There is a perpetual debate within training circles about whether it is better to train experienced people from within your own company or to hire people with the potential to become professional trainers and train them in your company products and policies. You'll probably have to do both.

You'll probably look inside your own company first. An outstanding salesperson who is nearing retirement or tired of traveling (and is flexible and open-minded) may find a new challenge in sharing his or her experience as a trainer. Or a bright young salesperson who has been successful in the field, but who really wants to move up, might jump at the opportunity to become a sales trainer.

Elsewhere in your company you may find a technical or service rep who has product knowledge, plus the ability to make a coherent, uncluttered presentation. Just keep in mind that many service and sales people are great in the field, but wholly undisciplined in their approach to training. The mechanic who can't see beyond the nuts and bolts or the salesperson who operates on gut instinct, anecdotes, and endless "war stories" (in which he or she is the hero), just won't succeed in training.

Outside your company there are three or four prime sources for people. For professional trainers you can look to organizations such as the National Society of Sales Training Executives and the American Society for Training and Development; training departments in other companies; and teachers in the education system, particularly at the high school and vocational school level. The professionals will be looking for challenge and satisfaction, as well as money. You'll have the most success with those who have a personal interest in your industry.

The young person with potential as a trainer can often be found in the graduating class of a university that offers courses in your field. He or she may have a good educational background, speaking ability, and perhaps some courses in your type of business. In some cases, high school and vocational-technical school graduates also have the potential to become trainers. To narrow down the area of search, start with the colleges that offer courses in your industry. This can form the basis for a recruiting list. Your personnel department can assist you with newspaper advertising in cities where there are concentrations of employees in your industry. You might also ask the personnel department to advertise in the training publications and other trade publications to attract the professionals in training.

The other department heads in your company may not welcome the idea, but departments that will use your training services are a good place to look for secretarial and clerical help. Along with experience in handling administrative detail and the usual secretarial skills, these people will bring to your training staff some understanding of the way your client departments operate. Staff assistants and secretaries in training departments are extremely important to smooth operation. The ability to organize work and have information available for instant recall is a prime requisite. If your department is small, you need a versatile professional who is able to do 50 things at once without getting flustered.

You'll spend the rest of your career determining the best way to find training personnel; and experience will show you that successful trainers have some common characteristics. The successful sales trainer is versatile, flexible, and sensitive to human concerns and needs. He or she will have the ability to relate to many different kinds of people inside and outside your company. The best of them are frequently described as "caring" people. Most of all, the good trainer is willing to accept a challenge that often is vague and undefined, certainly un-solved; and will develop solutions that meet your training objectives and support the operating departments of your company.

If you have decided to seek a trainer from the field sales force, you will have to secure recommendations from district and regional sales managers (unless your company already has an efficient system for early identification of salespersons who are qualified to be considered for promotion). In addition to a job description, field sales managers will be better able to help you if they have been provided with a "pro-file" of the qualities generally found in an effective sales trainer.

Once you have narrowed down the list, consider spending a day or two in the field with each candidate. How they deal with and relate to their customers will give you considerable insight as to how well they are likely to get along with (and be concerned about) sales trainees. If they do not have the capacity to earn the respect of trainees, a pro-motion to sales training could be a disaster.

Some companies postpone relocation of a new sales trainer until the completion of a three-month trial period. At the end of that time, it is readily apparent whether the move is appropriate. A probationary period also enables a new trainer to determine whether the job is one he or she really wants. The Personnel department can be of help to you in developing a trial program policy if applicable for your organization.

The characteristic ability to think in an organized way allows the trainer to gather, sift, and present quantities of material in a concise, memorable manner. It is a demanding job that requires a high level of initiative and creativity.

If the job is demanding, so is the good trainer. It's up to you to pro-vide a continuing challenge and an opportunity for growth.

CHAPTER 3

ADMINISTRATIVE ASPECTS OF
SALES TRAINING
CHARLES M. FIELD

Charles M. Field is Director of Sales Training for the Sterling Precision Corporation of West Palm Beach, Florida.

Prior to joining Sterling, Mr. Field held the position of Corporate Manager, Manpower Planning and Development for Levitz Furniture in Miami, Florida. Mr. Field has also been training executives at AMP Special Industries, the Oscar Mayer Company, and the Ford Motor Company. His present assignment includes responsibility for training and development throughout the Corporation.

Mr. Field received his B.S. degree from the College of William and Mary and completed his graduate work at Old Dominion University. He is a member of NSSTE and past Chairman of its Philadelphia Chapter. He has been a frequent speaker for sales and marketing organizations in numerous cities, as well as sales training clinics conducted by NSSTE and the University of Wisconsin.

If you recently assumed responsibility for sales training, by now you are probably more confused and less certain of your new duties than you were when you first accepted the challenge. That's a typical experience. The objective of this chapter is to sharpen your knowledge of the administrative side of sales training, provide some practical suggestions to make the job easier, and recommend guidelines which will allow the department to make a greater contribution to the organization.

VITAL—NOT EXOTIC

Administration of sales training is certainly not an exotic subject that sales-training managers want to discuss. In fact, most would rather leave the "paper-work" to someone else, so that they can be more involved with the actual running of programs, with being "up front." Nevertheless, you should appreciate that the administrative aspects of training are critical and vital, and you dare not overlook them in favor of "something else." The primary concern of most of us should not be running programs or giving presentations, but increasing the training department's total contribution to the success of the company.

USING ADMINISTRATIVE SKILL

To accomplish your objectives, you will be applying the skill of an administrator, not only in planning programs, but in recruiting, selection, development of budgets, controlling costs, establishing objectives, measuring results, and staff relationships. Your administrative responsibilities will take on increased importance and weigh heavily in the success of you, your department, and the company.

JOB DESCRIPTION

One of your first administrative tasks should be to write yourself a job description, if one is not already available. Writing your own description is worthwhile since it clarifies for you, your boss, and others general responsibilities and accountability. It also answers the question "What do you do?" One format you may find helpful is as follows:

Date _____

Position Description
Manager, Training

   I. *Broad Function:*
Responsible for the development, administration, and coordination of the company's sales and sales-management training and development programs.

   II. *Reporting Relationship:*
Reports to Vice President of Sales. Responsible for communicating corporate sales and sales-management activities and results accomplished.

   III. *Duties and Responsibilities:*
- To assist sales management in identifying training needs.
- To identify management problems to determine which are created in whole or in part in the sales sector and which of these can be remedied by sales-training efforts.
- To develop (or obtain) programs to meet the needs above.
- To organize, coordinate, and schedule the training.

- To determine who shall conduct the training, and to provide such personnel with what guidance is necessary.
- To evaluate the training and report results to operating management.
- To determine need for follow-up to insure continuing results; and to plan, organize, conduct, and administer such training.
- To coordinate with other personnel-development activities.
- To develop such long-range sales-management training programs as may be necessary to aid operating managers in developing and maintaining an effective work force.
- To coordinate and utilize the training facilities within the organization and to procure services of outside consulting services where available, necessary, and appropriate.
- To maintain an adequate system of records and progress reports.
- To submit an annual budget for approval. The budget is to contain an explanation of the need for each training program and the operating problem(s) it seeks to avoid or eliminate.

IV. *Relationships:*

Because of the staff functions of this position, there are ongoing relationships with all staff departments and the field organization.

V. *Education, Experience, and Knowledge Required:*

(Fill this section in to meet your requirements and protect your job.)

VI. *Acceptabilities:*

The primary measures of the Manager, Sales Trainee are:

1. The adequacy with which the total sales and sales-management training development is administered.
2. The degree to which the sales and sales-management expenses are controlled, kept under budget, and utilized.
3. The quality and timeliness of decisions and actions regarding all responsibilities of the position, including the quality and timeliness of his or her recommendations.
4. The quality of his or her leadership in developing and executing sales-training and sales-management programs.
5. The extent to which he or she achieves and exceeds results are measured against objectives.

This position description is intended only as a guide to assist in the preparation of your own document, and not a finished product. It will also be helpful to members of the department's staff when they are asked to prepare their own job descriptions.

GUIDELINES FOR STAFF EFFECTIVENESS

One thing which has been very helpful to me in managing a staff is to prepare a manual I call "Guidelines for Staff Effectiveness." The guidelines cover:

- Programming
- Administration
- Self-development
- Instruction
- Services
- Evaluation
- Contributions

This guideline is, in essence, a Management by Objectives document. All of us are uncertain and unsure of ourselves when we undertake a new responsibility. "Guidelines for Staff Effectiveness," established with your boss, eliminates questions as to standards of performance and what is expected, not only for yourself but for others as well. William Stillwell, Management Institute, University of Wisconsin shared this idea with me some years ago and it has been very useful.

PROPOSAL WRITING FOR TRAINING AND DEVELOPMENT

A question frequently asked is, "How do you sell your programs to management?" NSSTE member James Hageman, of the Dr. Pepper Company, Dallas, Texas, has written an excellent editorial entitled "Proposal Writing for Training and Development Requirements." This approach has been extremely successful for Mr. Hageman, as his proposals have gained approval and support for almost 90 percent of all requests submitted. His format is as follows:

- *Cover memorandum*
  - Summarizes the major benefit
  - Creates interest about how benefits can be obtained
  - Introduces the program concept
- *Program objectives*
  - Lists the objectives of the program
  - Makes the objectives supportive of company objectives
- *Program benefits*
  - Itemizes the benefits of the program
  - Outlines what management will receive for the investment

- *Current situation*
  - Lists all elements that prompted the program request
  - Reviews procedures used to analyze elements
  - Places estimated or real cost factors on each element
  - Indicates the total cost of present situation
- *Proposed program*
  - Lists all elements of the proposed program
  - Lists elements in direct relation to current situation
  - Places cost factors on each element of the proposed program
  - Indicates the total cost of proposed program
- *Summary and recommendation*
  - Summarizes the benefits of the requested program
  - Emphasizes return of assets managed
  - Lists recommendations for affirmative action

DIVIDING THE WORKLOAD

When the time finally comes to go to work, how do we divide the work-load when there is staff—or if we are working alone. The objective of every training department is first of all simply to survive, and then to make as large a contribution to the bottom line as possible. Not only do the efforts of the training department need to be worthwhile, but the results need to be visible so that the organization begins to utilize the training department appropriately, and to appreciate it.

Assigning priorities to training

Whether the work is to be performed by your staff or yourself, there is one fundamental principle that applies in each instance to dividing the workload. The principle is to develop a set of priorities for the work-load which is fully understood by your staff, your boss, and those requesting the work. That seems elementary; yet, it's not easy.

Priorities should be based upon contributions to the organization. The contributions should be, where possible, measured in terms of economic return to the company—profits. All too often we find ourselves doing things simply because we enjoy the task, or because it is easy for us to accomplish, or because someone asked us to do it. A system of establishing priorities will overcome this tendency and allow us to carry out tasks which make a really worthwhile contribution. Setting priorities can be performed by developing a formula which takes into consideration different variables or by a numerical weighting system [for example: a scale from (1) low priority to (10) high priority]. The question of how to divide the workload among your staff cannot be answered so easily. You should consider:

1. areas of competence, interest, or background;
2. position description or designation (sales, sales management, product, etc.);
3. availability of the individual; and
4. present status of workload of staff.

REQUESTS FOR TRAINING

Many trainers have found it helpful to have a form printed entitled "Request for Training." This form contains the request, the problem or situation which warranted the training, what the training solution will contribute to the organization, and the costs involved. The form also makes it easy to refer to the file number for an updated progress report. The file number can be easily tracked using a six-digit number, for example:

> 0 9 / 1 2 3 / 5
> mo. file no. yr.

Each request is numbered consecutively.

File no.————————————

Date————————————

FROM: ————————————

TO: Manager, Sales Training

SUBJECT: REQUEST FOR TRAINING

Training objectives: (end result desired)_____

_____

_____

Why? (need/problem/situation)_____

_____

_____

What will it do for the company? (benefits)_____

_____

_____

Costs:_____

....

Date_____

TO: _____

FROM: Manager, Sales Training _____

SUBJECT: Your training request for _____

has been considered and _____

_____
(Name)
Manager, Sales Training

Progress wall chart

Another way of handling program requests is to have a wall chart prepared which lists every one of them and traces the progress of the approved requests.

Training schedule wall chart

One of the most practical charts is a wall chart which covers all programs scheduled for the coming year, or a time frame which is most meaningful to you. For example, see Fig. 1.

SALES-TRAINING BROCHURE

After you have determined your needs, established priorities, developed programs, and arranged schedules, you may want to publish a

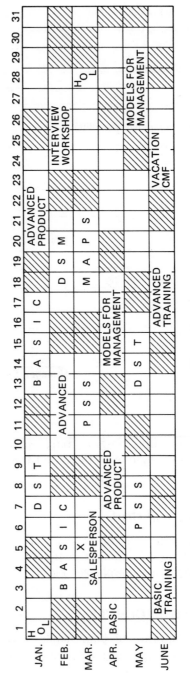

Figure 1

Table 1.
SALES AND MANAGEMENT PROGRAMS

PROFESSIONAL SELLING SKILLS	DIMENSIONAL SALES-MANAGEMENT TRAINING
Purpose: To teach salesperson how to probe, open, close, handle objections, use FAB, proof and support, statements.	*Purpose:* To improve interpersonal sales/management skills through sell-awareness and self-development.
Eligibility: Any salesperson, sales correspondent.	*Eligibility:* DST—Any salesperson with six months or more experience. DSM—Sales and Marketing Managers.
Description: PSS is a three-day program using programmed learning, audio cassettes, and role plays. It focuses on "how" to use the basic skills necessary for professional salespeople.	*Description:* DST/DSM—a 4½-day highly participative seminar that is based upon a behavioral model which emphasizes the development of self-awareness in sales/management situations and of persuasive communications and motivation skills for participants.
EXCEPTIONAL SALESPERSON/MANAGER	MODELS FOR MANAGEMENT
Purpose: To improve sales performance of participants by developing plans for increased sales through analysis of specific job objectives, activities, and accounts.	*Purpose:* To achieve a broad understanding of behavioral science which can be applied toward improving managerial effectiveness.
Eligibility: Any salesperson with six months or more experience. All managers.	*Eligibility:* All managers—line and staff.
Description: This highly participative three-day seminar focuses on the participants' analysis of specific job objectives, their activities, accounts, and territories. All of this is done to improve sales and management performance on the job.	*Description:* Highly participative 3½-day workshop which uses case studies, group problem solving, lectures, and feedback devices to improve management performance by creating awareness.

brochure which outlines the programs your department offers, and to whom. This brochure can also be used for recruiting purposes for yourself and your managers. (See Table 1.)

TRAINING AND DEVELOPMENT POLICIES

You may find it beneficial to develop a written training policy and philosophy, if one does not now exist. The policy is useful to guide your department's efforts to resolve questions regarding training, and to give wide exposure to the department's activities and contributions. Here is one example:

TRAINING—X-COMPANY

The Company provides training and development opportunities for all of its employees for the purpose of increasing its sales opportunities. The Company seeks to improve and perpetuate its human resources by recruiting personnel with above-average potential, and encourages them and others to develop themselves through practical self-development. The development and continuous growth of all employees is essential to the success of this Company.

It is Company policy that all managers are held directly responsible for the development of their subordinates. In the evaluation of each manager's performance, training and development responsibilities are every bit as important as production, sales, and costs. Organized training will be made available when it:

1. insures the efficiency of the organization,
2. is approved by the Company,
3. meets specific Company objectives,
4. is economically feasible, and
5. is consistent with Company policies and procedures.

TRAINING RECORDS

Many trainers keep a complete file of training records by program of enrollees, costs, etc. Another suggestion is to have a record of training and development included in each person's personnel folder. This record can be updated periodically as the representative attends additional programs.

These reports will help you recap costs and enrollees, as well as provide a roster for past program evaluations.

Name	C. Jones				
Location	Louisville				

Date	Present position	Program/ course	Completion Yes / No		Comments
8/74	Br. Mgr.	Legal aspects of interviewing	Yes		Satisfactory completion

RELATIONSHIPS WITH LINE AND STAFF DEPARTMENTS

The extent of your success in training and develoment depends upon a multitude of variables, all of which are vital to your performance and that of your department. Perhaps the greatest impact and influence on your success will be the effectiveness of your relationship with other line and staff departments. As a staff department, you are highly dependent upon the support received from others. No department is an island to itself, especially the training department. It is also true that it is relatively easy to isolate a training activity and end up without funds or support.

Approval and support for training activities will develop as other internal departments become involved and see firsthand the benefits of training. Your job as the "internal consultant" is to assist them in the attainment of their goals and objectives. Achievement here inevitably provides you with their necessary approval and support.

TRAINING COMMITTEE

One way to insure that training and development are "up front" and universally viewed as a valuable part of organization is to have a training committee. This committee should be composed of individuals from personnel, marketing, accounting, training, product development, quality control, general sales management, field sales management, advertising, legal (if applicable) plus at least one representative from the field sales force. Objectives of this committee are:

- Recognition that training and development is a *company* concern
- Identification of training and development situations
- Establishing priorities among training needs
- Securing of training funds
- Supporting the training function
- Acting as review board for new training materials

SUMMARY

Today's manager of sales training must be more than a motivational speaker or expert in training methodology. The individual must also possess effective administrative skills. Primary consideration must be given not merely to running programs, but also to how those programs contribute to the company's overall progress and effectiveness. Appropriate and realistic administrative policies and reports are essential to the accomplishment of the objectives of the company and the department. It is not exciting or glamorous, but it is essential. Success will depend upon a multitude of variables; line-staff relationships, accomplishment of objectives, contribution to the organization, and the sales trainer's administrative ability. You'll hit a home run if you cover all four!

CHAPTER 4

PUTTING TOGETHER YOUR
FIRST BUDGET

JACK M. HENDERSON

Jack M. Henderson, Manager, Sales Training, the Goodyear Tire & Rubber Company, began his career in the tire and rubber industry in 1937, in Canada. After 13 years in sales, he was named in 1950 to oversee a newly created Goodyear Sales Training Department in Los Angeles. Eight years later, he was named Manager of Sales Training in Akron. In this capacity he is responsible for the sales-training operations of all Goodyear product divisions, which include three Akron facilities and fifteen training centers in strategic locations throughout the country.

For the new trainer there is nothing more difficult—or intimidating—than his or her first budget. The only thing worse is being assigned the task of drawing up a training budget for a brand new department. It is a traumatic and boring experience at best. It is also very, very important.

Every once in a while we hear about a district sales manager or an outstanding salesperson who is called into the home office and told—with suitable ceremony—that he or she has been selected to head up a formal sales-training activity (heretofore nonexistent). Instructions are given (in almost the same breath) to "work up a list of programs, things you need, and a preliminary budget, and have it ready for submission, this time next week." When the shock—and the joy—have worn off, paralysis sets in. How does one begin?

If you are one of those unfortunates charged with creating an instant budget out of thin air—take heart. For whatever comfort it may bring, you are joining a select fraternity. This chapter should help you ask the right questions, and be aware of the myriad of items which should be included.

Before you can start on the numbers, however, you have some

thinking and planning to do. Start by establishing your goals. Do you want an improved attitude from field salespeople? Is your sales-training effort going to be measured over a predetermined period of time or are you expected to show an immediate increase in sales?

Are customer relations a factor? Is product knowledge what you are supposed to teach? Or have the basic fundamentals of selling somehow been overlooked in an effort to get on with order taking? When you have the problems identified, determine which you are setting out to correct immediately.

When your goals have been pretty well determined, establish a set of priorities. What do you want to do first? Second? Third? When do you want to see results? How do you expect to see results? What means do you expect to use to get these results?

Don't kid yourself. Nothing happens overnight—in a sales-training sense, anyway. And you can't afford the luxury of deluding anybody—especially yourself—that it does. Always give yourself a little extra time for those impossibilities that always occur.

After you set your goals, give yourself enough time to get the job done right. But you're still lacking a problem to solve and the sales-training means to do it. It's not quite time to begin putting the budget together—yet.

SHOW ME A PROBLEM . . .

Often, the faults that appear on the surface are only symptoms of what is causing them. If something is wrong, there's a reason. Find the reason, and you've established a basis for creative training programs and, incidentally, a definite need for money to do the job.

Go to line and staff management and ask how and where you are needed. Find out what's wrong, keeping in mind that different people will often view the same situation differently, from their own areas of responsibility. (The one common misconception is that sales training will solve any and all problems.) Then, having determined the problem and heard how everyone else thinks it should be solved ("Why, by sales training, of course"), it's up to you to solve it.

. . . AND I'LL SOLVE IT

What, within the wide range of training means and methods, will it take to solve your problem? Should you establish a training school and hold classes five days a week? Will an instructional film reach enough of your field sales force? Do slide presentations fit your business and its regional or territorial operations? Or is the printed word the most effective method—with regular reporting from those responsible for seeing that your training is held, understood, and effective.

You will need:

- Someone to research, develop, write, and oversee the production of your printed material.
- Someone to hold meetings—maybe in a training conference room or traveling around the country.
- Someone to oversee the myriad of operational functions that become burdensome in any training department.
- Someone to handle correspondence, typing, clerical, and secretarial duties.

In addition, each program you create frequently requires specialists outside the company—suppliers who take your thoughts and ideas and approved programs and give them professional polish. These people are:

- artists,
- radio and TV commentators,
- advertising agency account executives,
- printers,
- notebook sales representatives,
- consultants, and
- salespeople of every product you can possibly imagine who view you as a potential customer.

Where do you plan to do your training? No matter what media you decide to use to convey your messages, you need space in which to do it. You need a conference room with:

- adequate lighting—preferably rheostatically controlled;
- adequate ventilation—air conditioned;
- a pleasant, cheerful color pattern;
- a podium—preferably adjustable;
- a podium light;
- a sound system—microphone, amplifier, and speakers;

- desks, tables;
- chairs;
- extra chairs for visitors;
- a chalkboard—maybe many chalkboards;
- a movie screen;
- easels—several easels (and a supply of flip charts);
- water glasses;
- water pitchers;
- ash trays;
- writing materials—pens and paper;
- a slide projector;
- a movie projector;
- extra trays for slides;
- extra take-up reels for movies;
- films—motivational and instructional;
- a movable table for your projection equipment;
- enough tables for group or "buzz" sessions;
- a pointer;
- chalk;
- extra bulbs for all your projection equipment;
- cassette tape recorders;
- video tape players;
- closed-circuit television—(color);
- plenty of training materials—product brochures—anything that gets your message across.

This is a formidable list. But you must take all this into consideration when you plan a training budget. And remember, the more you intend to produce—the greater the need for your services becomes—the more items you need.

Cost figures change. Sometimes, you'll find yourself adding an item in one area and dropping another somewhere else. But the old cliche about going "first class" is never truer than in a sales-training department. If you want to be accepted as a professional—if you expect the people you train to realize the full benefit from what you are setting out to do—you must look professional and have the equipment to do it.

What about travel? You won't be staying in the office all the time. As a matter of fact, it is vitally important that you don't lose your touch with the field and what is going on out there. When you travel, you'll need:

- airfare,
- motel accommodations,
- food,
- taxi or rental car,
- entertainment money, and
- all the normal expense account items—because you have to see how your programs are working.

From this checklist, decide what you need tomorrow—and project through to the end of the year. As you can see, you need *lots* and *lots* of materials.

There is nothing more frustrating to a trainer than the realization, one month after your annual budget has been submitted and approved, that you forgot something important. One way to avoid this is to have complete budget-submission sheets. If they contain all the categories you need to include, you are not likely to forget anything critical. At Goodyear, training budgets are broken down into three major categories: Administrative, Programming, and Trainees. Each major classification is then broken down into subclassifications. Samples of three Goodyear budget forms are illustrated in Tables 1, 2, and 3.

Check with your boss. Find out what exactly you must do to prepare a formal budget. Include *everything* you feel you need. Be prepared to defend your requests with facts and figures. Remember, you're asking for money to improve the organization, to have a positive effect on sales and profits.

For the first time, you may want to meet personally everyone concerned with approving your budget. Perhaps the personal touch of having you there could be a deciding factor in getting your budget approved. If they have never before reviewed a sales-training budget, you'd better hand-carry it around—and be both informed and eloquent.

In arriving at a final figure, include a little extra for increased costs from suppliers. You're going to feel the inflationary spiral in your training costs, too. If you prepare for it now in your yearly estimate, the funds will be there when they are needed.

Table 1
ANALYSIS OF EXPENSE—BUDGET VERSUS ACTUAL
SALES-TRAINING ADMINISTRATION AND STAFF

July   Department

Code	Type of Expense	Total Actual Expense (Year) A	Budget Data		Actual Expense		
			Revisions (Year)	Total (Year) B	Month (Year)	Year-to-Date % B	Year-to-Date % A
	Salary, Personnel						
	Salary, Office, Permanent						
	Salary, Temporary Employees						
	Total Compensation						
	Travel Expense						
	Car Allowance						
	Total Travel						
	Telephone Expenses-Toll						
	Phone Equipment and Charges						
	Telex Expense						
	Total Telephone and Telegraph						
	Maintenance and Repair						
	Operating Expenses (including postage)						
	Trans on Supplies						
	Copy Machine Rental and Supply						
	Total Operating Items						
	Moving Expense						
	Dues, Associations, Membership						
	Meal Allowances						
	Stationery Supplies						
	Miscellaneous Unclassified Expenses						
	Total Office and Miscellaneous Expense						
	Hospitalization						
	Other Wage Benefits						
	Total Wage Benefits						
	Total Created Expense						

Table 2
ANALYSIS OF EXPENSE—BUDGET VERSUS ACTUAL
WHOLESALE AND RETAIL TRAINING PROGRAMS

July _____ Department

Code	Type of Expense	Total Actual Expense (Year) A	Budget Data		Month (Year)	Actual Expense	
			Revisions (Year)	Total (Year) B		Year-to-Date % B	Year-to-Date % A
	Travel Expense						
	Total Travel						
	Books, Publications, etc.						
	Conference Expense						
	Training Education Programs—inside						
	Training Education Programs—outside						
	Dues, Associations, Membership						
	Lecture Fees						
	Research Studies						
	Total Office and Miscellaneous Expense						
	Total Created Expense						

Table 3
ANALYSIS OF EXPENSE—BUDGET VERSUS ACTUAL
WHOLESALE AND RETAIL TRAINING PROGRAMS

July   Department

Code	Type of Expense	Total Actual Expense (Year) A	Budget Data		Month (Year)	Actual Expense	
			Revisions (Year)	Total (Year) B		Year-to-Date % B	Year-to-Date % A
	Salary, Personnel Compensation						
	Salary (Overtime, Regular, or Normal)						
	Salary, Temporary Employees						
	Total Compensation						
	Travel Expense						
	Total Travel						
	Meal Allowance						
	Total Office and Miscellaneous Expense						
	Hospitalization						
	Wage Benefits Other						
	Total Wage Benefits						
	Total Expense						

There may be some natural-born salespeople in the field, but over 99 percent are made the way they are. To really master the art and techniques of selling requires work and study. You—through your department and personal efforts—provide the means by which the sales force will become and remain professional. That's what the bottom line is all about.

The requirements are always changing, so your job is always growing. And as your job grows, your department, staff, and needs grow. This year's budget will become as obsolete as yesterday's news. But for tomorrow, when you submit it, you'll be on your way to building a good, solid sales-training department.

CHAPTER 5

THE TRAINING DEPARTMENT BUDGET

GEORGE J. LUMSDEN

George J. Lumsden is currently Manager, Sales Training, Chrysler Motors Corporation. He has worked as a salesman, an educator, a training supervisor (General Electric Company), and an advertising writer and account executive. Mr. Lumsden received his B.A. degree from Hope College and his M.A. degree from the University of Michigan. He has written several books and articles on communications skills and human relations.

Training directors are people whose interests lie, first and foremost, in the development and operation of training programs. Underlying this design and display effort is an ultimate objective of improving performance of salespeople and sales managers. Trainers, with all this interesting work to do, are unlikely to become enthusiastic over budget-making and budget-keeping. Yet it is the ability to make and keep a budget that often differentiates between the successful training manager and the mediocre one.

GENERAL CONSIDERATIONS

In any discussion of budget, there are several general considerations:

1. *Training costs money.* Anyone who has been in the training business more than ten minutes will recognize that without money you don't have much of a training program. This is important to understand because frequently a training director will be lured by the idea of operating out of someone else's budget, thereby hiding training costs. However attractive this approach may be, it's sometimes to the training director's disadvantage when the person whose budget is being used suddenly calls a halt to such expenditures. Top management has a right to expect a training activity to be productive, but it should also face up to the costs involved in it.

2. *Training is generally worth what it costs.* This is not to say the more expensive the training, the better it is. It means, however, that one cannot operate on a shoestring budget and produce effective training programs. Training done without financial support ultimately becomes a series of lectures or bull sessions. A good lecture or group discussion can be effective; but if that's all you can afford, it's like trying to play a piano using only the white keys.

3. *If you don't ask for money, you don't get money.* However sophisticated a company a training director may serve, it's unlikely that its management will voluntarily dump a fortune into the training treasury. Of course, training is a necessary expense; but it is one which many managers would prefer to do without. Businesses are at their best when all participants in that business are performing at top effectiveness. Since this is a dream unlikely to be fulfilled, training programs constantly seek to stamp out or minimize deficiencies. The first person to recognize the need for money to support the training activity should be the training director; and he or she will seldom (if ever) get more than requested.

4. *Ask for what you need, and use all you get.* This is a two-part consideration. Any training department that asks for funds in excess of realistic needs and at the end of a year turns back a portion of its budget has functioned as irresponsibly as the training department that consistently uses more than its budget allows. We do not save at the expense of the program, nor do we spend at the expense of the corporation.

5. *Training directors should be able to justify any money request by showing the productivity of a training department.* This consideration will receive more than its fair share of discussion in this chapter because it is a key factor in the submission of any worthwhile budget. It is a consideration of utmost importance because, year by year, budgets improve or deteriorate in direct proportion to justification.

6. *One thinks differently about new programs (new departments) versus old programs (established departments).* When introducing training to a function, tremendous care must be observed in order to establish the right kind of precedents. When picking up an established department, care must be given to justify changes in procedure and differences in spending habits. "How come old Harry didn't need all that money?" "Who's this new guy, anyhow?"

7. *Many corporate budgets are combinations of yesterday's mistakes and tomorrow's hopes.* Anyone who has butted his or her head against

the commercial wall or danced the corporate minuet knows that what is asked for and what is received may be two rather different things. We have seen managers who create budgets out of thin air, make enormous requests, overspend budgets, and are rewarded with bigger budgets the next year. Conversely, we have seen managers who are so careful in budget administration that they turn back funds at the end of the year and are penalized by a more stringent budget the following year.

These opposite and extreme examples both have one thing in common—poor budget administration at the top. But they are often triggered by substandard budget submissions and faulty internal controls. The budget-building procedure to be outlined in this chapter could forestall either of these situations.

A PLACE TO BEGIN

It is a personal belief that a good budget begins with good advance program planning. In other words, one should ask the question: "What do I aim to do that will require the money I'm asking for?" It follows then that before one mark is made on a budget request, advance planning of the coming year's activities should be well in hand.

As a specific example, let us consider one course to be offered in a sales-training department—call it Basic Sales Techniques. Quite apart from program content and teaching technique, a training director can anticipate the number of salespeople to be trained in Basic Sales Techniques and the number of meetings which will be required to train that many salespeople. Then it is easy to apply a cost factor per session for the physical handling of such a conference. In other words, how much are conference room costs, how much money is involved in luncheons, coffee breaks, cocktail parties, dinners? Does the training department pay for the travel and lodgings of conferees? Any expense involved in the physical handling of the meeting can then be considered and related directly to the number of people involved in such a training effort. The net result is the out-of-pocket cost per conferee.

Another thing that results from this kind of planning is a careful analysis of the instructional costs. If it is going to require 20 meetings, each meeting involving one week of an instructor's time, then there are 20 weeks of an instructor's salary to be considered just to handle that one course. As part of this analysis, you must also include the cost of traveling and lodging an instructor for that same period of time.

Training programs, as seen by the people who attend or participate, are merely the tips of icebergs. Behind every training session held is a considerable amount of development, planning, and production time and expense. If our course in Basic Sales Techniques is to be held at all, we will be incurring the expense of instructors or program planners as they develop the material. We will also be involving typesetting, printing, photography, slide making, motion-picture production, etc.,— all add to the costs required to hold that meeting.

And that's not all. For every day that an instructor works face-to-face with trainees, there are other people supporting him or her at home. Management salaries, secretarial salaries, and all the collateral expenses of maintaining the instructor in the field have to be considered as they apply to each individual program. These nonproductive people and expenses bear careful analysis, and what better time to do this than when evaluating budget needs?

Another consideration in budget building is the revenue potential involved. This, too, can be calculated on a per program basis. If certain training expenses are underwritten by the trainees themselves (Chrysler Corporation, for example, sets moderate charges for its dealers for the training provided to them, their managers, and salespeople), these revenues should be factored into the budget. Also, if a corporation operates training with a system of cross-charges against the department or division for which the training was performed, this should be included in the budget plan. A strong point is made here: *Fees and cross-charges should be considered as income and not as reductions in expense.* This is important because if we treat it as an expense reduction, we never really see the true cost of the training activity.

A final thought regarding revenue: When several divisions of a corporation are using a central training department, revenues may provide a handy measurement of training use. Also, it is very helpful to a training director to be able to point out that the $10,000 spent in the development of a program was recovered in time through its use by components of the corporation. (At Chrysler, some years ago, we went into a packaged training program which cost us some $47,000. We were relieved to show $62,000 in revenue from its sale.) Justification is important in any budgeting experience.

What we have at this point is an unusable collection of numbers— a sprinkling of instructional costs, a smattering of development expense, and a smidgeon of administrative expense. How much simpler it would be to take last year's budget, add a wedge for inflation, a pad for contingencies, and a float anticipating cut-backs. Wrong! Do that and you have missed building a workable budget—and a defensible one!

A WAY TO GO

Good budget planning begins not with a budget-submission sheet, but with a planning sheet that lets you see exactly what each component is and where it fits into the program. Table 1 is such a sheet, as currently used by the training department of Chrysler Corporation.

This is strictly a worksheet, and it contains space for information of specific interest to the training department—not to the budget department. It includes a descriptive title for each training program or project. It then proceeds with the status of each program and/or action plan required. This is followed by an estimate of number of conferences, enrollments, fee per student, and projection of revenue. If revenue is not involved in your budget effort, these last two columns are superfluous, but the number of conferences and the number of people involved will, as the worksheet progresses, be very important.

The next column involves estimated development manpower. A current program, for instance, requires no development manpower. On the other hand, a new program may require a great deal. What is more important, some new programs will require development effort considerably out of proportion to the number of students involved or the number of conferences to be held (at Chrysler we have developed quickie conferences that have played before several thousands of people. Development for this kind of program may have taken as little as one month of a person's time. On the other hand, we have developed programs aimed at perhaps one hundred people that have taken months of a developer's time.) Judgment regarding development manpower rises out of experience and a knowledge of the capabilities of development personnel.

The next column allows for an estimate of instructional manpower. This estimate can be extracted fairly accurately from the number of conferences to be held. A three-day conference very nearly takes up a full week of an instructor's time, whereas a two-day conference scheduled back-to-back with another two-day conference makes better use of an instructor's time. This figure should be entered into the worksheet as a percentage of full-year involvement.

We are faced in nearly every training program with some kind of production costs. There is a space on this worksheet for that. Included in this estimate would be any of the mechanics required to bring ideas into being. Also included in this estimate would be the cost of free-lance writers and artists—labor costs but not payroll costs.

Another column allows for an estimate of travel costs. This is generally most carefully estimated if it is related exclusively to the travel

Table 1
MARKETING TRAINING DEPARTMENT
Chrysler Motors Corporation

Training Program or Project—_____ Model Yr.	Status and/or Action Plan	Number of Conferences Planned	Estimate of Enrollments Per Year	Fee Per Student	Projection of Revenue Per Year
A	Current	100 (1)	1,200	25	30,000
B	New/Jan.	50 (1)	500	35	17,500
C	New/Mar.	200 (1)	2,000	35	70,000
D	Current	10 (3)	100	100	10,000
E	New/Apr.	60 (1)	720	35	25,200
F	Update	30 (2)	300	50	15,000
G	Current	250 (1)	3,500	25	87,500
H	New/July	100 (1)	1,200	35	42,000
I	New/Oct.	20 (1)	400	50	20,000
J	New/Nov.	40 (2)	800	—	—
K	New/Dec.	0	2,000	25	50,000
Totals		860	12,720	X	$367,200

of instructors. Experience reveals an average cost of keeping an instructor in the field per day. Travel, lodgings, food, and related expenses can be calculated on a per diem basis and readily applied using the conference count and the days per conference (Chrysler instructors travel out of Detroit to locations all over the United States, Canada, and Mexico. We keep a log of monthly travel costs and throw out extreme travel expenses—either high or low—in order to produce average daily costs.)

A final column provides for an estimate of conference cost. This would include conference-room rentals, luncheons provided to trainees, lodging supplied for trainees, and any other on-site costs (projector rentals, for instance). These costs will vary from location to location, but here again it is possible through experience to make a fairly accurate determination of this on an average daily basis.

Table 1
MARKETING TRAINING DEPARTMENT
Chrysler Motors Corporation

% Development Manpower Needed	% Instructional Manpower Needed	Estimate of Development Production Cost	Estimate of Travel Cost	Estimate of Conference Cost
0	.50	0	10,000	12,500
.20	.30	8,000	5,000	6,250
.40	.90	15,000	20,000	25,000
0	.30	0	3,000	3,750
.30	.30	7,000	6,000	7,500
.10	.30	3,000	6,000	7,500
0	1.20	8,000	25,000	33,250
.30	.50	8,000	10,000	12,500
.40	.10	10,000	2,000	2,500
.30	.70	4,000	0	0
1.20	0	21,000	0	0
3.20	5.10	$84,000	$87,000	$110,750

Putting it all together

If we look at Table 1 we see an example of how this may work out. (The examples given simulate a year in the Chrysler training experience.) Here are training programs with all the above-described extensions. Data, for the most part, is self-explained. Certain exceptions demand clarification.

For instance, programs A, D, and G are current—they require no development manpower or expense. Program G, however, requires reprinting of materials, so expense is anticipated there.

Numbers in parentheses in the Conferences column indicate the number of days per conference. This helps explain extensions of estimated expense in all categories.

Program J is an internal program—no revenue; and it is taught at the home office—no travel or conference costs. Program K is a packaged home-study course—no instructors and no travel or conference expense, but plenty of development cost.

As examination of this example will reveal, even in a revenue-supported program there are some real losers. Program B is a good example. This involves limited enrollments, but is aimed at a vital audience and is well worth the expense.

Development and instructional manpower estimates are calculated and rounded *up*. (In the illustration used, we'd probably go for nine training specialists.) Estimates are based on 44 weeks of work, allowing 4 weeks for vacations, 2 weeks for holidays, and 2 weeks for schedule mismatches.

The worksheet does not include supervisory or clerical salaries and expenses. These are accumulated separately because they do not relate so specifically to program plans. They are folded into the final budget submission.

SUBMITTING, JUSTIFYING, PARING

Budgets submitted will pick up the totals listed here. That's a simple step. Now comes the fun—if you've planned properly.

A challenge to your budget request has its reply based on your worksheet. Can you explain why you asked for what you did? Of course you can. Can you show management what it gets for what it spends? It's all there on your worksheet.

In spite of your good preparation, your asking budget is trimmed by, let's say, one person and $50,000. By going back to the worksheet, you can eliminate a program or limit its offering. Money and people come out of budget requests exactly the way they went in.

This system of planning has value in the ongoing control of expenses, too. As each program is developed and conducted, pluses and minuses are noted. Also, if emergency programs are required, other programs give way. Going in or coming out, your planning is helpful.

The illustrations given in this chapter cover a fairly large sales-training activity, but the same kind of budget planning can work equally well in a much smaller one.

The writer has used this system for nearly a decade. It has been helpful in build-ups and in cut-backs. It takes work and it isn't always perfect—but it beats guessing, wishing, and worrying. It puts the manager in charge of the budget rather than under its control. Give it a try!

CHAPTER 6

LOCATING, DESIGNING, AND EQUIPPING THE IDEAL TRAINING FACILITY

JOHN R. PERRY

John R. Perry joined Procter & Gamble in 1957, after graduation from the University of Missouri. During his career with Procter & Gamble, he held field sales management assignments in Kansas City, Minneapolis, and Omaha. In 1966, he was transferred to the General Offices in Cincinnati, Ohio, where he is responsible for initiating and developing training programs and materials for sales and sales management.

Mr. Perry worked with Skidmore, Owings & Merrill, and a visual communications consultant, Hubert Wilkie, Incorporated, in designing, constructing, and equipping a 10,000-square-foot Training Center in the General Offices' Building. In recent years he has conducted training in facilities such as the Trans-World Airlines Breech Training Academy, conference centers on both coasts, and in major cities in the U.S., Canada, Venezuela, and Germany.

Like all training activities, locating, designing, and equipping a training facility should be based on your needs and objectives. Good facilities cannot make up for weak training programs, but bad facilities can weaken and detract from the very best training program.

The following questions, with some comments, are intended to help you work through your needs, and develop your own answers.

What facilities are you using for training now?
Answer:
 Most managers want to start from a known base.

What is wrong with the current arrangements?

Answer:
> Are you spending too much for outside facilities? Too much time setting up and tearing down? Competing for space with other departments in the company? How much time, effort, and expense could you really save if you had the ideal facility?

What do you feel you need that you don't have now?
Answer:
> At this point you may be saying, "I picked up this book to get the answers to my questions, not more questions or a checklist." Unfortunately, every situation is different, and there is no right answer for the ideal training facility. What's right for you today, when your training groups average 18, may be too crowded three years from now when growth of your company builds your average group to 27, and you develop new training activities to meet new needs. The list of questions could go on to infinity. You should recognize that you will not have "one answer" to most of the questions, but should at least consider the implications as you develop your plans.

> The "ideal facility" for you must depend on a number of factors.

Where are the people located who will participate in the training?
Answer:
> If they are all within a couple of hours of your home office, it's easy to assume that the headquarters city is the best location. But this is not necessarily so. Sometimes it is desirable to get away, go to a new location, or combine activities. Do you ever plan recreation or other events as a part of your training? How good is the transportation to your headquarters?

How many different types of training are you currently doing?
Answer:
> What will you be doing three years from now? Do you plan some training activities in the field near your salespeople? Do you need to go to a plant or laboratory for product training? Do you need provision for "hands-on" skill training?

Who will be doing the training, and in what setting will the trainer be most effective?
Answer:
> If you are going to use academic people, you may want to plan

that training program at one of the many conference centers on university campuses.

If you are using "home-office" facilities, you may find it helpful to take the trainees around to various locations where they can see and do, rather than bringing the "trainers" and training to a central facility. For an extreme example, let's suppose that you are dealing with an aspect of product training where a chemist shows what happens when two products are mixed in the wrong proportions, producing a bad odor. It's a lot better to have that aspect demonstrated in the chemist's lab, where the setting is "right" and everyone can immediately recognize the odor. More importantly, you and the group being trained can move on to another location, another subject, and leave the odor behind.

CENTRAL FACILITY

For the next few paragraphs, let's assume that your immediate need is to develop a central training facility in your "home-office" city, if not in the home office itself.

In most instances, the job of convincing management of the need for a training facility will be yours alone. The sales presentation you employ to secure corporate approval of what you really need should follow the same proven techniques you generally use and are comfortable with in selling your own products.

Unless you have a truly unique situation, you will probably not be able to keep the "ideal facility" you want, dream of, and will really need five years from now occupied 100 percent of the time. To get what you want, you may wish to find out if there are other groups in your company who have compatible needs, and could support your recommendation. If you do this in your initial planning stage, you can incorporate their needs and yours. The danger in this approach is that you may wind up competing for the space with the others. This can be minimized by mutually agreed upon planning and guidelines.

You may be concerned about tailoring a room to fit several different objectives and groups. While it may be hard to compromise on this initially, if your plans are well thought out, it may be a real advantage in the long term. The more flexible a facility is, the longer it will stay up-to-date. Few companies can afford single-purpose training rooms. Even more important, if your facilities are flexible, you can be more innovative in your training techniques.

FIVE BASIC AREAS

There are five basic areas to consider:

1. *Space:* How many square feet do you need, based on the numbers of people, types of seating, room for demonstrations, break areas, storage, etc.?
2. *Sound:* How do you control the sound in the room, and keep outside sounds from interfering?
3. *Ventilation:* Can you keep the room comfortable for 5 people, or 20 people? Can you get rid of smoke, and adjust the temperature for women in sleeveless dresses and men with coat and vest?
4. *Lighting:* Can you vary the light from low enough to project slides or pictures to high enough to make color videotapes? Will you need that flexibility? Would you like to have it?
5. *Equipment:* You need to consider everything under this category from convenient restrooms for men and women, to coffee and coke facilities at break time, to your actual training aids.

As you read the five areas, you probably thought of even more things to consider.

Unless you are a true "renaissance" person, you probably do not have the expertise to write the specifications for each of these areas. You may find within your own company people who can be of help to you. If you are planning a major facility, you will want to employ the services of a communications facility consultant. A good consultant will help you answer all of the questions, and help you with many more details. Technology is constantly changing, and you will seldom know of all the newest developments in equipment. A consultant will be able to help you with the "benefit and costs" points necessary to convince your management of the need for what you propose.

Just as it is difficult to specify the ideal facilities, it is also hard to get management's agreement to an unlimited budget. If you cannot hire an outside consultant to help, and have no inside resources, here are a few tips on how to do it alone.

Space

Space is the most important element. If you have enough square feet, you can handle some shortcomings in other areas. If you are really cramped, though, all of your other problems multiply themselves.

- Do you need a central meeting room for group presentations, and smaller rooms for workshop sessions or videotape-recorded role plays? How many, etc.?
- Do you want to keep everyone in one central room, but have enough space so that they can conduct table discussions?
- What size tables or chairs will you be using? How much floor space will be taken up by other equipment?
- Do you need to provide space for:
  - breaks?
  - luncheons?
  - storage of props, displays?
  - speaker rehearsal while the main meeting is in progress?
  - equipment storage?
  - equipment repair?
  - extra phones or desks in the break areas?
  - coat and briefcase storage?
  - luggage storage on the last day?
  - extra chairs and tables that are not always used?

You need to determine exactly what you have now, and then measure how much more you need. It's smart to think of all your meeting participants as long legged, heavy set, slouching-down people. If you measure your table size and chair space on this basis, you will not have uncomfortable people who are more concerned with their leg room than your latest sales technique.

Another key part of space is the entry/exit areas. Can you get in and out of the room without disturbing the group? Can you plan space where coffee breaks are set up and cleared up without interfering with instruction?

Sound

If you are planning to use a variety of audiovisual aids (slide projector, film projector, or anything that makes a noise), you should provide space and arrangements so that the noise can be kept out of your meeting room, and in a projection booth. This also gives you the opportunity to perform such necessary tasks as rewinding and changing trays without disturbing the meeting.

Sound problems and room acoustics are a major concern in the design of any facility. In most situations involving groups of 20 persons or more, some means of voice amplification should be available. Maybe you are confident of projecting your voice, but not everyone can, especially for any length of time.

Outside noises are also a problem. Some facilities minimize this by putting up signs in outside hallways that say "Meeting in Progress."

You can also design a room that sounds great for a single speaker, but sounds terrible when five or six table discussions are going on. Some compromise is generally necessary.

Ventilation

Ventilation is a science in itself. Key concerns about ventilation are:

- Can you control it in each room independently?
- Is the air change sufficient to handle smoke if everyone in the room lights up a cigar?
- Is it quiet enough so that the air or blower noise does not detract from the meeting?
- Can you avoid drafts?

Getting a system designed to do these things is difficult. In this situation the audiovisual consultant works with the general contractor and the mechanical engineer. They will work out the best solution based on your persistence and the amount of money available for the job.

Lighting

Whatever the size of your room or type of lighting, room dimmers or rheostats are important. You cannot dim fluorescent lighting, so you should consider having incandescent lighting in most situations. You should also plan for light tracks to allow you to spotlight and back light areas.

If you have natural sunlight, you need to be able to control it from just shielding the glare for discussions, to total darkness if you need it for projection.

It should be noted that you seldom can plan more power outlets than you need.

Equipment

Some very effective training has taken place in rooms with a chalk-board, bare walls, straight chairs, and a table. Total cost for equipment, including the chalkboard and an extra eraser—$50.00. There are also custom-designed facilities with color-coordinated decor and furnish-ings, swivel armchairs, adjustable solid-wood tables, concealed screens, suspended color-television monitors, and every conceivable remote-controlled audiovisual device, where very little training or behavior change takes place.

Your equipment shopping list should be based on what you need to accomplish your current training objectives. Don't buy something you think you "might" need later. Plan for it, make provision for it, but don't buy it until you are going to use it. Chances are that if you are looking two or three years into the future, there will be better equipment available when you really need it. If you want to try it, rent it or work out a demonstration period with your supplier.

Seating is a very important consideration. Most of the time the people will be seated. In some instances, fixed auditorium seating is best, where you want all attention focused at a central point. Many meetings today try to involve people in questions, discussions, and communications with each other. For this, you need swivel chairs so they can easily turn to face one another. It is also helpful to have roll-ers on the chairs to position them where you want them.

Tables are a second item. You may want some sessions in class-room style, where you have chairs facing the front of the room behind tables (Fig. 1). Many training applications use discussion tables (Fig. 2). This works well when your training objectives call for some group problem solving, role playing, or teamwork. Other sessions involving the whole group work well in Conference "U"s (Fig. 3) where each per-son can face and communicate with the others. The "auditorium" or "lecture" setup (Fig. 4) works well for a movie or brief lecture, but does not work well in involving the participants.

As you can see, there will be applications for each in your facility. You need to have easily moved furniture for this flexibility, and a place to store what you are not using.

After you have the group seated, they need to hear something. A good sound system, for voice amplification, your movie sound track, and even background music are essential.

How elaborate the system is should depend on your needs. Many people find it helpful to have remote tape equipment to play music as

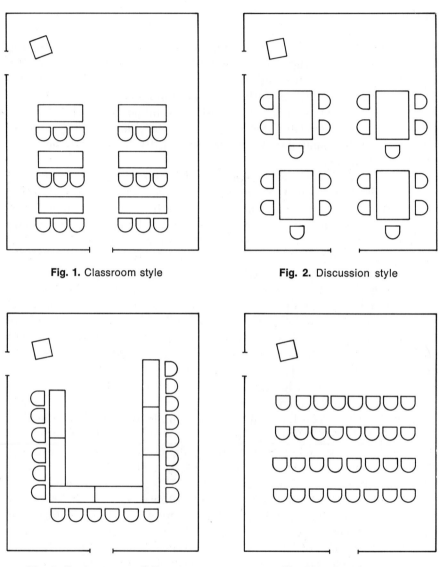

Fig. 1. Classroom style

Fig. 2. Discussion style

Fig. 3. Conference or "U" style

Fig. 4. Auditorium style

a group enters a meeting, or leaves at the closing. If you can control it remotely, it is even better.

For voice amplification, we often find a microphone permanently attached to a lectern. All mikes should have well marked off-on switches, so the speaker has some control.

If you want to get your speakers more involved with your group or to use such equipment as a chalkboard you need to provide a lavaliere or neck mike so they can move around. Have you ever experienced a speaker booming through the mike at the lectern, who goes to a chalkboard and tries to talk with his or her back to the audience? A neck mike will get all remarks across.

Visual illustrations add to almost every presentation. Slides, movies, overhead and opaque projectors, video tape, closed-circuit television—all can make an important contribution. The only limiting factors are money, time, and your own creativity.

As you plan your "ideal facility," and make up your list of equipment, ask yourself the following:

- How often will I need this?
- How will I use it?
- Will anyone else use it?
- How will we store it, repair it, and keep it operating?

If in doubt, rent it until you can prove to yourself you really need it. There are advantages and disadvantages to both "front projection," and "rear projection" systems. You need to determine which best fits your needs. You may want to incorporate both.

At Procter & Gamble, our larger "assembly room" is front projection since it will hold over 130 people in a space 34 feet x 55 feet. The small training room is rear projection, for a space 30 feet x 40 feet. The layout provides for a break area with vending machines, four group-discussion rooms 13 feet x 26 feet, a control room, and storage space.

We feel that controlling all of our visual equipment, projecting the right image or movie at the precise moment, is very important.

Our lectern has controls for:

- Programmer cue,
- Slide projector,
- Filmstrip projector,
- Movie projector,
- Audiotape player, and
- Technician-call button.

A slide-out drawer contains a Random Access Control for a second projector which the instructor can use to answer questions or go back to review points at the end of a program, or during a question and answer period.

Videotape is an important part of training today. One important consideration is to make it movable. This can be accomplished by a cart for easy portability, which gives you control in a single discussion room. If you are planning to play videotape to larger groups, suspended 25-inch monitors can provide clear viewing and do not take up valuable floor space with carts or wires.

You will often want to start a tape at a specific spot. For this you need a digital control to insure precision editing and starts, and to let you skip and repeat to any part of a tape cassette quickly and accurately.

All of these devices can help you save time and money, and give your instructors more flexibility and creativity in their training presentations. Some are custom designed, others are readily available. A key principle in planning your own facility is to get out and see what others are doing and using. Most training people are like new grandparents when they are asked about their own training facilities—they like to show them off. They are also happy to tell you their facilities' shortcomings, and what they would do differently.

Publications on training carry many stories and illustrations. If you see something that is similar to your own needs, a phone call or letter will usually result in a lot of specific information and often a personal invitation to visit.

Your local audiovisual supplier will also be happy to arrange for you to visit installations recently made; or, through a manufacturer, you may visit new facilities that incorporate the latest in equipment and design.

OUTSIDE FACILITIES

Let us now assume that you have sold your management on the need for a facility, worked with a communications facility consultant and equipment suppliers, equipped the ideal training facility, and feel you are set for the next five years. You've had six training sessions in your new facility, and everything works great. You are certain you will never have to tape another power cord to the floor because you have it all built in. That's the day when the sales manager calls and tells you he needs a special three-day training program using all the visuals you use in your training center, put on 2,000 miles away from your location.

Your problems really aren't starting all over again. First, you know about what size room, tables, etc., you need. You also know the types of equipment you will have to have on hand. With this information, you can give a hotel or conference center the specifications you need. Most major hotel chains have planners who will work with you. Most hotels work with local audiovisual suppliers who can rent and install any type of equipment.

Unless you have a lot of time to travel and personally inspect sites in advance, you may wish to turn over your specifications to a local manager to carry out. But remember, you are still responsible for what goes right or wrong and should stay as involved as you can. It certainly pays off to get good scale drawings of any facility before you commit yourself to it. These should include ceiling heights, sound and ventilation arrangements, and any obstructions (such as pillars or low chandeliers).

Trade publications are full of ads and listings of hotels and conference centers who are anxious to cater to your needs. Taking the show on the road and finding the right facility is no longer an impossible task. You may even find other companies, with training facilities similar to your own home-office facility, who will let you rent them for a few days, or on a regular basis.

In fact, if you have planned your own facilities well, and corporate policy permits, you may find it possible to rent them on a day-to-day basis to other noncompeting companies, which will help defray operating costs.

SUMMARY

The psychological impact of a superior training facility can improve your training effectiveness.

- It frees you from such worries as equipment setup and room arrangements, and lets you concentrate on program content and the trainees.
- It allows you the flexibility to illustrate and use audiovisual techniques appropriate for your training objectives.
- It provides the trainees with an atmosphere where they can concentrate totally on the learning situation they are in, without worrying about their own personal comfort, straining to see a slide, or trying to shut out distracting noises.

By applying good training principles to your design of a training facility—

- thoroughly defining your needs,
- identifying possible resources,
- developing objectives and plans to achieve them, and
- communicating the benefits to your management

—you should be as pleased with your new facility as you are with the results of your training.

SECTION III

DIRECTING AND COORDINATING
TRAINING

CHAPTER 1

TRAINING TECHNIQUES
ROBERT P. DIES

Robert P. Dies is Manager of Training and Communication for the B. F. Goodrich Tire Company. He is responsible for the design and development of all B. F. Goodrich Tire Company Training programs. A native of Akron, Ohio, Mr. Dies attended the University of Akron and Northwestern University. He joined the B. F. Goodrich Advertising Department in 1951 and for a period early in his career served as a Market Planning Specialist where he developed Marketing Programs and Strategies.

Mr. Dies is a seminar leader for the Sales Trainer Clinic conducted by NSSTE and in courses conducted by the Department of Business and Education, the University of Wisconsin. He is a qualified instructor for both the Dimensional Sales Training Program and the Managerial Grid Organizational Development Program. He has received several awards from the NSSTE for the excellence of his Editorial Contributions. Mr. Dies is the author of numerous magazine articles and is widely recognized as a skilled and persuasive speaker and seminar leader in motivation, communications, and sales techniques.

TRAINING TECHNIQUES ARE NOT SOLUTIONS

One of the first concerns of any trainer is the means by which he or she proposes to teach trainees. What training techniques are available? How difficult are they to administer? When should they be used? How often? Will assistance be needed to present them? How will I know when they're working?

There are a number of often-used sales-training techniques. In this chapter some of the more common ones, their applications, and tips on how to use them will be briefly described. But the skilled sales trainer considers techniques only as *tools* by which he or she achieves an *end result.* Consider for a moment this true story:

Once upon a time ... there was a sales trainer who successfully used role play to solve a particular training problem. He became so enamored with role playing as a technique ... from that day forward ... role play became his *only* solution to every sales-training situation. He neglected to consider that role play is an excellent *sales-skill training tool,* but a poor one for subjects which require memorizing, like product knowledge. Alas, that sales trainer was soon replaced by one with more creativity.

Sales-training techniques are as varied and as numerous as the creativity of the trainer and the needs of a specific situation. However, the experienced sales trainer will only allow this creativity to become an influence *after* a proper *needs analysis* has been made and a set of reasonable, attainable behavioral *objectives* developed. Furthermore, no *one* training technique by itself ever solved a training problem.

So, sales-training techniques can be considered as the *link in a chain,* leading to a successful learning experience. To achieve a behavioral objective is the real concern of the professional sales trainer. Many factors must be considered in determining how these "links" of techniques will be formed and connected to achieve the objective. Let's look at some of them, before we discuss some of the more common techniques.

Since it represents the first formal approach to training in this country, a good place to start considering training techniques is to take a look at all the elements of the Job Instruction Training JIT method developed during the early 1940s. While it was originally developed for factory workers, it is equally effective—on a modified basis—for sales trainees. (See Table 1.)

JIT may not seem very profound in light of some of the more sophisticated training techniques available today, but it is still fundamentally sound. Nothing has ever come along that has taken the place of the value to the trainees of initial observation (JIT step 1); and the "curbstone conference" (step 2) is—or should be—used after every call. This in turn is followed by further observation (step 3) and the opportunity to practice (steps 4, 5, and 6).

TRAINING TECHNIQUES ARE THE "TOOLS OF THE TRADE"

A good worker does not use a sledge hammer when a ballpeen would do the job. Nor does a skilled sales trainer use a lecture when a learning exercise will best enhance the learning experience. The selection

Table 1
JOB INSTRUCTION TRAINING (JIT)

In the early stages of World War II, the Job Instruction Training (JIT) program was developed to train housewives and others who had never been in a factory to do production jobs they had never dreamed of doing. These are the steps of the JIT method and how a sales trainer might apply them to a new trainee:

1. *Show how you sell.* Let the new salesperson observe as you make sales calls. At the beginning of the call, *explain* the trainee's presence as a "learner" or an "assistant."

2. *Explain the key points of the sale.* In a "curbstone conference" (after you have left the customer) carefully review the critical stages of the call. Be candid about how you feel the sale went, what you could have done better, danger signals to watch for, how the presentation flowed from opening to conclusion.

3. *Let the trainee continue to observe as you sell.* Do this until you both feel the trainee can adequately perform on his/her own.

4. *Somehow, let the trainee get into the act by doing a noncritical task.* Pick understanding customers. Let the trainee get started by making the Feature, Advantage, Benefit or other kind of presentation. Be prepared to help when necessary.

5. *Help your trainee do the entire sales job.* Let the trainee carry the load with an understanding customer and get involved yourself only when absolutely necessary.

6. *Let the trainee make complete sales calls.* Stay out of the act, unless absolutely necessary; but observe carefully, and continue curbstone critiquing after each sale.

7. *Put your trainee on his/her own.* But, be available to answer questions—the "throw 'em in and let 'em swim" technique loses more good trainees than it saves.

and linking of the appropriate sales-training techniques depends on many factors:

1. *Numbers of salespeople involved.* The classic one-on-one JIT approach might be best where only one person is involved, as is often the case with individuals new to the sales assignment where initial field training is mandatory. On the other hand, if a group of salespeople are involved, the most appropriate technique might be the presentation of a motion picture followed by a group discussion, followed in turn by role play in subgroups.

2. *Salesperson's initial understanding of the subject matter.* When a

group is to be trained, the sales trainer must ascertain how to bring those with a little bit of knowledge about the topic to be taught to a level somewhat close to those who already know more, so that the learning experience can begin at a common point for all.

3. *The time and place where the sales training will take place.* "There is a time and place for everything." And so it is with sales training. For instance, a "morning" topic that requires alertness, but somehow gets slotted into an afternoon time might determine the technique to be used. One that might have been appropriate in the morning may very well bomb if attempted in the afternoon. People do tire, and especially trainees!

Another important consideration is the training facility and the equipment available when sales training will be conducted. Very often these factors greatly restrict the variety of techniques from which the trainer can construct the learning experience.

4. *Number of trainers available to assist in the sales training.* A one-person training department, or a situation where only one sales trainer is available presents a completely different set of circumstances than is the case where there are a number of trainers to assist.

5. *Past experience of the learners.* The techniques used with "old hands" usually are structured differently to teach the same material to the trainees. Another consideration of the sales trainer is ... do the group members have 10, 20, or 30 years of experience, or do they have 1 year of experience repeated 10, 20, or 30 times?

PARTICIPATIVE VERSUS NONPARTICIPATIVE TECHNIQUES

In devising the links of the learning chain (the learning techniques that lead to an end result), it might be wise to consider the Scientific Method Model of Learning as presented by Blake and Mouton.* (See Fig. 1.)

Blake and Mouton explain this model very well in their book. The purpose of presenting it in this chapter is to show the relationship of certain techniques, some of which *do not* necessarily require active participation by the learner (theory-generalization) with those that *do* call for participation (action-critique-application). Note in Fig. 1 that the "action-critique-generalization-application" flow is almost a direct

* Robert R. Blake and Jane S. Mouton, *Corporate Excellence Through Grid Organizational Development, A Systematic Approach* (Houston, Tex.: Gulf, 1968), pp. 347–351.

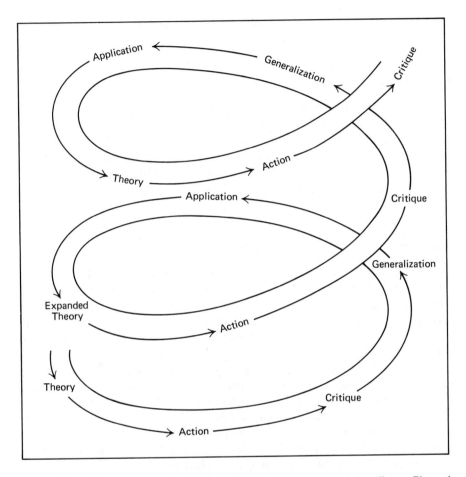

Fig. 1. The Scientific Method Model of Learning from *Corporate Excellence Through Grid Organization Development: A Systems Approach,* by Robert R. Blake and Jane Srygley Mouton. Houston: Gulf Publishing Company, Copyright © 1968, page 282. Reproduced with permission.

parallel of the sequence in the principles of the JIT formula (see Table 1).

Nonparticipative techniques are those which require the learner to see or hear but *not actively* respond to the input information (theory-critique-generalization). Participative techniques require *active* involvement by the learner to help discover the real usefulness of the knowledge or skill being taught (action-application).

There are a number of excellent idea sources for a wide variety of proven sales-training techniques.

Nonparticipative techniques

Do not require the learner to respond actively to an input of information. Nonparticipative techniques are generally utilized for theory and generalization inputs and, hopefully, are coupled with participative techniques, which assure complete understanding of the information. Some of the more common nonparticipative techniques are the lecture, various kinds of audiovisual presentations, reading assignments, and dramatic presentations.

The lecture

A cornerstone of our educational system is the lecture. Unfortunately, all too many lecturers feel that as they drop pearls of wisdom the students are supposed to absorb the information as if their minds were sponges. The strength of the lecture is that it permits the instructor to pick and choose his or her words and meanings, and weigh them carefully before they are delivered.

Many sales trainers, however, feel that the poorest use of their time or the learner's time is to lecture on subjects better taught otherwise. Yet, all too often, many sales trainers choose this technique over all others. Why? Because it's easier! But ask yourself *how many times you really understood what someone has told you, the first time they told you.* Very, very few times does one really understand the *first time* around. This is the problem with the lecture.

One of the simplest models upon which to construct an effective lecture is the time-proven three-step approach:

- *Step 1*—Tell your listeners *what you are going to tell them.*
- *Step 2*—*Tell them.*
- *Step 3*—Then tell them *what you told them.*

When many subjects are covered in the same lecture, the "3T" technique can be applied by simply recycling through the 3Ts as new topics are introduced. The 3T formula, when combined with an awareness on the part of the lecturer of the need for a warm-up at the beginning and a feedback at the end of the talk, can be an excellent model

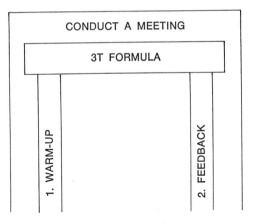

Fig. 2. A model for giving a lecture

for any lecture (see Fig. 2). The warm-up and feedback activities assure that the lecturer has properly prepared the audience, has delivered the message effectively, and has confirmed this by means of a question-and-answer session (or testing or discussion). Lectures can be further improved by the use of slides, overhead projectors, flip charts, blackboards, etc.

Audiovisual presentations

Nonparticipative techniques include the general field of audio and videotapes, sound-slide films, slide-script presentations, motion pictures, and recordings. The advantage of the presentation technique is that the message can be "canned" so that every listener or viewer is *exposed* to the same message every time. Note the careful use of the word "exposed." It was chosen to point out that usually there are as many different messages delivered from an exposure as there are people exposed to it. (The audiovisual has yet to be created that achieves that sense of satisfaction for either the teacher or learner that a well-structured form of participation elicits.)

The audiovisual presentation is useful for just that—the presenting of information. But to be effective, the message must be reinforced and shown to be useful on the job through the use of participative techniques. The audiovisual alone cannot be depended on to accomplish sales training.

Any audiovisual presentation should cover the following steps:

1. *Prepare to use the audiovisual.*
   a. Light levels okay?
   b. Sound levels okay?
   c. Seating arrangements okay?
   d. Power supply adequate?
   e. Screen size okay?
   f. Has the motion picture been prescreened? Any breaks or ripped portions which need repairs?
   g. Extra bulbs on hand?
2. *Prepare the audience.*
   a. Properly introduce the subject of the audiovisual—pointing out the need of the salespersons to be aware of the message they are going to hear/see.
   b. Alert the salespeople to points of interest which will require them to pay particular attention.
   c. Let the trainees know that there is going to be a feedback session (test-discussion-question and answer).
3. *Present the audiovisual.*
4. *Feedback.*
   a. Ask various individuals to relate the message of the film in terms of their jobs, or
   b. Use a test followed by book answers and discussion, or
   c. Conduct a discussion on how the principles of the film can be applied on the sales job.

Reading assignments

Reading assignments, like any other nonparticipative technique, can help prepare learners for participative training or further reinforce a different kind of nonparticipative technique.

Skits—dramatic presentations—sales shows

The pluses and minuses of "show business" techniques for sales trainers are legion. But unless the skit or presentation has an element of role play involving the learner, it must be considered as a nonparticipative technique, differing from the lecture only in that it has dialogue and presents dramatized examples.

Many times referred to as a "dog and pony show," this kind of activity is all too often relied on to "jazz up the troops." Just as often, the effect is so transitory that it barely registers with the audience! Under certain circumstances, it's a palatable way to present a message, and usually a lot of fun when it's happening.

In the early days of sales training, skits (dramatic presentations) and sales shows were considered an essential part of the sales-trainer's repertoire. A sales meeting was not a sales meeting without a "right" and "wrong" presentation; and the wrong presentation was usually a comedy skit which either got a big laugh and taught nothing or fell flat —usually the latter. Comedy is extremely difficult to do well. It should be approached with extreme caution: it is the rare amateur who can succeed with comedy—especially with today's sophisticated sales forces. High production costs have made the dramatized sales show impractical for many companies. Also, enlightened trainers have learned that participative sales training is much more productive.

The 3T design for a lecture discussed earlier is just as valid for this type of technique. Follow the steps of "warm-up—3T—feedback," and you'll have the basic format for a sales show.

Participative techniques

Probably one of the earliest recorded uses of the participative technique was by the greatest of the Greek philosophers, Socrates (469(?)–399 B.C.). He taught by *questioning* his learners about their opinions and then asking further questions about their answers. By this means he was able to show them how inadequate their opinions generally were. Then, he helped them go beyond opinion and search out essential meanings.

Professional sales trainers are making ever-increasing use of a variety of participative techniques to improve the results of their training. As was pointed out in the discussion of the Blake and Mouton Scientific Method Model of Learning, the need for participative training is vital if the sales trainee is to put the training provided to effective use.

Of all the participative techniques available, the most common are: the role play and critique, coaching and counseling, team grouping, and instrumentation.

Role play and critique

Role play was originally developed by Dr. S. L. Mareno as a psychotherapeutic tool to help people gain better insight into their own behavior. It was soon recognized by sales trainers as a powerful technique which allows a trainee to try out and experiment with various sales styles without endangering sales in a real-life situation. Role play provides the trainer with hard evidence of the salespersons' mastery of the sales function—the ability to make Feature, Advantage, Benefit (FAB) presentations and close a sale. There are many variations of the role-play technique—some utilizing audio and/or videotape—but generally role plays are conducted as follows:

1. *Define the sales problem.* It can be a written or verbalized structure with complete market and other background; or it can be presented with a minimum of structure.

2. *Establish a situation.* This is sometimes referred to as the "critical incident." Polarize a situation for the participants in forms of specifics that can be dealt with in the "here and now."

3. *Cast the characters.* If possible, it is prudent to let the characters play themselves as much as possible to avoid side issues such as strange names and unfamiliar personalities. Many times it is wise to prepare written descriptions of the customer, the salesperson, and the situation.

4. *Brief the salesperson and the customer.* Assure yourself that the "actors" know their roles. Some trainers brief the salesperson player separately from the customer player. When this is done, it assures a more spontaneous role play. It is wise to assign observer roles to all who will witness the role play. Make sure everyone has a task.

5. *Act out the situation.* The first few minutes of a role play are vital to the players losing themselves in the process. If they get off to a poor start, there is nothing wrong with asking them to start again. Once the action starts, the success of the role play is almost assured.

6. *Stop the role play at the appropriate time.* Experienced trainers set a time limit so that the role play does not drag on endlessly. Most experienced trainers do not let the role play exceed ten or fifteen minutes. Many restrict it to fewer than five minutes.

7. *Critique—analyze—discuss the situation and behavior of the actors.* Most sales trainers feel it makes sense to ask the audience observers to give their views of how it went *before* the actors give theirs. However it's done, the critique is vital to the learning experience. In a sense, it's more important than the role play itself.

8. *Decide how to use the sales insight gained.* This is the critical point that is missed so often. A good question to ask the salesperson who played the sales role is, "How will you use this experience in your very next sales effort?"

Coaching and counseling

The very heart of participative sales training is that done by the sales supervisor out on the job—in the real world. It is the "guts" of real sales training, and can only be done effectively by the salesperson's boss. Many supervisors forget that, for better or for worse, the salesperson is constantly being trained—or should be. It is a process that never ends, so long as the supervisor-salesperson relationship continues. Entire books have been written on the sales coaching and counseling process.

The techniques for training sales supervisors so that they can become more effective in coaching and counseling are discussed in other chapters of this book. (The JIT sequence discussed in Table 1 is an excellent model). Sufficient for the reader at this point is the knowledge that supervisor's coaching and counseling is one of the most powerful techniques available to the sales trainer. It is the very essence of sales training and, to the frustration of many sales trainers, is sometimes beyond their power to make effective.

Team grouping

Often referred to as "buzz" groups, or brainstorming sessions, or "subgroups"—these types of experiences, in which small groups of four to seven people get together to confront a problem, are enormously effective participative exercises. These techniques are particularly useful where "peer" exchange is important to the learning experience. And peer learning is a powerful force.

Team-grouping exercises can be structured in a variety of different ways, and are especially desirable where involvement of each individual is critical. The usual instructions for team groups are as follows:

1. *Make sure that the task of the subgroup is crystal clear.* Many trainers write the task out and make copies of it, then read it to the subgroups before they are released to carry out the task. They also give them a copy of it so that it can be reviewed in the subgroup, prior to the exercise. If this is not done, the tendency is for a lot of confusion to exist, with the group losing a lot of time that should be spent

on the task while trying to figure out what they are supposed to be doing.

2. *Instruct the group to appoint a captain and/or a recorder.* It is wise to have the group do this as a first step before they get down to business. It is normal to provide flip charts for the recording of the thoughts of the group which can be used later for feedback to the entire group of the teams' conclusions and/or recommendations.

3. *Precede the exercise by some input on "synergy."* Remind the group that the result of thinking by many minds is far better than the individual thinking of single minds. Remind the group that each person has a responsibility for insisting that every other member of the group be heard.

4. *Set specific time limits for the exercise.* Follow this up by looking in on each of the subgroups occasionally and reminding them of their progress against the allotted time.

5. *Regrouping for summary.* Always conclude the exercise by reforming the entire group and having the team captain report the group's results. Where practical, attempt to resolve the various team reports into one major summary.

Instrumented training

Blake and Mouton introduced the use of instrumentation for evaluation and critique as a part of their Management Grid Program.* They later applied the same techniques to the sales situation in their program "Sales Grid Training." Instrumented training allows the trainer to manage the learning experience with minimum involvement on his or her part. A good instrument is not easy to prepare—it requires much sound thinking and perception to prepare properly. Nevertheless, the results are almost invariably rewarding, particularly where it is important for peer exchange to take place.

The use of multiple-choice-question instruments combined with teaming and subgrouping has become a valuable tool for sales trainers when used as follows:

1. The salesperson completes the multiple-choice instrument. Answers are then "set in concrete" and cannot be changed. Often these instruments are completed prior to the training session, and are based on reading required by the trainer.

* Management Grid Program—Scientific Methods, Inc., Austin, Texas.

2. The salesperson subgroups with others who have completed the instrument, and the group is instructed to complete an instrument *for the team as a whole.* This causes much discussion and argument for points, leading to real learning as peers discuss the reasons for their particular answers.

3. The subgroups are reassembled, and the trainer provides the book answers. Many times it is possible to show that the average score of the individual team members is much lower than the team group effort. A skilled trainer in this technique can make many useful behavioral observations from an analysis of the results of such an effort.

Programmed instruction

The modern use of programmed instruction stems from research originally done by Dr. B. F. Skinner and his associates at Harvard. They demonstrated that learning could be enhanced by presenting small bits of information at a time, and reinforcing positive behavior and penalizing negative behavior. The initial application of this technique in modern training was to present the learner with small bits of information—in "frames"—in contrast to the reading of a page or an entire chapter of a text. Learner response was asked for immediately in the form of a question about that bit of information. If the learner answered the question incorrectly, this was known because the correct answer was immediately supplied. The learner was not supposed to proceed to the next bit of information until he or she understood why the question had been answered incorrectly.

The initial forms of programmed instruction were complex and tended to be exceedingly boring for many students, because each bit of information was repeated—tested and reinforced in four separate frames.

The programmed-instruction technique has survived its growing pains, and has been greatly refined and improved. It is a valuable tool for bringing a group of salespeople to a common starting point for further training where a body of knowledge is necessary. Although attempts have been made to use programmed instruction to teach selling skills, it is basically a tool to convey information. The beauty of it is that each trainee proceeds at his or her own speed and is motivated to move on because of the immediate feedback provided.

Many new and exciting programmed-instruction techniques have been developed since the early days of straight "linear" programming. The most common of these is "branching," which allows the learner, if he or she responds correctly, to move more rapidly through the program. Only when an error is made is the subject required to go back and restudy the data incorrectly learned. Branching is often referred to as "mixed book," "gating," or "fast tracking." What this means is that each individual is able to determine his or her own entry level, and is not compelled to waste time covering information that is already known. Salespeople are notoriously poor (and reluctant) readers. When they are provided with a mechanism that permits them to study only that which they do not already know (rather than wasting their time on data that is old hat) they are grateful.

New training techniques are constantly being developed by creative trainers. One way to keep yourself up to date is to join organizations such as NSSTE when you are qualified, or the American Society for Training and Development. Association with other trainers will inspire you to learn, innovate, and create new training techniques on your own.

CHAPTER 2

DEVELOPING TRAINING PROGRAMS
WILLIAM J. BRYAN

William J. Bryan is Manager, Education and Training for the Glidden-Durkee Division, SCM Corporation. This 21-member training staff provides sales, sales-management, research, manufacturing, and financial training for the SCM Corporation. Mr. Bryan is a Chapter officer in the American Society for Training and Development and a member of NSSTE. He has spoken to many groups on the subject of training and development, and is currently authoring a book on manpower planning and development.

What do you do—when you've been a sales trainer for two weeks and someone "up top" decides you must conduct a sales seminar within the month?

Your first sales seminar within the month? It sounds absurd, but the fact is that it really happens. Once top management has decided sales training is a worthy undertaking, they frequently see no reason why their new sales trainer shouldn't start to train—and soon. If you happen to be one of those charged with performing such a miracle, see if you can't buy a little more time. If, however, the practical realities make a postponement an impossibility, you have a lot of ground to cover in a breathlessly short period of time.

Since you are going to need a lot of help—on short notice—you should ask that a memo from someone high up be circulated to all those whose participation you are probably going to need, informing them of the importance of the seminar and of the urgent need for their assistance. Such a decree has a magical effect on the degree of cooperation extended by individuals who might normally be expected to beg off because they "just haven't the time."

Simultaneously, you must telescope a number of developmental steps and chores which are normally strung out in a more sequential and orderly fashion. Major steps include the following:

1. Determine exactly who your audience will be and how they are to be selected, as well as notified, about the session.

2. Determine where and when the seminar will or should be conducted, and make all necessary arrangements for the meeting room—and accommodations.

3. Discuss with the appropriate managers what they feel are the organizational and training needs which must be covered in the seminar.

4. Determine how, when, and *who* should cover these needs.

5. Determine whether the seminar will consist of selling skills, product knowledge, or a combination.

6. If it is to consist of product and product-application knowledge, merchandising, product programs, etc., determine what specifically should be covered (what are the deficiencies?); and decide who would be the best person to conduct that portion of your program.

7. After step 4 is completed, meet separately with these individuals and discuss their role, ascertain what sort of visuals, if any, they will require, and get someone working on them.

8. Send each session leader a letter which reviews your meeting with him or her; summarizes your understanding of the subject matter to be covered; and confirms the length, time, and date of his or her presentation.

9. If you need support people, other than actual session leaders, contact them and outline what you expect them to do. (An example might be a buyer for a role-play situation).

10. Send each individual contacted in step 9 a letter reviewing your meeting with him or her and the exact nature of his or her assignment. Be sure to include specifically when and where this person will participate in the seminar.

11. If selling skills are to be part of the program, and you don't have time to develop your own framework, determine which "off-the-shelf" program might best fulfill your needs with *minor* changes.

12. If time permits, develop your own "framework" for selling skills. Topics you should consider are Features, Advantages, Benefits; various questioning techniques which can be used to develop customer needs; ways of handling customer objections (and why they might object); how to close the sale; and territorial planning. Always remember that

participants in a seminar enjoy and benefit most from participation. In a sales seminar, this means the participants should have an opportunity to practice their newly acquired skills as much as possible—and to express their views.

13. Make arrangements for audiovisual-equipment needs.

14. Arrange for handouts to be duplicated, collated, etc.

15. If VIP appearances and words of welcome (and/or wisdom) are appropriate, be sure to line them up (and don't forget anyone!).

16. Consider the "ceremonials" which can be very important, especially if you will be bringing in experienced salespersons from the field. These might include a welcome cocktail party and dinner on Sunday night, and/or a "graduation cocktail party" the last night to be attended by key company executives.

Conclusion. Having done all of the above, you should not overlook the power of prayer.

SEMINAR DESIGN

Develop and implement training programs for first-line field-sales supervisors, experienced salespersons, new salespersons, and then field sales training programs.

The basic concepts in seminar design

Any seminar, whether it is designed for management or sales, should be developed to fulfill specific individual and/or organizational needs. These "needs" should further take the form of skills and/or knowledge *deficiencies.*

A *skill* is what a person needs to be able to do to fulfill the performance requirements of his or her job. *Knowledge* is what a person needs to know to apply the required skills effectively. Examples of skills requirements for management are counseling skills, communication of task skills, and decision-making skills. Examples of skills requirements for selling are handling customer objections, closing, and questioning techniques. Examples of knowledge requirements for a salesperson are product knowledge, product mix, and how to maintain profitability. Hence, a seminar design should focus on supplying the participants with skills and knowledge *which they presently do not have or are presently doing incorrectly.*

Since a skill is something one must do, the seminar participants should have an opportunity to *practice* the skill as well as discuss it. Practice sessions can take the form of business games, case studies, role plays, etc. A specific session in a seminar would contain four ingredients:

- knowledge needed to apply the skills,
- skills discussion and demonstration,
- skills practice, and
- skills critique.

Skills building becomes another important design consideration. Simply, skills building means a logical acquisition of related skills. In other words, some skills a salesperson performs are interrelated. Handling customer objections is a skill. But, maybe part of this skill is questioning technique (which is also a skill). In designing a seminar, new skills should be built on ones already acquired. For example, the skills involved in questioning a customer should be acquired by the seminar participant before any attempt is made to discuss, acquire, and practice the skills involved in handling customer complaints (if questioning skills are part of your procedure for handling customer complaints.)

Designing a seminar is similar to developing a programmed-instruction text

It is one thing to be concerned about skills building; it is another to apply this principle in seminar design. Skills-building techniques are very similar to the techniques used by someone developing a programmed-instruction text.

After *need identification,* the programmer determines what total skills and/or knowledge will be needed by the reader. Then, he or she *writes the last page of the program first.* This page is called a criteria page. It either consists of test questions or directions to demonstrate skill acquisition. The programmer then asks the question, "For the reader to answer these questions or demonstrate these skills, what must he or she know and what additional skills must he or she have?" Graphically, this is represented as shown in Fig. 1.

For each subskill, sub-subskill, sub-sub-subskill, etc., the programmer develops a criterion page. This page is actually a test that will tell the programmer *and* the reader if he or she has acquired that necessary skill or knowledge. If not, more reading and/or practice are needed. You can use these same techniques in designing seminars.

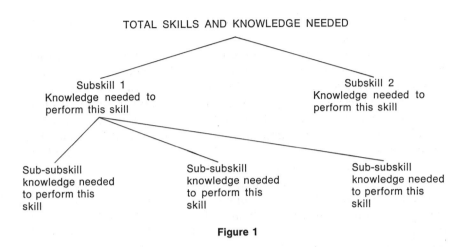

Figure 1

"When your participants leave the seminar, what will they need to know and what will they have to do (different from what they already know and can do)?" From this question you can begin developing sub-skills and knowledge requirements. These subskills become the basis for the various sessions in your seminar.

In designing your seminar, how long should it be?

"I have a good idea!... Since I'm bringing in our regional managers for a three-day meeting, why don't we extend it to five days and add some management training!!" That might be a good idea if: There is a *specific* need for management training for regional managers, and if this need can be fulfilled in the two days allotted to you. A fateful mistake in seminar design is to begin the design by determining the number of days for the seminar first. A more logical sequence would be to:

- conduct a needs analysis to determine skills/knowledge deficiencies;
- determine the most educationally sound and efficient way to impart needed skills and knowledge;
- determine the sequence (skills building) and time requirements for each skill/knowledge deficiency;
- construct a master agenda for timing;
- determine the number of days necessary to impart the needed skills and knowledge.

In other words, *determining the length of the seminar should be the last thing you do.*

In reality, however, operations management might dictate exactly how much time you will have. If the time allotment is not enough, establish skills/knowledge needs priorities with operations management and eliminate part of your program. Do not attempt to fulfill all identified needs if you don't have the time to do it. It would be more educationally sound to use the time to remove just a few deficiencies than to present a smorgasbord of ideas and concepts that no one could possibly absorb or practice in the time allotted.

On the one hand, management might reduce the time you have for a seminar. On the other, they might say, "Look, instead of bringing them in for three days, bring them in for five!" This leads to another don't: Don't *expand* your programming to fill the time available. Instead, determine what additional subjects should be added. Once an individual has learned the knowledge and concepts to support a skill, demonstrated ability to perform this skill, and practiced the skill until it becomes second nature, it would be detrimental to spend more time on the subject. Adults recognize when someone else is wasting their time—so don't.

THE FIRST-LINE SALES SUPERVISOR

What should you consider including in a basic first-line sales-supervisor's seminar? To answer this question, two other questions must also be answered:

1. What "problems" do your first-line sales supervisors say they have?
2. What performance standards, used by management to measure the effectiveness of a first-line sales supervisor, are these people presently not meeting?

Other questions which might help you in seminar design are:

1. How close did the supervisors' "units" come to meeting unit profitability (measured in placements, sales quotas, dollar quotas, bottom-line profitability, gross profit, etc.)?
2. Why, if it be the case, did they miss unit profitability? In other words, are there any evident skills and/or knowledge deficiencies?
3. How well is each supervisor able to get people involved in and dedicated to profit-producing objectives and activity?

4. If they have "problems" in these areas, could these problems exist because of skills/knowledge deficiencies?

5. What are these skills/knowledge deficiencies?

Your design of a first-line sales-supervisor's seminar should focus on *skills* and *knowledge* which will assist the manager in overcoming supervisory deficiencies. But these deficiencies should have a direct relationship to profitability; how they can make themselves more effective, and how they can make their people more effective.

The skills and knowledge necessary for a supervisor to meet the first criteria can be discussed using a lecturette, a business game, or similar training device. The intent would be to permit supervisors to acquire a better understanding of business controls and how they can interpret and use the controls available to them.

The second criteria is based on the "behavior" of a supervisor in relationship to subordinates. To meet this standard, a supervisor must be aware of:

- his or her present behavioral impact on subordinates;
- individual differences between people;
- why people work;
- the supervisor's "developmental role";
- how to communicate effectively tasks with both development and motivation in mind;
- how to control the activities of subordinates through the objective-setting process;
- how to have effective, "one-to-one" discussions with subordinates (career counseling, performance reviews, performance problems, job accountabilities, etc.);
- how to manage and control subordinates' time and supervisors' time.

The following first-line sales-supervisor's seminar agenda focuses on these two criteria. *No attempt is made to discuss functional business problems in this seminar.*

TYPE of Seminar: GENERAL CONCEPTS OF MANAGEMENT

First day: 8:15 A.M.   Opening Remarks and Administration
              9:00   Action Maze designed to test supervisor's "feelings"
              9:15   Functions and Activities of Management

		(What are the differences between being a supervisor and working in a nonsupervisory capacity?)
	11:30	Discussion of Management Style (Role play is used to describe various styles. Mainly used to develop a structure for the remainder of seminar.)
	12:30 P.M.	Lunch
	1:30	Management Styles Discussion
	4:00	Management Styles Case Study (To test the understanding of concepts and to permit participants to apply concepts.)
	5:30	Close
Second day:	8:15 A.M.	Planning, Forecasting, Objective-Setting Process (Various exercises and cases are used to apply theory to actual practice.)
	12:00 noon	Lunch
	1:00 P.M.	Delegation (The emphasis is on the "how to" of people development.)
	4:00	Motivation Discussion (Review preseminar reading assignment on motivation. Participants ask questions about reading assignment and apply it to "everyday problems.")
	5:30	Close
Third day:	8:15 A.M.	Motivation Presentations (By participants—critique is made by other participants on feasibility of plan.)
	11:30	Management Decision Making (The decision-making process—group dynamics.)
	12:30 P.M.	Lunch
	1:30	Management Decision Making
	4:30	Questioning Techniques (skills for counseling)
	5:30	Close
Fourth day:	8:15 A.M.	Counseling (Counseling sequence is presented, then role plays are used to demonstrate and practice counseling skills.)
	12:30 P.M.	Lunch
	1:30	Sales (A discussion of the sales representatives' seminar—subjects covered, etc. Purpose—so each supervisor is prepared to give operational follow-up to any sales representative sent to a seminar. Also, gives them background knowledge for field coaching.)
	3:30	Field Coaching (discussion and role plays)
	5:30	Close
Fifth day	8:15 A.M.	Interpersonal Communications (Exercises, case studies, role plays, to demonstrate individual differences, impact of behavior, how to deal with interpersonal relationship problems, etc.)
	12:30 P.M.	Lunch
	1:30	Repeat of Action Maze (Measures if participants have understood seminar concepts.)

2:30   Implementation Assignment and Follow-Up (Participants prepare *specific* objectives based on their newly acquired skills and knowledge.)

4:00   Session Evaluation, Closing Remarks

4:30   Close of Seminar

Suppose you had to design a seminar for a "Distribution Unit" sales manager. Not only would current management concepts be discussed; but, also, functional business "problems" and knowledge deficiencies. The following seminar was designed for a distribution unit manager in a coatings-sales business function.

First day: 8:15 A.M.   Welcome and Introduction

9:00   Discussion of the Corporation
(A major corporation with five operating divisions)

9:30   Accountabilities/Responsibilities of Unit Manager
(His/her position description)

10:15   Effective Management of Time

12:00 noon   Lunch

1:00 P.M.   Motivation

2:00   Delegation

4:30   Establishing Objectives Based on the Seminar

Second day: 8:30 A.M.   Credit and Credit Collection

9:30   Legal Aspects of a Unit Manager's Job

11:00   Security

12:00 noon   Lunch

1:00 P.M.   Accounting and Financial Control (Use of control input and output.)

4:00   Territorial Planning

5:00   Dinner

6:00   Special Product Application Discussion

Third day: 8:30 A.M.   Market Segment and Product Discussion
(Products, promotions, problems, competitive activity, control, profitability, etc.)

11:00   Tour of Research Facilities

12:30 P.M.   Lunch

1:30   Product Roundtable (Discussion of present products, product problems, future product needs, etc. An idea exchange.)

4:30   Close

Fourth day: 8:30 A.M.   Management by Objectives and Performance Reviews

9:15   Counseling

12:00 noon   Lunch

	1:00 P.M.	Market Segment Discussion (Products, promotions, problems, control, profitability, etc.)
	5:00	Close
Fifth day:	8:30 A.M.	Market Segment Discussion (Product, promotions, problems, control, profitability, etc.)
	10:15	Recruiting and Selection
	12:00 noon	Lunch
	1:00 P.M.	Description of Training Resources Which Can Be Used by the Manager in the Development of People
	2:30	Summary, Seminar Evaluation, Objective Setting

Designing a sales seminar

The concepts used in the design of a sales seminar are very similar to the concepts used in designing a supervisor's seminar:

- present skills deficiencies of the sales force,
- present sales knowledge deficiencies of the sales force,
- present product-knowledge deficiencies of the sales force,
- the most effective method for imparting specific sales knowledge,
- the most effective method for imparting specific skills, and
- designing the seminar around the concept of skills building.

Product knowledge, pros and cons. One question which must be answered before you attempt to design a sales seminar is, "Where and how should a sales representative learn product data and product-application information?" In other words, should the representative learn this in a seminar or in the field from his or her supervisor? To answer this question, several others must be asked:

- Do product knowledge deficiencies exist within the sales force?
- What specific products are the least known by the sales force?
- Why?
- Is it logical to assume the supervisor can impart this product knowledge to the sales representative?
- If it is logical, why doesn't this happen in the case of specific products?
- Are there specific products which should be discussed in a national seminar?

- Why? (For example, would it be helpful for the participants to discuss specific products, product application, product-merchandising techniques, etc., in order to learn from each other's experiences?)

Obviously, the design of your seminar will depend upon whether it will address itself to just selling skills, product knowledge, or a combination of the two. *It is possible to teach product knowledge and selling skills at the same time!*

Assume you have decided to design a sales seminar which encompasses selling skills and product knowledge. Product knowledge can be taught while discussing and practicing selling skills.

For example, suppose you are designing a seminar for a consumer-sales representative. To be effective, this salesperson must understand and be able to communicate "related merchandising" concepts to store buyers. Knowledge about related merchandising can be presented to the participants in a seminar using the traditional techniques of: a roundtable discussion, an idea exchange, a lecture, case study, films, slides, etc.; or this knowledge can be incorporated into a selling-skills session. An example of how this might be done is seen in the following *evening* assignment.

> Tomorrow, you will call on the XYZ Company and discuss related merchandising techniques with their buyer. Your objective is to acquire more store facing and additional shelf extenders to display your product. Presently, this store buys a minimum amount of spices, extracts, and gravy mixes. Attached is information on the related merchandising concept. Please read this material, prepare your sales presentation which will permit you to use all the selling skills discussed to date, and be prepared to make your presentation to a buyer. Your presentation will be videotaped for your personal critique . . .

This procedure permits you to expose the seminar participants to related merchandising techniques and knowledge; gives them an opportunity to *practice* their selling skills; and gives you and them an opportunity to critique both selling skills and product-knowledge acquisition.

Sell your products and services—not a briefcase, window fan, or martini shaker. When developing or explaining selling skills, make sure your exercises, examples, case studies, and role plays express your products or services *and* sales environment of the representative. In other words, everything you do should be as "real life" as possible.

You are asking a representative to apply concepts and skills to his/her present situation. Hence, you shouldn't ask them to sell a briefcase to practice a skill *unless* you do, in fact, sell and market briefcases. The sales process is also important. It would be foolish to design a "brief-case" role play for an industrial sales representative; especially if the sales effort requires a considerable amount of product development time, product-application study time, testing time, etc. Such sales do not happen on the first or second call. The sale is completed after maybe two or more years of work with a specific customer. The sales environment should also be an important consideration. A consumer-sales person might *never* sell a product to a buyer in an office. The primary job is to "run down" a busy store manager and use his or her skills to acquire more facings or product exposure. In this case, practice of selling skills should take place in front of a simulated store rack, not in a private office. Make the process of skills acquisition and skills practice as realistic as possible.

Should someone, other than a sales trainer, be permitted face time in front of your group? Whenever questions such as "What products, product programs, product-application techniques, etc., should be discussed in the seminar?" are asked, the question of "*Who* should present this information?" is also usually asked.

Who should be responsible for discussing the products in a specific market segment? The product manager? The market-segment manager? You? In some cases, it is logical to have a product manager, a staff representative, a line manager, or other knowledgeable person present a segment of your sales seminar. *This is especially true when you are looking for someone to play the role of a buyer in a selling role play.*

If, however, you give a precious block of time to someone, don't abdicate this time to them. In other words, don't say to a product manager, "Would you spend two hours on Thursday morning discussing Products X and Y?" Instead:

- discuss with the individual the overall seminar objectives,
- discuss how his or her segment will fit into the overall objectives,
- discuss the *specific* objectives of this segment,
- give "hints" on techniques which can be used to obtain two-way communication and participation,
- give information on how to use audiovisuals effectively,

- after the individual has prepared the segment outline, review it for educational soundness,
- if possible, have the person practice the segment with you for critiquing purposes.

The following is a typical seminar agenda for an industrial sales representative. (The emphasis of the seminar is exclusively selling skills.)

SEMINAR: CONCEPTS OF SELLING (THE INDUSTRIAL SALESPERSON)

First day:	8:30 A.M.	Introduction—Administration
	9:30	An Overview of the Corporation
	10:30	How to Listen Actively
	12:00 noon	Lunch
	1:00 P.M.	The Sales Process (A comparison of three types of sales processes, i.e., stimulus-response, formula selling, and need satisfaction.)
	1:45	Questioning Techniques to Determine Need/Feelings
	4:00	Features, Advantages, Benefits (Lecturette, exercises)
	5:30	Close
		Evening Assignment: Preparation for sales call-handling objections.
Second day:	8:30 A.M.	Handling Objections (Use of videotape feedback-role-play situations)
	10:30	Sales Planning (Movie, exercises)
	12:00 noon	Lunch
	1:00 P.M.	Psychology of Selling (Buyer motivation and psychology of the sale)
	3:15	The Close—Introduction
	5:00	Close
Third day:	8:30 A.M.	Closing (Role play with customer objections)
	11:00	Selling Skills Practice (Videotape feedback on one-to-one sales situations)
	5:00 P.M.	Adjourn
	6:30	Attitude Adjustment and Banquet
Fourth day:	8:30 A.M.	Selling Skills Practice
	10:30	Interpersonal Relationships
	12:00 noon	Lunch
	1:00 P.M.	Interpersonal Relationships
	3:00	Inspirational Film

3:30	Development of Objectives Based on Seminar Content
4:00	Critique of Seminar
4:30	Adjourn

As stated earlier, this seminar emphasizes selling skills. Product is only mentioned or discussed in case studies, exercises, and role plays. The following agenda is for a salesperson who sells in the painter-maintenance coatings marketplace. Both selling skills and product are emphasized in it.

SEMINAR: PAINTER-MAINTENANCE COATINGS SALES REPRESENTATIVE

First day:	8:30 A.M.	Welcome and Introduction
	9:00	Corporation Overview
	9:30	Review of Responsibilities and Accountabilities of the Painter-Maintenance Salesperson (Position description)
	10:00	A Discussion of the Sales Process
	11:00	Videotape Presentations (To become accustomed to the medium)
	12:00 noon	Lunch
	1:00 P.M.	Listening
	2:00	Features, Advantages, Benefits
	3:00	Role-Play Sales Situations
	5:00	Close
Second day:	8:30 A.M.	Psychology of Selling
	10:00	Questioning Techniques
	12:00 noon	Lunch
	1:00 P.M.	Handling Objections
	2:00	Closing the Sale
	3:00	Selling Skills Practice (Videotape feedback)
	6:00	Close
Third day:	8:30 A.M.	Product Discussion—Market Segment
	12:00 noon	Lunch
	1:00 P.M.	Product Application Techniques (Discussion and "hands-on" practice)
	6:00	Close
Fourth day:	8:30 A.M.	Territorial Planning
	10:00	Product Discussion—Market Segment
	12:00 noon	Lunch
	1:00 P.M.	Product Programs and How to Sell Programs

	4:00	Open Discussion on Any Topic to Product Managers (Idea Exchange)
	5:30	Close
	6:30	Banquet
Fifth day:	8:30 A.M.	Prospecting for New Accounts
	10:00	Product Information Presentation
	12:00 noon	Lunch
	1:00 P.M.	Practice Selling Skills
	3:00	Development of Objectives Based on Seminar Content
	3:45	Seminar Evaluation, Critique and Close

Who should sit in the back of the room? One problem, faced by every sales trainer, is the "well-meaning" operations manager who "just wants to sit in on a few sessions." Another variation of this theme is the manager who says, "Give me a rundown on your evaluation of the participants," or, "I want to see the videotapes of the sales presentations!"

A training seminar should be developed around the theme of "WHAT WE SAY HERE ... STAYS HERE." So, how do you handle this type of manager?

• Point out the effect a stranger in the room has on the flow of communications. Like it or not, meaningful exchanges will be dampened considerably by this "intruder."

• If someone just "happens" to walk into one of your sessions unexpectedly, stop what you are doing, and introduce him or her to the group. Then, continue with the discussion. Probably, discussion will be dampened. At the first opportunity, ask the person to leave, pointing out the effect his or her presence is having on the group. Nine chances out of ten, the individual will "feel" the tension in the group and cooperate fully with your request.

• If someone asks you to see such things as videotapes of practice sales situations, say, "I'm sorry. I gave my word that these would not be shown to anyone ... and, I won't show them," or, better, "I'm sorry, they're already erased!"

Telling people what happened at a sales seminar or showing tapes of individual presentations can come back to haunt you. If, after you assure everyone that your lips are sealed, you then discuss or show individual presentations to someone in line management; this same, well-meaning line manager might make a point of saying to a participant during a banquet presentation, "I understand you really had a problem closing today, Jim," or, "Jane, I saw the tape of your close. You did a good job!" The next day the word will get around, and you will have a "dead" session. More importantly, future attendees will hear the familiar phrase, "Watch what you say . . . it's all repeated to management." The credibility of any training department is based on development of a real trust relationship with all trainees.

Suppose an operations manager "demands" time with the group. Give him or her the time (especially if the department is paying your bills)—but, designate this block of time as "a chance to exchange ideas with the boss." It should not be called "a chance for the boss to evaluate your performance!"

You may also encounter the manager who will ask for your evaluation of the participants. How do you handle him or her?

- Point out the differences between a learning experience and an assessment center.
- Discuss the differences between involvement and participation.
- Discuss the fact that there is often little correlation between classroom performance and actual field performance (or, some people were born to be outstanding, professional students).
- Review the material presented in Chapter 7, "Trainee Performance Evaluation," and outline what the training department can and can not do in the way of evaluation.

A SEMINAR FOR NEW SALESPERSONS

The design of a seminar for new salespersons will depend on the type and degree of initial training they received from their supervisors. In fact, instead of using your precious time to design a sales seminar for new salespersons, it might be more appropriate to use some of this time to:

- determine how a new sales representative is presently trained in the field,
- determine what changes are needed in his or her initial indoctrination and training (for example, should there be some type of training at headquarters before the first territory assignment?),
- design a program to assist sales supervisors in their training function,

• design a follow-up system to assure your program meets the needs of the newly appointed salesperson.

The above activity can take place while you are conducting seminars for managers and supervisors. Again, part of their training might include selling skills. Knowledge of selling skills is invaluable to a manager or supervisor while field coaching, counseling, or training a salesperson.

Assume you establish an initial field-training program for salespersons. Further, assume you want your salespersons to have at least six months' field experience before they attend a seminar. This last requirement would permit them to apply seminar concepts to actual "problems" in their territories. A sales seminar for a new (six-months' experience) salesperson would probably emphasize both selling skills and product knowledge.

The following agenda was designed for Consumer Foods salespersons with six months' experience.

SEMINAR: CONSUMER FOODS SALES SEMINAR

First day: 8:30 A.M. Introduction and Administration
              9:15   Corporate Overview
              10:30   How to Listen
              12:00 noon Lunch
              1:00 P.M. Territorial Management
              3:00   Sales Process and Psychology of Selling
              6:00   Adjourn

Second day: 8:30 A.M.   Questioning Techniques
            10:45   Features, Advantages, Benefits
            12:00 noon   Lunch
            1:00 P.M.   Handling Customer Objections
            3:00   Closing
            5:00   Adjourn

Third day: 8:30 A.M.   Product Discussions
             11:45   Lunch with Product Managers
             1:00 P.M.   Product Discussions
             2:00   New Products
             2:45   Customer Relations
             3:00   Point-of-Purchase (Concepts and application)
             4:00   Administration (Forms completion, reports, etc.)
             6:00   Adjourn

Fourth day: 8:30 A.M. Selling Skills Practice (Videotape feedback)
           12:00 noon Lunch
           1:00 P.M. Buyer's Side (A presentation by an actual buyer of a major retail chain—discusses what a buyer looks for in a salesperson—reinforces the use of selling skills.)
           6:30 Banquet
Fifth day: 8:30 A.M. Merchandising and Merchandising Techniques
           12:00 noon Lunch
           1:00 P.M. Closing Administration
           2:30 Adjourn

FIELD SALES SEMINARS

Where should you conduct your sales seminars? This is a very important consideration, and there are some questions which can help you decide.

1. Are there enough potential seminar participants in a specific geographic area to make a field sales seminar worth considering to decrease transportation and lodging expense?

2. If you conduct a field sales seminar, who must be excluded from your agenda (or, what subjects will be excluded)? It might be impossible to have the same staff and management support away from a headquarters location.

3. If the subjects which must be excluded are *essential* to the seminar, can they be presented without the session leader being present? (Can media such as filmstrips, videotapes, etc., be used instead?)

4. If you are going to have selling-skills practice, who will be your buyers?

5. What tours (such as plants, research labs, etc.) will not be included in your agenda if a field seminar is conducted?

6. Is there a meeting location central to the participants?

7. Is it possible to obtain all needed audiovisual equipment (videotape, projectors, etc.) at the meeting site? If not, what effect will this have on your agenda?

8. What are the true cost savings for an in-the-field seminar? Answering the following will help you determine actual cost savings.

1. HEADQUARTER SEMINAR COSTS

   a) Cost of participant travel (ground/air to/from national headquarters) $_____

   b) Cost of meeting room (if applicable)   _____

   c) Travel cost (manager's reimbursement) for seminar support personnel other than training staff   _____

   d) Rental cost for audiovisual equipment (if applicable)   _____

   e) Cost of participant lodging at seminar   _____

   f) Cost of participant meals at seminar   _____

   g) Cost of participant ground transportation while at seminar
(to/from hotel/motel, etc.)   _____

   h) Cost of any seminar materials   _____

   i) Banquet costs, if applicable   _____

                   j) *Total Headquarter Seminar Costs* $_____

2. FIELD SEMINAR COSTS

   a) Cost of participant travel (ground/air to/from seminar site) $_____

   b) Cost of training staff travel (ground/air to/from seminar site)   _____

   c) Cost of support personnel travel (ground/air to/from seminar site)   _____

   d) Cost of lodging and meals for training staff   _____

   e) Cost of lodging and meals for support personnel   _____

   f) Cost of lodging and meals for participants   _____

   g) Cost of group meals during seminar   _____

   h) Cost of meeting room at seminar site   _____

   i) Cost of equipment rental   _____

   j) Cost of participant ground transportation at seminar   _____

   k) Cost of training staff ground transportation at seminar   _____

   l) Cost of support personnel ground transportation   _____

   m) Cost of any seminar materials   _____

   n) Banquet costs, if applicable   _____

                   o) *Total Field Seminar Costs* $_____

        1.(j) − 2.(o) = Cost Difference

1. (j) *Total Headquarter Seminar Costs* $_____

2. (o) *Total Field Seminar Costs*   − $_____

                  Cost Difference   = $_____

At first glance, a field seminar might seem less expensive. But, if
you already have a national training room, audiovisual equipment, ne-

gotiated hotel/motel rates, etc., the cost difference might be minimal. In fact, what you gain in cost reduction, might be lost in seminar effectiveness.

SUMMARY

As a training director you are responsible for the knowledge and skill level of the sales force; although the front-line manager is ultimately held accountable, you must provide the meaningful training. So design your programs with a view toward maximizing sales efficiency. Resist the temptation to try to cover every subject in one meeting. Develop your programs, present them, and carefully evaluate the results back in the field when it counts.

CHAPTER 3

PRETRAINING HOME-STUDY PROGRAMS

JOSEPH F. BOVA

Joseph F. Bova is with Smith Kline & French Laboratories, Division of SmithKline Corporation. His first experience in training was as an instructor in the U.S. Army Medical Department. Following graduation from St. John's University (N.Y.), he became a Professional Sales Representative for SK&F Labs. While studying for an MBA at New York University, he was promoted to District Sales Manager of Manhattan. Four years later, in 1963, Mr. Bova moved into the home office to reorganize sales training. He is a charter member of the National Society of Pharmaceutical Sales Trainers and a member of NSSTE since 1970.

An efficient and economical way to prepare your new hire for formal or centralized training is by means of a Pretraining Home-Study Program. We will give you some solid and proven thoughts on how this may be accomplished. We'll cover frequently asked questions, such as:

- What material should be covered?
- Who should get the program?
- When should the program be given?

And if you need further ideas on why to have a home-study program at all, we've listed some too.

How successful you'll be with your use of home study will surely depend on factors such as money, timing, and product complexity; and who approves and who administers your program will certainly affect its implementation. WHAT material to cover will be your most difficult decision, followed closely by HOW to implement it. WHEN the program is to be given will be affected by your hiring formalities and timing, as well as the scheduled start for formal training.

What you cover in the Pretraining Home-Study Program should have a very close relationship with what has to be done on the job in the real world. All three kinds of training should, therefore, be in close alignment: Home Study, Formal Training, and Field Training. They should all be preparing the trainee to face reality. The Pretraining Home Study gets the trainee "off and running" in the right direction. If much of home-study time is spent on material that is not needed later in the formal training, this may, in turn, cause the trainee to wonder how much of the formal training is a waste.

If you've come up through the sales ranks in your company, you'll have some idea of the material that needs to be part of the home study. But whether you're old or new in the company, don't take for granted that you are aware of the kind of background material the new salesperson should know. Get out and spend some time with people in the field. If someone needs a reason why, tell them you're doing a "task analysis in preparation for designing the Pretraining Home-Study Program." Whatever you call it, do it!

When you were selling or supervising, your ears were tuned for certain verbal information. Now that you're a trainer, you should be listening for additional information. Do you hear a mispronounced word? Do you sense a lack of basic information? Is there some hesitation to refer to backup material? Is there improper basic information? Perhaps one customer doesn't catch the errors or omissions; maybe the next one will. What kind of questions are the customers asking? What kind of information do they assume the salesperson should have? These are the sort of questions you should be asking as you spend time with salespersons.

If your home office is in the Chicago area, don't just contact salespeople on the Minnesota-to-Ohio and the Michigan-to-Iowa axis. These are all midwestern states, and the customers in these states will share certain similarities. Get out and see what the salesperson in Louisiana and Florida faces. Check out accounts in southern California and Washington state. Customers in Massachusetts are just not the same as in Atlanta. They often think and act differently, have different needs, may even express themselves differently, and are concerned with different problems. Your program should provide basic information that will prepare the salesperson for the specific information needed to sell in any territory.

WHAT THE NEW SALESPERSON SHOULD KNOW
WHEN REACHING THE FORMAL CLASSROOM

It's probably best if you don't assume the new hire, regardless of education or experience, knows anything about your product line. What is common terminology in your industry may be Greek to someone else. You may hire someone who was formerly with a competitor who'll need only learn a few essential differences. Or you may hire a person who has heard of neither your company nor your product.

The Pretraining Home-Study Program is the best time to familiarize the new hire with your industry and product-line terminology. This is an area where audiotapes are a great help. It's one thing for the new salesperson to recognize words and know their meaning, but what puts a couple of strikes on a new person calling on customers is the incorrect pronunciation or usage of your industrial terminology. An audiotape is an excellent way to be sure your new person recognizes the word verbally as well as in written form.

Initial training should provide basic background on your industry and types of products. The more technical and scientific your business, the more important this becomes. If, for example, your product is made of metal and it's important that your customer know your product is better because of the metal in it, home study might be the right place to describe the general area of metals from which your products are derived. Perhaps a review of how the metal used in your product and similar products was discovered, how it's produced, who produces it, foreign or domestic, and why that metal is an advance over similar formulation could be prepared so your new hire gets a feel for your product area and accompanying technical information.

In pharmaceutical home study, for example, we teach Medical Terminology using audiotapes, describe how drugs are administered, and then cover selected material on anatomy, physiology, pharmacology, and microbiology. This last subject is important because in talking about our antibiotics, we feel it's essential to know about the organisms that cause diseases. We leave the learning about our specific products to the formal classroom course.

Some of the questions on the new salesperson's mind, or perhaps the spouse's mind, might include: What sort of company am I joining? What are the benefits? Insurance, etc.? How often is pay day? Part of the pretraining material can easily and quickly cover this area. Don't forget that spouses are often unpaid members of the sales force. They often take messages, forward requests, or even perform minor services for the customer when the salesperson is unavailable. What better way to get them thinking positively about the new company than by giving them some information in an impressive programmed package?

DECIDING HOW TO IMPLEMENT YOUR PROGRAM

Set the tone for your formal training by putting together a well-designed home-study program—including estimated times to complete. The new person will really appreciate a program that tells exactly what is expected and then provides adequate time to complete it. At the start of your home-study program, the field person who may assist new representatives will not know your program very well, and may not be able to put the kind of emphasis on the training material you would like. Perhaps the old home-study training program was, "Read the catalogue and be familiar with pricing, if you have a chance, before you come in for the formal training." In this case, the new program will be quite a change, and the people who administer it for you will have to adapt.

Since you will have to use the first-line supervisors to administer your program, *be sure they know what you are trying to do!* Get out and meet as many managers as possible. Sell them on how important the home-study program is. Show them that the formal training will be better and more advanced and, therefore, will send a better-prepared person back to them to train and supervise further. If possible, and this isn't always feasible, get managers or experienced salespersons to go through the home study and your formal training course as it is revised, so that they will reflect the more sophisticated approach you are bringing to training. If you do this, they will be more cooperative, will boost your program, and will be certain the new hires complete the pretraining material properly.

Don't get hung up on hardware! Eventually there will be laser-motion holograph projectors that will allow you to project in 3D the most sophisticated product. This technique will allow an image to be projected in mid air in such a way that all sides can be seen in great detail. What a boon that will be in training for the big-ticket items. When this equipment is available, and regardless of the cost, there will be someone selling a training package utilizing it as the best way to train one-on-one or to a group!

Right now you can "only" choose from audiotapes and cassettes, sound on slides and on text sheets, slides synchronized to tape and discs, filmstrips synchronized to tape or disc, and super 8mm and

16mm motion-picture projectors, some capable of single-frame projection as well as the motion-picture mode. There are also reel-to-reel videotape, videotape cassettes, and video discs. There are computer terminals for computer-assisted instructions with readout on a screen, and some that prepare hard copy on paper. And, of course, there are old-fashioned books, hard- and soft-covered manuals, loose leaf and bound. This doesn't cover all the hardware available, but it gives an idea of what is available.

The decision of what hardware to use will be a substantial and difficult one to make. Often your budget will be the determining factor. The larger the budget, the more difficult the decision. Your task, after the budget considerations, is to select the most efficient way of communicating your training message.

While I believe that audiovisual equipment has much to offer, it should be used only if it will do the training job better or more efficiently. Its principal use should not be to make the program more entertaining or more impressive, to add "pizzaz," or to keep the audiovisual people busy making slides and tapes.

In deciding on hardware for your Pretraining Home-Study Program, there are five factors you should consider:

1. Most important—decide what is to be taught. Prepare a complete written text of the objectives and actual course material.
2. Let the material to be taught govern which teaching or audiovisual equipment will be used. Don't buy equipment and then try to fit what's to be taught into it.
3. Look at your budget for the program. Be sure this is the third item, for if you consider budget too closely at first and then unexpectedly have plenty of funds available, someone will want to get some "really impressive" equipment that may not do what you want it to do when the time comes.
4. Consider who will have the equipment between use; in other words, will it be readily available in a nearby company office, or will it have to be shipped to the trainee with consequent delay and possible breakage?
5. How much time between hire and start of formal training? If a hire is made on a Friday, and the home study starts the following Monday, equipment availability will be essential.

Perhaps the most efficient and economical way to have a trainee achieve agreed-upon learning objectives is by means of a well-written programmed instruction. The completion of a properly tested or validated program will ensure that your new trainee will come to the Formal Training Program with the specified knowledge. Simple, pen-and-pencil programmed instruction is not as exciting as many audiovisual techniques, but it can probably teach more material in an equal amount of time, at a tiny fraction of the cost. Don't overlook programmed instruction, and be sure to include it in a varied home-study program.

Part of the program should include testing devices to see if the new person is having any special problems or is not "getting" what you're teaching. By having the manager involved hold reviews throughout the home-study program, it also conveys the importance that is attached to proper effort to complete the material.

DECIDING WHEN THE PRETRAINING HOME-STUDY PROGRAM SHOULD BE GIVEN

The program should begin just prior to formal training, and the new hire should be allowed the necessary time to complete the home-study program. If you do this, you'll have participants who will remain very interested in preparing for their new career. If the hiring decision is made and the new hire isn't actually taken aboard for some time, then wait and give the home study just prior to attendance at the Formal Training Program.

This admonition is based on the idea that a new hire should not represent your company in any capacity until he or she has completed formal training. I strongly urge you not to do what some companies have done in the past: give the new hires some product brochures on a small number of products and a day or so to study them, then tell them to call on a few customers to "get the feel of the job." This seems to me to be a good way to hurt your company, your customer's feelings, and maybe, most of all, your new salesperson. What has to be a nonprofessional performance casts doubts on your company's image. The customer may feel insulted by being sent this untrained salesperson, and the new hire may feel let down at being "thrown to the wolves" with so little preparation. If the new hires must get the feel of the job, let them do it through observing experienced salespeople.

Another reason for starting the home study while enthusiasm is running very high is that you may have to ask the newly hired salespeople to complete some of the study on their own time, in the evening or on weekends. Your program may be well planned, but because of problems in leaving a present job, it may have to be done on a weekend.

Some companies who ask the new hire to complete the pretraining program the week before the formal training starts use the day they start the home study as their hiring date for personnel purposes. Others pay the new hire's expenses and per diem salary, preferring to use the first day of formal training as the official starting date.

Depending on the complexity of your company's selling situation, the new hire should ride with one of your better salespersons. This can easily be done in the middle of the home-study program; it will provide a break in the study routine, and also allow the new salesperson to hear some of the material being studied used in the sales situation. The field experience also provides a good frame of reference during the formal training class as to what happens in the real world.

Riding with another salesperson, however, can be a double-edged sword, as some bad habits can consciously or unconsciously be conveyed to the new trainee. So be sure that a "field trainer" is selected carefully, receives training on what role he or she is expected to play, and is briefed on the trainee's learning objectives. Senior salespeople who are being considered for future managerial positions are usually good choices for field trainers. It gives their managers an opportunity to evaluate their ability to develop people.

DECIDING WHO SHOULD RECEIVE
PRETRAINING HOME STUDY

This is very easy—everyone! No matter what experience the new hire has had, it has not been for *your* company, selling *your* product. Every new hire should know as much about your company as possible, so start with the home-study course. Here is the first place you have to be aware of that old sales trainer's admonition—don't "assume" the new hire has certain knowledge.

We have good examples of this. We've hired salespeople from other companies that sell antibiotics. A salesperson may come from one company and have a deep knowledge of the subjects relating to antibiotics and, therefore, find our course almost a review. But there have been other times when new hires with previous antibiotic experience have had only a very perfunctory knowledge; they really had to study to master our material. You simply can't be sure how much a new hire knows when joining your company. Your Pretraining Home-Study Program, if properly produced with appropriate tests, will help you and the trainee determine exactly what needs to be learned.

Another thing the home-study course does for the new hires is give them a "feel" for the kind of company they are joining. They are looking to see what sort of an outfit it is. Your home-study course gives an impression that may last for years. You'll want to be sure the program is well thought out and professionally prepared, and that it covers the material in the proper depth to prepare them for the formal course.

Also, you should get marketing people (such as copywriters and promotion people) to take the program. They'll better understand what the salesperson goes through in getting ready to sell your company's products.

SUMMARY

The Pretraining Home-Study Program can be the most important part of your training program. Its influence will be felt for months or years in the salesperson's attitude and knowledge. It is while taking this program that many of your new hires' impressions of your company are formed. So you should:

- select material for them to learn that will stand them in good stead;
- present it professionally, using media or a blend of media that accomplishes the job, without complicating the new salesperson's life with gadgetry;
- provide the new person adequate time to complete the program;
- be sure there is some guidance from field management during reviews;
- build in a chance for the new hires to ride with an experienced salesperson;
- give the course to all new hires (Don't "assume" a new person doesn't need it.), and
- not let anyone represent your company without having both the Pretraining Home-Study and the Formal Training Programs.

In retrospect, perhaps the title of this chapter is all wrong—the terms Pretraining and Home Study are probably mutually exclusive. I feel that there is nothing "pre" about home study—it should be considered an integral part of any training program. The success of the total program begins with the care and attention paid to the home-study material.

CHAPTER 4

TRAINING THE NEW SALES TRAINER
DONALD W. FRISCHMANN

Donald W. Frischmann, CLU, is Vice President—Agency for the State Farm Insurance Companies in Bloomington, Illinois. He is currently head of State Farm's Agency Manpower Development Division, which is responsible for the creation, maintenance, and administration of the sales and sales-manager training and development programs for State Farm's more than 12,000 agents and 900 agency managers country-wide. He served on the Agent Training Committee of the Life Insurance Agency Management Association, the Content Committee for Disability Income Course of the Life Underwriter Training Council, Chairman of the Sales Trainer Clinic Committee of NSSTE, and is currently the President of the Midwest Training Directors Association.

Mr. Frischmann majored in Business and Educational Administration, receiving a B.S. degree from State Teachers College, Indiana, Pennsylvania, and an M.A. degree from George Washington University, Washington, D.C. He has done additional graduate work at the University of Maryland and at Illinois State University.

The manager of training, regardless of the exact title which may be assigned to the position, generally has one of two functions, or a combination of the two. One function may be that best described as the "program putter-together." The other function may have the manager of training involved in the day-to-day, actual, front-line training of the sales or marketing person. Some training managers perform a combination of both. Major emphasis in this chapter will be directed primarily to that individual who has the responsibility for creating the training program(s), maintaining and revising them, and at some point in the future eliminating or discarding and replacing them with that which *currently* meets the objectives of the marketing program. The trainer's role with the trainee on a day-to-day basis in the field will not be neglected, since the program "putter-together" must have a valid understanding of what happens "out there in the real world."

If this describes your responsibilities, there are perhaps nine major areas of emphasis, consideration, and involvement necessary on your part. The amount of involvement or attention to any one of the individual areas may well depend on your past education, experience, current interest, and whatever is top priority in your job assignment and in your company.

So you're going to put training programs together? Then it seems that you'll have to get a handle on the following:

1. Learning or determining how to find out what the trainee is expected to do.
2. Finding out how people learn.
3. Learning how to teach knowledge and skills.
4. Learning how to administer a training program.
5. Learning how to create a positive climate that encourages trainee self-development.
6. Learning how to evaluate and reinforce correct performance.
7. Learning how to apply post-selection criteria in training.
8. Learning how to monitor a training program and furnish feedback to the developers of the program.
9. Learning the art of self-development and keeping up to date in the training arena.

How do we get all this accomplished? Let's take the nine previous points apart, one by one, and identify some activities, resources, and insights to help us get started in our careers as professional trainers.

Learning or determining how to find out what
the trainee is expected to do

If we're going to create a training program to teach a salesperson to sell our product, it probably makes sense to find out some of the following:

1. Has the company defined what is expected of the salesperson?
   a) Prospecting required or leads furnished?
   b) Sells only to established customers or also opens new accounts?

    c) Obtains order only or also schedules delivery and services customer in the future?

    d) Specific sales quotas established? *Who* sets quotas?

2. What degree of technical knowledge of the product does the salesperson need?

3. What field assistance will be provided for the salesperson?

    a) Field sales manager whose only emphasis is getting the sale closed?

    b) Technical help provided on the spot by sales manager or other person?

4. Previous experience, specific educational background, or other prerequisites for the individual hired into the sales position?

    a) What kind of trainee will enter your program?

    b) Is trainee selection made by some other function or will you have some responsibility in the process?

This is not intended to be an exhaustive list, but rather to stimulate your thinking. If you don't have this kind of information, you have to obtain it. It will have to be secured from your company management (both in-house and in the field), from current salespersons (or others knowledgeable of what real life is out there on the firing line), and from other accepted authorities. If this doesn't provide the necessary input, then you just have to go "out there" and find out for yourself. While all this is taking place, there are some cautions to observe.

1. For the program "putter-together":

    a) Don't assume that only the person with past or current sales experience can provide the desired or correct information.

    b) Don't assume that *you* can put the program together because of your past sales experience or previous background in teaching or allied fields.

    c) Get a clear understanding of your company's objectives. An excellent, workable, valid training program may fall by the wayside because it is designed to meet some *other* set of objectives.

2. For the field, front-line, day-by-day trainer:

    a) Don't assume that because you're out there on the firing line that you know everything there is to know about the product, how to sell it, or what the prospects really want.

b) Don't assume that your past sales experience qualifies you to "teach" someone else how to sell. That experience may also be harmful. How long ago was it that *you* were selling? Are the product, prospects, and economic conditions now the same?

Once again, this list of cautions could be greatly expanded, but if we're to secure an eagle's eye view of this total "train the trainer" subject, we have to keep flying onward. Most of what is required of you, the trainer, in this first subject area has to be secured from and related to your own organization.

Finding out how people learn

When we know what it is that the trainee is expected to do, then we have to turn our attention to acquiring some knowledge about how that trainee actually learns. Some people spend their lifetime in this vocation, but right now you and I can't do that. If we don't really know how people learn, how do we find out?

1. We could start out by reducing to writing our own experiences in learning.
   a) *What* did we learn?
   b) *When* was *it*?
   c) *How* did we learn what we learned?
   d) *What* procedures, tools, and influences were involved?
   e) *What* was the climate or atmosphere prevalent during this experience?
2. We can do some reading on the subject. Some specific references are identified in the list of references at the end of this chapter.
3. We can ask other people and we can do some observing of the training process in action.
4. We can enroll in some college or university courses on the subject; we can attend short seminars or programs on the subject; and/or we can hire an outside consultant or authority to come to us and put on a program.

You have to acquire this information or knowledge if you don't already have a working familiarity with it. While you're doing this, these cautions might be considered:

1. For the program "putter-together":

   a) Keep in mind that the objective is the ultimate development of a training program to meet your company's objectives—not to develop a late twentieth-century Horace Mann of you, the company manager of training.

   b) Consider the audience you'll be trying to reach, your trainees, and the general level of the subject matter—whether the objective is to teach them how to look at the moon through a telescope or how to maneuver a rocket to the moon and back will determine the depth of what *you* need to know about learning.

2. For the field, front-line, day-by-day trainer:

   a) Be able to distinguish between "*Can* the salesperson do it?" and "*Will* the salesperson do it?" As a general rule, it won't be done if it's not known *how* to do it. And it won't necessarily be done because you give orders to "do it," or because you knew how to do it when you were the salesperson. You, too, have to know how people learn in order to be able to do some diagnosis if learning is not taking place.

In addition to the resources already indicated, there are professional training organizations to which you can belong. Affiliation with some of these can provide you with regular contact with other trainers and thus provide a source of information, ideas, and answers to problems. Some of them publish periodicals and other material from which the same kinds of information may be secured. There are independent publishers who also publish regular periodicals devoted exclusively to training. Some of these organizations and resources are indicated in the list of references at the end of this chapter.

Learning how to teach knowledge and skills

It's at this point that the information and knowledge we have acquired have to be considered in terms of starting to create/construct our training program. Assuming that we've never performed this kind of activity before, how do we get started?

1. Professional help and/or information becomes quite important at this point. Not only do we need to know *how* to write effectively, we also need to know how to put it together, how to organize it, and what objectives we are trying to achieve.

a) There are many resources upon which to draw in this subject field. (A limited number of specific references will be listed at the end of this chapter.)

2. If you are the "program putter-together," you have to know how to write valid objectives for every individual piece or component of your program. An objective explicitly spells out what it is you want the trainee to be able to do when he or she has completed each little piece of your program. You *cannot* put any program together until you have defined objectives in this manner.

3. Once we have defined our objectives, then we can investigate other programs or materials that may be available (for a price) from outside vendors, within your industry, or from some other source. Generally speaking, these "outside" programs or materials may or may not ideally match your objectives. But if they're within the ballpark, purchasing this kind of material and adapting it to meet more specifically the needs of your company and your trainees may be much simpler and less costly than attempting to create a new program from scratch.

4. If there is nothing available on the outside, or nothing with which you can be satisfied, your only alternative is to create the program and associated materials yourself. Chances are fairly good that you can secure examples of other programs that you can use as a basis for reference right within your own organization. Someone will be able to inform you about the good and bad points of those programs or materials. You're probably not going to have to "invent the wheel." That has already been done, and your task will be that of modifying the wheel to meet the objectives you have established. This shouldn't be oversimplified, but you'll probably find that it is not as difficult as it seems on the surface.

In this area, too, there are some cautions to be observed:

1. For the program "putter-together":
   a) As you build your program, do your best to separate the skills, information, and all other related things that the trainee "*needs* to know" from those which it would be "*nice* to know." Build your program on the "need to knows."
   b) Don't be reluctant to test or try out the pieces of your program with real trainees before you cast that wonderful creation of yours in bronze. This can be done with a limited number of trainees, and you'll find out a lot of things you need to know. Of course, if you have the time, the financial resources, and

trained researchers at your disposal, you can embark on a very scientific research study with control and noncontrol groups. You and I can't resolve that in these pages, but you will have to resolve it on the job based on your own priorities, objectives, and resources.

2. For the front-line, day-by-day trainer:
   a) Concentrate on what the trainee needs to know in the market at this point in time versus what you needed to know when you were the trainee. There may be a major difference.
   b) Listen to the program "putter-together." If that person is spending full time or a major portion of time doing this kind of thing, perhaps he or she really knows a lot more about how to teach knowledge and skills than you do.

Learning how to administer the training program

Given an excellent training program developed by competent individuals to meet specific objectives of the organization and a continuing supply of reasonably qualified trainees, that program still has to be administered (conducted, put into operation). Except perhaps for individual sections or pieces of a program, there are few, if any, totally self-administering training programs.

If you are the "putter-together," an important part of your work is the consideration of and final decision as to how your masterpiece will actually be put into operation. Who actually conducts it; when; where; with what materials, equipment, and other resources; and how does that person secure all the information and expertise required to do all this effectively? These are only a few of the considerations that have to be included in your thinking and action as the manager of training.

One of the most important cautions you have to observe is that you cannot assume that any program will administer itself nor that it will be conducted the way you think it should be conducted in every respect. This part of the training activity has to be monitored and observed; and it's one of your responsibilities that may not have been spelled out well, if at all, in your job description.

If you are the front-line, day-by-day trainer of the trainee, you have to be reasonably familiar with all of the considerations taken into account by the program "putter-together." In other words, you have to know "how to do" out there in the real world. If that is your responsibility, then you have to do whatever is necessary to fulfill that responsibility.

Assuming that you have the greatest training program ever devised to use with your trainee out there in the real world, then you are accountable for seeing that it gets done, and gets done effectively and on schedule. Don't blame the trainee or the program if you're not fulfilling your job responsibility. Your point of view should be that the trainee becomes "trained" because of you, not in spite of you.

Learning how to create a positive climate that
encourages trainee self-development.

There is an important concept which relates to everything you do as a manager of training. Simply stated, the concept is: "All development is self-development." Perhaps it's a restatement of the old adage "You can lead a horse to water, but you can't make him drink." You have to embrace this concept and must also do whatever is necessary to assure that everyone else accepts it—the trainee, the field trainer, and all levels of management in your organization. If this acceptance does not occur, then you are placed in the unfortunate position of being expected to do the impossible—making the horse drink.

Acceptance and understanding of this concept place a greater responsibility on everyone involved than may be readily apparent. If learning is to occur, it is those who are to use the training program that must accept it for the purpose intended. If your objectives and those of your company are to be met, then everyone involved has a major responsibility for creating a positive climate so that all these things can happen. A number of the references listed at the end of this chapter speak to this subject.

Here, too, there are cautions to be observed:

1. For the program "putter-together":
   a) Don't assume that the trainee has accepted the concept of self-development.
   b) Don't assume that all this will happen because of your magnificent program.
   c) Don't assume that the positive climate that is being talked about means that everything is always "sweetness and light." Life isn't that way. There are times when hard-nosed management must be applied in order to attain objectives that are ultimately beneficial to everyone in the organization.

2. For the front-line, day-by-day trainer:
   a) If this positive climate is to be created, you have a major responsibility that you can't abdicate or delegate.

b) This positive climate can't be legislated from the home office, nor can it be created by edict or by memorandum. It's an all-encompassing attitude, and you have to make a major effort to see that it is accomplished.

Learning how to evaluate and reinforce correct performance

It's at this point that you and I have to take a good hard look at whether or not our training program is *results-oriented*. Perhaps this is an expanded way of saying that our emphasis has to have been placed on what the trainee needs to know, not on what it would be nice to know. Most companies have marketing objectives. If you and I have built the training program properly, it's designed to meet those objectives. We should have built into each training assignment a specific method by which the trainer *and* the trainee can evaluate the performance and understand what is required if performance is not at the required level.

The program designer has to build these checkpoints into the program; the trainer has to accept the responsibility for checking these bases periodically and in the manner prescribed. The trainee must understand why this is necessary. Specific materials and tools must be designed to assist in the process so that it becomes routine and easy to accomplish. Someone has to keep score!

The following cautions must be observed:

1. For the program "putter-together":
   a) Don't assume that the field trainer will automatically keep score so that the evaluation and reinforcement process will just naturally take place. You have to provide the rules and the tools to help the field trainer perform this function.

2. For the front-line, day-to-day field trainer:
   a) Don't assume that all discrepancies in performance can be corrected by training. If performance is not as required or expected, be sure to identify all of the influences that may have a bearing on nonperformance. Understand that the training program cannot be and is never intended as a be-all, end-all process.

Learning how to apply post-selection criteria in training

If a business is to operate at a profit, it must have personnel that perform regularly to meet the company's objectives, which in turn will help them meet their personal goals. The individual who is involved on a daily basis in the selling process has to meet some sales objective in order to continue to earn the right to stay in that position. In your company, you have to know what that sales objective is. All people are not qualified to be in selling. Thus, everyone who enters your sales-training program must receive a report card at some point. If the trainee can't pass muster, that person must not perform in the selling end of your business—for the sake of both the company and the individual. At the start of the process, everyone involved must know what "grades" are required to graduate and/or continue actively in the selling end of the business. At the risk of oversimplification, these few points are essential to the training manager at this point in the training process:

1. Agreement must be obtained, in the beginning, from company management, field trainers, and sales personnel as to what criteria will be established for acceptable performance from salespeople in your organization. *Everyone* needs this information. If I am to become a trainee in your organization, I can legitimately ask you how you can evaluate my performance if I do not know at the start what it is supposed to be—and, if you can't tell me, then I can rightfully assume that you don't know.

2. Once the standards of performance are established, then everyone needs to know what will happen if the standards are not met.

3. With standards established and consequences defined for nonperformance, the next step is to delineate the responsibility for identification of the trainee who does not meet these standards. Generally, this is out of the hands of the training manager; but the training manager has to be involved in the process if the training program is worth its salt, so the training function has to exert its influence in this direction.

Learning how to monitor a training program and furnish feedback to the developers of the program

This is a two-fold responsibility. The manager of training must:

1. Establish a system or process for getting a regular reading on how effectively the training program is:
   a) Being used in the field.
   b) Being accepted by the trainee.
   c) Being accepted by the field trainer.

d) Meeting the marketing needs of the company.

e) Meeting the needs of the trainee in the real world.

2. Be willing and capable of accepting the information being received and adapting the training program to meet changing needs.

The field trainer must:

1. Be capable of interpreting the program in terms of its ability to meet the needs of all those functions involved.

2. Assume responsibility for giving intelligent feedback to the program "putters-together" so that needed changes, modifications, and/or additions are intelligently discussed and related to agreed-upon objectives of the company. As a result, realistic information feedback from the real world will enable appropriate follow-up action.

Learning the art of self-development and keeping up to date in the training area

At this point, it becomes rather academic to state that you and I, as trainers, must also accept the concept that "all development is self-development." We have the same responsibility as does the trainee and the front-line, day-to-day field trainer. We have to become proficient in our responsibility. How is this accomplished? There is no exact formula, but it requires all of the following activities on the part of the training manager:

1. Acceptance of the concept of self-development.

2. Willingness to study available literature and information in the training field.

3. Willingness and ability to listen to the experts, wherever and whoever they may be, and to sift out that which makes sense in terms of helping to meet the objectives of your company's marketing program.

4. Willingness and determination to exert influence of the training function into higher company-management deliberations and decisions—being a "proactor" rather than only a "reactor."

5. Understanding of the value and responsibility of the training function in your organization.

6. Ability to see the training function as a viable part of the organiza-

tion of the company, essential to the development of the human resources involved, and not as a mere stepping stone to some other real or imagined responsibility in your company's management structure.

Sales training may or may not be glamorous, depending on your point of view. Its rewards, although sometimes delayed, are great. I wouldn't trade it for any other function in my organization.

REFERENCES

The following references will provide the reader with additional information related to the nine points presented in this chapter. Numbers following each reference identify the specific points about which the reader may find further information in that specific reference.

Books

Flesch, Rudolf. *The Art of Readable Writing.* London: Collier-MacMillan Ltd., 1949. (3,5,9)
Friesen, Paul A. *Designing Instruction.* California: Miller, 1973. (2,3,5,9)
Kirkpatrick, Donald. *Evaluating Training Programs.* Wisconsin: American Society for Training and Development, Inc., 1975. (6,8,9,)
Knowles, Malcolm A. *The Adult Learner: A Neglected Species.* Houston, Tex.: Gulf, 1973. (2,3,9)
Mager, Robert. *Developing Attitude Toward Learning.* Palo Alto, Calif.: Lear Siegler, Inc./Fearon, 1968. (2,3,5,9)
———. *Preparing Instructional Objectives.* Palo Alto, Calif.: Fearon, 1962. (2,3,9)
Mager, Robert, and Pipe, Peter. *Analyzing Performance Problems.* Palo Alto, Calif.: Fearon, 1970. (1,2,3,5,6,9)
Mager, Robert, and Beach, Kenneth M., Jr. *Developing Vocational Instruction.* Palo Alto, Calif.: Fearon, 1967. (1,3,6,9)
Warren, Malcolm. *Training for Results.* Menlo Park, Calif.: Addison-Wesley, 1969. (2,3,4,6,8,9)
———. *ASTD Professional Development Manual,* Wisconsin: American Society for Training and Development, Inc., 1974. (1,2,3,4,5,6,7,8,9)

Periodicals

Sales Training and Development
Myers Publishing Company
381 Park Avenue South
New York, New York 10016

Training
Ziff-Davis Publishing Company
1 Park Avenue
New York, New York 10016

Training and Developmental Journal
American Society for Training and Development
P. O. Box 5307
Madison, Wisconsin 53705

Professional organizations

American Society for Training and Development
P. O. Box 5307
Madison, Wisconsin 53705

Life Insurance Marketing and Research Association
170 Sigourney Street
Hartford, Conn. 06105
(This organization has a "sponsorship" relationship to a number of regional training director groups.)

National Society of Sales Training Executives
1040 Woodcock Road
Orlando, Florida 32803

CHAPTER 5

THE CARE AND FEEDING OF TRAINEES

C. ROBERT APPEL

C Robert Appel is Director of Sales and Training, International Ortho Diagnostics, Inc. He joined Ortho Pharmaceutical Corporation as a sales representative in 1953. He was promoted to Division Diagnostic Representative in 1958, and received the Diagnostic Representative's Award in 1959. He was subsequently promoted to Division Trainer in 1967, Manager of Sales Training in 1968, and Director of Sales Training in 1972. Mr. Appel was awarded his company's "Distinguished Contribution Award" in 1975, the highest honor which Ortho Diagnostics, Inc., can bestow on any employee. Mr. Appel is a member of the American Society for Training and Development and NSSTE.

How do you treat trainees when they are with you for formal training? How do they feel about you as a result? What are the things you can do—outside of the classroom—which will help make them proud, loyal, and long-term employees from the very outset? Do they go back to the territory feeling ten feet tall and bursting with excitement? Or do they give a silent prayer of thanks that the miserable ordeal is over?

The home-office training of newly hired sales representatives puts a severe demand and responsibility on the sales trainer. Obviously, the trainer must teach the technical information, the product knowledge, and the sales skills necessary for the sales representative to perform well on the job. If the home-office sales-training department does not impart the proper attitude to the sales representative, and does not conduct home-office training programs so as to motivate the trainee, the effectiveness of the training will be marginal at best. Thus, a real challenge to the sales trainer is to establish in the trainee the proper attitude toward the sales-training department, the company, and—most of all—the job. Development of a proper attitude, pride in being chosen, and the assurance that the trainee has made the right career decision are firmly in the hands of the sales-training department.

What are some of the things that contribute to making the new trainee happy and proud to be part of the organization?

Transportation of the newly hired sales representative to the location where the training is to be conducted should be the first consideration; this is particularly true if the home office is located in or near a large metropolitan city that requires the trainee to fly into a complex airport in a strange area.

Taxis, limousines, rental cars, and public transportation are among the possibilities for transporting the trainees to the hotel/motel where they will be housed. With so many companies having moved from central-city locations to the suburbs, public transportation and taxicabs are not always the best means of transportation. Obviously, we want to transport the trainee economically, but, at the same time, not overlook convenience and ease.

If costs permit, consider having the trainees met at the airport by a contracted limousine or taxi service, and given help in getting their luggage. Some companies have found that the cost of a limousine service is not much more than taxis or car rentals, and the reaction of the trainees to being met and transported in a chauffeur-driven car is one of profound gratitude. They are also pretty impressed (if not downright astonished!). It is difficult to put a price tag on the effect on the person who has been met at the airport and chauffeured in comfort and luxury. We have done it for years at Ortho, and view it as one of the best investments we could possibly make.

The living accommodations for the individual's stay during the training program are, of course, exceedingly important. The choice of housing should be made from the viewpoint of the trainee rather than the trainer. Many companies will pick a hotel/motel for housing the visitors simply because it is close to the home office of the training center rather than considering whether it will be the best and most comfortable place for the trainees. The size, decoration, condition, and brightness of the rooms are extremely important. Food service, attitude of the staff, and available services and recreation facilities should also be considered. Obviously, the longer the period of training, the more important the services and the comforts. Is it close to stores, theaters, and good restaurants? Even a restaurant serving outstanding food can become dreadfully tiresome if all meals must be eaten at one place for an extended period of time. Variety is still the spice of life; and this certainly holds true for food when one is away from home.

The decision to put the individuals into single or double accommodations must be considered from several viewpoints. The first, obviously, is cost since it is more expensive for single accommodations than double accommodations.

There are many benefits to teaming people up—provided they get along! They learn to study together and help each other. Frequently, the friendship established with their roommate during initial training lasts throughout their careers and possibly their lifetimes. If your sales candidates are predominately college graduates, most have already lived with other people, so doubling up presents little or no problem (unless a personality conflict develops). Many people think that if the candidates are male, there is no problem about doubling. The same people, however, become concerned about doubling up women. We have found no reason why two women cannot successfully live together.

Obviously, an indoor pool and perhaps a sauna or gym (and a pool table) are a real plus for the hotel/motel accommodations. This will give the trainee an opportunity to relax and exercise, and clear away the cobwebs.

If the initial training is longer than a week, a hospitality room for trainees should be considered. Frequently, the motel will provide one at no extra charge. The advantage of the hospitality room is that it gives the trainees some place else to gather, talk, play cards, etc., besides their own bedrooms. A living-room type of hospitality suite that, perhaps, is set up with refreshments and snacks can also serve as an ideal area for either group discussion and learning or study activities.

It is important to remember that the new trainee is not only entering a new job and a strange area, but he or she is going to be involved for a period of time with a new peer and management group. For this reason, it is important for training department personnel to be at the hotel to greet the trainees as they arrive. If the trainers sit down informally with the trainees and help develop a relaxed atmosphere, nervousness and fear evaporate. Here, again, the value of a hospitality suite for the class pays off. It can be used for a quiet cocktail party, but in an atmosphere more like a home living room. The most important aspect of the evening is the realization by the trainees that the trainer is an individual who is truly interested in them and who truly wants them to succeed.

Following this ice-breaking session, a dinner is held in an attractive restaurant in a private dining room. At the dinner the "ground rules" for the training period can be outlined, the training schedule handed out, and an opportunity given for questions and answers. As a result, the trainees retire that first night with a clear idea of what training has in store for them.

The location of training facilities will vary from company to company. Some have a training center or classroom facility in headquarters. Others reserve space at the local hotel/motel. Each location has advantages and disadvantages. Training in a hotel/motel complex permits casual dress and the absence of travel. The disadvantage of a hotel—and it is a significant disadvantage—is that the trainee does not get to feel part of and identify with the organization.

Make certain that the room used for training is large enough so that the feeling of "the walls closing in" does not develop as the day progresses. It should also be well ventilated, have adequate temperature controls, and be properly lighted. A possible disadvantage to a classroom in the home office is the need to conform to the company dress code.

The major advantages of a training facility at the home office are the feeling of belonging and the opportunity to meet all of the company's key executives, as well as the people who will be servicing the representatives once they are back in their territories. It represents an unparallelled opportunity for the trainees to feel welcome and important. After all, every company is dependent upon its sales force to sell its products; so it is fair to say that every individual within the home office or plant is dependent upon the sales representatives for his or her livelihood. Recognition of this reality should be conveyed to the trainees during their stay. It does wonders for their sense of commitment.

A small but important touch that has tremendous impact on trainees is the chance to meet and talk with the president of the company. A simple gesture such as having coffee in his or her office can create a lasting effect on the trainees' future motivation. Others who should be given an opportunity to meet and talk with trainees are the vice president of sales and the vice president of marketing.

Lunch periods and morning and afternoon coffee breaks are excellent times for other members of the marketing team to meet and get acquainted with the trainees. It can be helpful to provide all those who are to meet the trainees a list of their names, and the location of their territories. It means a lot to sales representatives back on the territory to be able to match faces with voices when they are obliged to call the home office.

The feeling on the part of trainees that "they really care" can be further reinforced at the conclusion of training by having all the key executives drop in the last day. It sends them off on "cloud nine," which is just as it should be.

Under certain circumstances, it is well to consider having one of the members of the training-department staff on hand at the hotel/motel in the evenings to answer questions and provide special help or counseling necessary to bring the slow learners up to the rest of the class. If the training program has trainees preparing a sales presentation for role playing, the following day the in-resident trainer setup can be extremely effective. Not only is the trainer there to assist, but he or she can also use part of the evening for necessary additional instruction.

One method that works well is to assign a sales situation and a particular competitive product for each trainee to prepare to sell against in the role play the next day. If every trainee is assigned a different competitive product, they will study that product in depth for their presentation. During the evening, the trainees can be brought together for 30 to 40 minutes in the hospitality suite and asked to tell the rest of the group about the features, advantages, and disadvantages of the competitive product assigned to them.

It goes without saying that cars should be made available for the trainees so that they are not motel-bound during their stay. This gives them the opportunity to shop, go to different restaurants, and move around on weekends.

The training department should set guidelines on meal allowances. The amount will vary in different parts of the country, but it is pennywise and pound-foolish to be overly frugal with meal allowances. When one is away from home, attending classes all day, and studying until late at night, the evening meal in particular becomes a very important time for relaxation and enjoyment.

There is always the possibility that after a successful career in field sales, the trainee could be promoted to the home office, so it is always useful to give trainees an opportunity to get to know and appreciate the home-office area. You may well consider encouraging them to utilize weekends for casual sightseeing so that they can become acquainted with the residential and shopping facilities available to inplant personnel. In that way, they learn that it is a nice place to live (should they ever be promoted!).

A graduation dinner for the trainees at the conclusion of their training is really a must. It can be a formal banquet attended by top-management personnel, or an informal affair with training-department personnel. Some companies conduct formal ceremonies with handsome engraved "diplomas." They are always appreciated—and almost always framed and hung with pride. If the initial training is only the first stage of a long-range training program, a certificate of recognition should probably not be presented until later on.

What about the cost of telephone calls home during training? If trainees are expected to pay for the calls themselves, this may create a serious morale problem. Many companies pay for two calls a week. Any more are on the trainee. That seems to satisfy everyone.

Laundry is another consideration. The trainee away from home should not be expected to be responsible for dry cleaning and laundry. Even though the expense for hotel laundry and cleaning is generally higher than a neighborhood shop, the convenience for the trainees is usually well worth the extra cost to the company.

So far we've only talked about the external factors that can have influence on the trainee's attitude and motivation. There is no question that the key person or persons are the sales trainers.

The teacher teaches but the student learns. And, as we all know, learning is markedly affected by the manner and the quality of the teaching. It is vital that the trainer establish from the very beginning that his or her responsibility is totally to the trainee. The only justification for the trainer's existence is to make the learning process as easy and as effective as possible. The trainer must become a friend and develop a genuine trust relationship with each trainee. The trainer should truly love to see learning occur and growth take place—because that's what training is all about.

In summary, it is important to recognize that many little things markedly affect the success of sales training. The trainer must have empathy for the feelings and needs of each trainee. Obviously, costs are important, but if you add up the cost of recruiting, selection, and training itself, the price paid for these important extras is small indeed. The major cost to consider in comparison to all expenditures for training is the price of failure, lost business, turnover, damage to the company's reputation, and replacement of the sales representative. What is the return on investment? A successful, productive sales performance. For the trainee to return to the territory excited as well as prepared to do the job is the only feedback the trainer needs to know to insure that the company's training objectives have been fulfilled. It's a rewarding feeling.

CHAPTER 6

FOLLOW-UP TRAINING METHODS
RICHARD H. SCHOENLANK

Richard H. Schoenlank is with Vick Chemical. His responsibilities include the development and implementation of marketing staff and sales force training programs.

After graduating from Wagner College in 1950 with a B.S. degree in Mathematics and Business, Mr. Schoenlank began his career in sales with Campbell. Over a period of 12 years, he held various positions, including Salesman, Key Account Manager, Institutional Specialist, and Line Manager. For two successive years (1962–3), Mr. Schoenlank earned the Salesman of the Year Award. With R. J. Reynolds Foods, he served for six months as a Line Manager, and then was promoted to Manager of Sales Training. In that position, Mr. Schoenlank developed and implemented a full program of training for all levels of the sales force as well as for manufacturing, plant superintendents, and front-line supervisors.

Mr. Schoenlank has been a lecturer for the American Management Association, and is currently an active member of NSSTE in which he is serving as cochairman of the New York Chapter of the NSSTE as well as Assistant Editor for the Society's new book of *Sales Training for the Sales Manager.*

Many interesting and brilliant sales-training programs have been administered over the years for the purpose of improving skills and changing behavior. Regrettably, not many of them are followed up effectively to insure achieving maximum results. Permanent behavior change cannot take place unless the new skills are practiced continually. But how can you be certain this will take place, and what steps can be taken to make sure those skills *are* practiced? This is one of the most critical and difficult aspects of your total training activity.

The burden of follow-up training is and always will be on the field sales supervisors. If they are not fully cognizant and in total support of home-office training, follow-up of a meaningful nature is not likely to happen. On the other hand, there are many things that can be done by the training staff, in concert with others in marketing, to support and supplement the follow-up activities of field sales supervisors. Let's review some of the follow-up techniques which have been successfully employed over the years. Hopefully these will serve as thought starters for you to develop your own reinforcement methods.

BUILDING REINFORCEMENT CONTINUNITY AS YOU PLAN AND DEVELOP YOUR TRAINING PROGRAMS

The first consideration is to build in appropriate reinforcement techniques, when you are initially developing your sales-training programs. This should include how, when, why, who, and where reinforcement will be accomplished. In other words, if your training is based on specific selling techniques, you should plan specific reinforcement activities to precede and follow all group training sessions. Your activities can range through the many proven techniques covered here and others you are now using. Training reinforcement can be applied through written, verbal, or audiovisual forms. The key point is to plan something to precede your formal training and something to follow up once the training has been completed.

PREMEETING ASSIGNMENT

Prior to a national sales meeting/district sales meeting, a premeeting assignment dealing with the skills to be performed (at the forthcoming meeting) by each participant can be sent out. During the meeting these assignments are carried out and discussed in small in-team sessions. This serves two purposes: first, it generates interest in the forthcoming meeting; and second, it lets participants know what to expect at the meeting so they will be better prepared.

POSTTRAINING SESSION ASSIGNMENTS

To keep the skills and the how-to fresh in the minds of the trainee, practical experience in development of these skills can be given in the form of a postworkshop assignment, such as exercise questions, tests, case situations, etc. The postworkshop assignment should force the participant to think clearly through what was learned at the training sessions and apply it.

Another effective means of follow-up is a series of individual assignments, with deadlines set in advance, for the completion and return of each. These assignments, based on material covered during a formal training program, should be returned to the sales-training department, with a copy sent to each trainee's manager. This keeps the field sales managers involved and up-to-date on training being given.

CONSISTENT FIELD TRIP FOLLOW-THROUGH BY FIRST-LINE MANAGERS

Field follow-up is best accomplished by work-with visits on a regular basis by the field sales supervisors. Also effective are similar field visitations by top field sales management and sales-training staff members. They can observe and further reinforce the skills presented and practiced during previous group training sessions.

The advantage of these trips is that they are strictly one-on-one, so the needs of the individual salesperson are the sole objective. But— how can you be certain that the field sales supervisor is doing an effective job of reinforcement during visits with the salespeople? One way is to have a sales manager or sales-training department staff persons observe a field sales supervisor working with one of his or her salespeople. It calls for considerable sensitivity—and a real trust relationship—but what is learned can be of great benefit to the field sales supervisor and, in turn, to each of his or her salespeople.

If handled correctly, such visits represent effective reinforcement of previously learned skills, as well as a way to evaluate the strengths and weaknesses of field sales supervisors and their salespeople.

FIELD CONTACT PROCEDURE BETWEEN TRAINERS AND SALESPEOPLE

As mentioned previously, one of the best methods of follow-up is actually to work with salespeople in the field. Such visits, however, should be carefully planned and coordinated with the field sales managers. On-the-job training is the responsibility of the field sales manager, so your role is really to assist in this activity. The following is a suggested agenda for such a visit.

TRAINER CONTACT PROCEDURE WITH SALESPEOPLE

1. *Preplan:*
   a) Review territory operation and coverage.

    b) Bring pertinent documents to discuss with salespeople.

    c) Review past objectives and results, and set specific training objectives. (Set only a few, not many.)

    d) Coordinate purpose, time, date, and duration of visit with the responsible field sales manager.

2. *Training contact:*

    a) Beginning of the day discussion:

        1) Organization,

        2) The day's plan,

        3) Specific training objectives for the day.

    b) Prior to each call discuss:

        1) Account knowledge,

        2) Salesperson's account knowledge,

        3) Specific presentation plan,

        4) Role play and anticipated problems.

3. *Observing the salesperson's call:*

    a) Explain to customer why the trainer is there—such as, to gather information for future training which will help the customer.

    b) Observe but do not interrupt.

4. *Evaluation:*

    a) First get the salesperson's comments.

    b) Give your observation.

    c) Get agreement on areas needing improvement and how to implement.

5. *End of day review:*

    a) Salesperson's review and estimate of needs.

    b) Trainer's review and estimate of needs.

    c) Agreement on needs and action to be taken to accomplish them.

    d) Identify training objectives for next contact with salesperson.

RELATING THE TRAINING TAUGHT TO REAL-WORLD OPPORTUNITIES

One of the first complaints of many salespeople concerning skills taught during group training sessions goes as follows: "These skills sound just great, but I have to deal with the real world out there, and my customers simply can't be handled that way."

Does that sound familiar? If so, you might ask yourself whether the comment is made to rationalize their unwillingness to try some particular skill on customers. Salespeople hate to be coerced or forced to try something new. However, by practicing the new skills in real-world situations during training, and then on a one-on-one basis with their customers as soon as they return to the field, they soon see them as successful and productive. The critical thing is to make absolutely certain that both the sales situations and the skills involved are indeed "real world."

The following is an example of a typical real-world role-play situation description to be used during training.

Case L—customer background

Publix Markets in Lakeland, Florida, is the customer. Using the account knowledge in your possession, sell Howard Bremmer, the buyer, the ARGO Sixth Event Promotion. Before doing this, relate the product history and history of calls on this account to the rest of the group. Be sure to pass on any specifics about the buyer's personality and habits.

This type of role play allows the salesperson to describe an actual customer, and a problem which may exist. Whoever plays the role of the buyer should follow the real customer's profile in making responses.

LINKING UP SALESPEOPLE WHO ARE SUCCESSFUL AT HANDLING THE SKILLS WITH OTHERS WHO ARE NOT, AFTER FORMAL TRAINING

One productive technique of reinforcement is through the formal linkup of individuals who are successfully handling the sales skills with salespeople who are having difficulty implementing them in the field. They can, at specific intervals, talk with one another on the phone, and, better yet, meet and discuss their successes and opportunities in the field. The learning experience will be greatly enhanced if they work with one another in one or both territories and/or handle a specific assignment together dealing with those skills, applied to a particular customer or customers.

Needless to say, the way in which the concept is presented to the salesperson in need of help can make or break the whole thing. Also, the way in which the more experienced salesperson approaches the task is equally vital. There has to be a genuine desire to help—not merely correct or demonstrate. Successful salespeople are usually more than willing to help a new salesperson since it gives them a feeling of importance plus a chance to demonstrate potential managerial skills. In choosing a successful salesperson as a coach, be sure to check with the field sales manager and get his or her approval. The manager who has intimate knowledge of the people involved may be able to offer additional suggestions on how to maximize your results.

RETRAINING SESSIONS FOR FIELD SALES SUPERVISORS

It is obvious that with the myriad of problems and demands faced daily by the field sales supervisor that the skills taught during formal training can deteriorate rapidly. Therefore, skills to be followed up in the field need to be reinforced with the field sales supervisor at special training sessions, or at regular sales-management meetings. You should never overlook an opportunity to obtain a priority position on the agenda of these meetings. One way to get their attention is to present a "status report" on the special needs of the field sales force.

The obvious objective here is to refocus on the need to reinforce skills previously taught. A refresher program should then be given to the field sales managers covering reinforcing sales skills in the field. Proper and continuing emphasis on the training support needed by the field sales supervisor is considered by many as the most productive means of reinforcing sales training.

THE USE OF REINFORCING PHONE CALLS

Personal phone calls placed to the regional sales managers, reminding them of the importance of personal follow-up on their part, as well as their field sales supervisor's part, are essential to the reinforcement process. A planned frequency of such calls should be a definite part of the action-oriented ongoing reinforcement of sales training.

Calls directly to recent workshop participants or salespeople you have worked with in the field can also help reinforce training given. Besides showing them that you are really concerned about their progress, such calls offer an opportunity to counsel with them and answer any questions they may have concerning application of a new sales approach.

THE USE OF WRITTEN BULLETINS
FROM THE SALES-TRAINING DEPARTMENT

A series of sales bulletins should follow sales-training programs dealing with specific skills. These should be aimed at both the salespeople and their field sales supervisors. One way to put those skills to work *now* is to ask for success stories from those using the newly developed skills.

Keep the format of the success stories as simple as possible. All you really need is a description of the selling situation and how the new skill was used to close the sale. The function of the sales bulletin is to give recognition to the salespeople and to share their success with all others, proving that the techniques really work. We all like to see our names in print, and this need is recognized by your successful sales bulletin.

USABLE HANDOUTS ON SALES SKILLS INVOLVED

Handout materials given during formal training sessions or supplied afterwards can be helpful to reinforce sales training. The key point to keep in mind when developing such material is that it must be produced in a usable format. Loose sheets of paper or odd-sized aids are quickly discarded. Find out what your salespeople normally have with them on a sales call and design your handouts to fit with other needed materials. You may find that a laminated card, a calendar planning guide, or a well-done brochure may be just the thing they will use.

Always try to get feedback from the salespeople, concerning how they are using the selling tools you have provided. You can do this by a questionnaire or, better still, by observation in the field. Suggestions from salespeople concerning future handout formats can really make your material a valuable part of their selling kits.

Companies spend lots of money developing sales aids which far too often wind up unused in the trunk of a car. With a little thought and a consideration for the wants and needs of your salespeople, you can avoid this and really provide valuable handouts.

USE OF AUDIO CASSETTES FOR REINFORCEMENT

As an alternative to written bulletins, audio cassettes can be produced at headquarters, distributed to the sales force, and played back as they ride between calls or in their homes. Their use at district/division/area sales meetings can also be effective. Generally speaking, cassettes provide a more effective training tool than a written bulletin. They can be produced as informal, personal messages giving examples supporting sales techniques which have been taught.

USE OF VIDEO CASSETTES FOR TRAINING REINFORCEMENT

Another effective method of handling sales-training reinforcement can be through the use of video cassettes, if you happen to have this capability. For instance, let's say you are planning a series of training workshops on specific sales skills, whether they be Management by Objectives, team building, benefits selling, or others. As part of the original training sessions, the sales-training department might produce a series of video training cassettes and then provide for each sales zone/region/division. These can be used during the field training sessions to practice the skills demonstrated on the video cassettes.

The video cassette is a positive and effective sales-training tool, and a natural to help accomplish sales-training goals as well as reinforce sales-training skills.

ACCOUNTABILITIES DEVELOPED AND CONTROLLED BY THE SALES DEPARTMENT

Obviously, all the skills training in the world cannot possibly be implemented properly without accountability. Much of the momentum built up during a formal training session can be lost unless a way is found to set up a form of accountability for the sales techniques just learned.

To make sure this does not happen specific goals should be set up for each person. For example, upon completion of a program stressing "benefit selling," the following might be established as an individual goal for each participant. "Develop written benefits-oriented presentations to be given to the top ten accounts and send copies of these to the sales-training department when completed." You can then track the results of those presentations and do everything possible to see that each individual succeeds. Make sure each responsible field sales manager also receives a copy so he or she can help you track the results.

REINFORCEMENT THROUGH PERFORMANCE EVALUATIONS AND MBO

Performance evaluations of some kind are used by most companies. Not many performance evaluations are aimed at the full development of specific sales skills, however. Since the performance evaluation is important to the salespeople involved, it can be a good tool for sales-training reinforcement.

If, for example, a sales-training course on benefits selling has just been concluded, a performance evaluation concerning use of the specific sales skills by the salespeople should be developed. New objectives can be added to established ones specifying measurements of ability to perform new sales skills. This way field sales managers reinforce the value of the new skills and measure progress. Also, by having the accomplishment of a new technique as a goal, the salespeople will strive to improve.

INTEGRATION OF SALES SKILLS TAUGHT IN PRODUCT MANAGEMENT—MARKETING PLANS

It is a tragic fact that many sales-training departments and marketing departments work independently of one aother. They usually do so even though their ultimate objectives really are the same—an increase in sales and profits on the entire line. What a waste of time this condition can cause when it occurs. What can be done about it? First, all major company meetings should present and discuss sales training and overall marketing objectives. In the planning of their content, a procedure should be followed to include input from both departments. An example might be the following situation in which each department has a definite objective for a particular type of meeting:

- Sales-training department—objective is to teach benefits-selling skills.
- Marketing department—objective is to accomplish the orientation of first-quarter sales promotions on their brands.

As a result of these two objectives, an integrated meeting format might be planned using selling-skills training, followed by specific product-promotional presentations to accomplish the marketing objectives. Then, to integrate both objectives completely, trainees could be divided into small groups and given case situations to practice their newly learned sales skills in support of the promotions presented.

CONCLUSION

All the methods outlined in this chapter can be effective and are being used today by many companies to help reinforce sales training. A very real part of the reinforcement procedure is to sell your company sales manager and people on the need for the reinforcement of sales training. If there is difficulty achieving this, it is safe to assume sales management is not really sold on the validity of the sales training taught. They may need to be resold if they are not convinced of its importance—or the sales-training activity may need upgrading!

CHAPTER 7

TRAINEE PERFORMANCE EVALUATION
J. DONALD STAUNTON

J Donald Staunton is Director of Manpower Resources Development for National Starch and Chemical Corporation, Bridgewater, New Jersey. He received his B.S. degree from Niagara University, and his M.B.A. degree from New York University Graduate School of Business Administration.

Mr. Staunton was Assistant Basketball Coach at Niagara University from 1948–1949, a Lecturer in Personnel Management at the Fordham University School of Business from 1949–1950, and an Instructor in the Management Department of the School of Business Administration at Seton Hall University from 1950–1951 (full time) and 1951–1954 (part time). He joined National Starch and Chemical Corporation as a Personnel Assistant in 1951, became Director of Training in 1954, and assumed his staff coordination of employment, training, and management development efforts throughout the Company in sales, research and development, manufacturing, and administration. He is also responsible for coordination of internal and external communications.

The objective of training in any situation is to change the behavior of the trainee. The evaluation of the trainee is a broader process, however. It will happen inadvertently even if not formalized.

Evaluating the trainee takes place both in one-on-one situations and in group situations. Group situations, however, are more dynamic and give a broader range of ramifications. Key areas in which trainees will be rated include participation (within group sessions), ability to express themselves, degree of learning exhibited, and social interaction with peers. Obviously, all four of these skills are highly relevant to the general effectiveness of the trainee.

It should first be made clear that there are four levels involved in training evaluation in general: *reaction, learning, behavior change,* and *results.* A detailed chart (Table 1) indicates that all four can be mea-

Table 1
TRAINING EVALUATION

CATEGORIES	DEFINITION	CONCEPTS INVOLVED	METHODS OF MEASURING
Reaction	How well the trainees *liked* the program.	• Program enjoyment • Identification therapy • Supportive and encouragement • Status enhancement • Attitude building • Sense of growth	• Evaluation sheets at end of program • Post evaluation on *follow through* evaluation • Evaluation discussion sessions • Daily evaluations • Improvement suggestions
Learning	How well they learned the *facts*, principles, and techniques.	• Specific facts retained • Actual usable information that can be applied • Mandatory operational information • Fundamental base for advanced learning	• Daily summaries of material covered previous day • Tests—feedback reports • Buzz-session summaries • Programmed learning exercise • Case study analysis • Role playing and evaluation
Behavior	What changes in on-the-job behavior have occurred as a result of training.	• Unless acquired information is *used*, it is lost • On-the-job-performance is essential to ultimate learning; unless applied, reaction and learning are meaningless • Human performance improvement must result	• Precourse survey and post-course follow-up by immediate supervisor • Complete *follow through* exercise with copies to boss and training department • Periodic follow-up in the field • Support of program for *execution* deficiency control
Results	Specific evidence that the effort produced improvement to the organization.	• Must meet pragmatic *objectives* of overall effort—*Examples: cost savings; increased volume;* reduced inventory; faster decisions; improved communications; credibility, etc. • Effective *use* of new *learning* must contribute *value* in terms of profit improvement	• Analysis of before and after costs, volume, etc. • Clear distinctions between D_K and D_E in beginning analysis of problem. • Postprogram comparison with specific, clear-cut objectives of program set in beginning.

sured, but effective *results* is the only one that really pays off and justifies the training effort.

It is this results measurement that is highly relevant to the evaluation of the trainee. It is the *presentation effort** of the salesperson that justifies the function; interpersonal effectiveness is critical to the success of anyone in selling.

Accordingly, the early measurement of the trainee's performance in interpersonal effectiveness seems highly relevant. It also seems apparent that the trainee should be made aware of this given adequate time and preparation to make his or her best "presentation effort."

To accomplish this, instructions and assignments should be given to the trainee prior to arriving on the "training scene." Along with this, training-need analysis can also be implemented by seeking the salesperson's inputs to higher individual training needs. This can help in determining the "initial repertoire" (the knowledge and skills and/or lack of these that the trainee has prior to training). Tables 2 and 3 give

Table 2
ADHESIVE PRODUCT TRAINING SURVEY

CONFIDENTIAL

CODE 1—Very Important
2—Next Important, Etc.

Product Application	Order of Importance to You											
	E	E	G	W	R	R	O	J	W	R	D	D	F
Case Sealing—Aqueous	3	12	2	10	1		1	15	3	1	2	16	—
Case Sealing—Resyn	4	9	2	10	2		4	15	3	1	2	17	—
Carton Sealing—Aqueous	2	10	2	9	2		2	14	2	1	2	10	—
Carton Sealing—Resyn		4	2	9	1		2	14	2	1	2	7	—
Box Mfg.—Folding		5	3	8	1		1	7	2	1	2	3	—
Labeling—Bottle		8	2	14	1		2	6	2	1	2	14	—
Labeling—Can		1	2	15	1		3	13	2	1	3	15	—

* "Presentation effort" is a term coined by Dr. Leavitt of Harvard in his study of "Communications in Industrial Purchasing Behavior" which refers to the impact and influences the salesperson has on a specific customer. Division of Research, Graduate School of Business, Harvard University, Boston—1965.

Product Application												
Tube Winding	16	2	3	1	4	9	2	1	2	11	—	
Laminating and Mounting	2	1	13	1	3	5	2	1	1	1	—	
Bag Making—Paper or Glassine	3	3	7	1	4	1	3	2	2	9	—	
Bag Making—Wax Bags	14	3	7	2	4	1	3	2	2	2	—	
Cellophane and Acetate Film	11	3	1	2	4	8	2	2	3	6	—	
Envelope Gums	13	4	2	1	5	3	1	1	1	—	—	
Glued Lap	15	4	11	1	5	10	2	1	3	8	—	
Heat Sealing	18	4	4	2	4	12	3	2	3	5	—	
Hot Melt Adhesives	17	3	12	2	5	17	1	2	1	4	—	
Blister and Skin Packaging	6	2	5	2	5	16	1	2	3	12	—	
Extended Resyn Adhesives	7	1	6	2	4	11	2	1	2	13	—	
Cups—Drinking					2	2						
Straws—Drinking						4						
Vinyl Laminations												
Struct. Prods.—Instant Lok												
Box Manufacturing—Setup				4								
Book Manufacturing				4								
Structural Adhesives						1						
Food Starches						2						

Table 3
ADHESIVE PRODUCT TRAINING SURVEY

CONFIDENTIAL

CODE		
	1–2	Need Max. Help—Know Little or Nothing
	3–4	Need Additional Knowledge
	5–6	Fair or Adequate Knowledge
	7–8	Good Knowledge
	9–10	Very Good Knowledge

Product Application	Degree of Knowledge											
	E	E	G	W	R	R	O	J	W	R	D	D	F
Case Sealing—Aqueous	7	8	6	5	5		8	7	6	3	4	6	9

Case Sealing—Resyn	4	6	6	6	6	6	7	6	3	4	6	9
Carton Sealing—Aqueous	4	7	5	6	5	7	7	3	3	3	5	9
Carton Sealing—Resyn	4	8	5	6	3	7	7	3	3	3	5	9
Box Mfg.—Folding	5	3	3	6	4	8	4	3	3	4	4	9
Labeling—Bottle	7	6	7	4	4	6	6	5	3	4	6	8
Labeling—Can	5	9	8	3	5	5	6	5	3	3	6	8
Tube Winding	3	2	6	4	3	4	6	3	3	3	4	9
Laminating and Mounting	2	3	3	5	2	4	6	3	2	4	3	7
Bag Making—Paper or Glassine	5	6	2	6	2	3	5	3	3	4	4	8
Bag Making—Wax Bags	6	7	2	6	2	3	5	3	3	4	4	7
Cellophane and Acetate Film	3	6	3	7	3	3	3	3	1	3	3	6
Envelope Gums	3	2	2	8	2	3	10	7	1	3	1	6
Glued Lap	6	4	2	8	5	5	3	7	3	3	4	7
Heat Sealing	2	3	2	6	1	3	4	2	3	3	2	–
Hot Melt Adhesives	3	7	2	2	3	3	3	3	2	4	3	6
Blister and Skin Packaging	3	1	3	6	1	2	4	3	2	3	1	8
Extended Resyn Adhesives	3	8	3	7	1	5	5	4	2	3	3	7
Cups—Drinking						3	6					
Straws—Drinking							6					
Vinyl Laminations	4											
Struct. Prods.–Instant Lok		3										
Box Manufacturing—Setup						4						
Book Manufacturing						3						
Structural Adhesives								7				
Food Starches								3				

an example of how such a pretraining survey can help tailor a product training program.

In our experience, we have also found that precourse assignments, surveys, and instructions add considerably to the trainee's psychological preparations and get him or her very involved in content and objectives of the program; which maximizes the probabilities for productive results of the training effort, as well as setting up an objective climate that can "fairly" measure the trainees in action.

AREAS TO BE MEASURED

In forming an evaluation of trainees the following areas should be measured.

1. *Participation.* Since one *learns by doing,* the trainees must involve themselves totally in the content discussions to reach maximum comprehension. Most training programs are designed to involve the participants to a maximum effort and give each individual every opportunity to get involved in the program.

Three dimensions of evaluating participation are;

a) indications of *attention*—nonverbal signs of conscious awareness of what is going on with full control of preoccupation and distractions,

b) *constructiveness*—verbal participation that clearly moves the discussion forward with relevant inputs, and

c) *objectiveness*—avoidance of participating for participation's sake, control of emotional projections into the discussion.

The best way we have found to measure this area is through "peer ratings" compared with instructor ratings. Participants are asked to rank their peers, and this accumulative ranking is compared with instructor's ratings for a composite rating. (See Table 4.)

2. *Ability to express self.* In our programs we give an assignment to all of our trainees called an "Idea Mint." (This is a well-used concept in the NSSTE organization and a mandatory requirement for new members.) The details of this assignment include instructions on preparation, delivery, and ideas for content. At the subsequent group sessions each participant gives the ideamint which is rated by the peer group, and ultimate winners receive prizes, etc. This peer rating can be very useful in the combined ratings. (Also see Table 4.)

3. *Degree of learning exhibited.* The most objective way to do this is by that increasingly controversial method, *tests.* Testing asks the trainee to reproduce the knowledge he or she has been exposed to and asked to study. This serves two important purposes in training:

a) it reinforces the key material that will hopefully be retained, and

b) it screens out key areas in which full comprehension has not been achieved so a relevant review can be effected.

Table 4
PRODUCT INTENSIVE TRAINING COURSE

COMBINED RATINGS

	GRADE QUIZ	SPEECH	PARTICIPATION	TOTAL
D	8	3	1	12
B	7	4	2	13
F	1	8	4	13
R	3	2	10	15
B	5	5	6	16
E	2	12	3	17
B	9	6	5	20
D	4	9	11	24
G	6	10	9	25
B	12	7	7	26
O	13	1	12	26
B	10	11	8	29
J	11	13	13	37

PERSON-TO-PERSON RATINGS

PRODUCT QUIZ GRADES (As Scored By Tech. Dev. Dept.)		SPEECH CLINIC (Delivery, Content, Amount of Preparation, Visuals) (As noted on by group)		PARTICIPATION (Amount of, Objectiveness, Constructiveness, Attention)	
1	S	1	K	1	R
2	C	2	O	2	H
3	O	3	R	3	C
4	S	4	H	4	S
5	F	5	F	5	M
6	G	6	M	6	F
7	H	7	H	7	H
8	R	8	S	8	K
9	M	9	S	9	G
10	K	10	G	10	O
11	L	11	K	11	S
12	H	12	C	12	K
13	K	13	L	13	L

More recently formal testing (as indicated on Table 5) has come under criticism because it allegedly "threatens" the learner and creates barriers to learning by inducing emotional blocks to some learners.

An alternative to traditional training would be a method that could screen out areas of noncomprehension without creating a threatening or inhibiting climate. This can be accomplished through the process of programmed instruction. In working through a programmed text the trainee works at his or her own pace and supplies answers or completes statements in the text. Correct answers are acknowledged by the text and the trainee is encouraged to continue. Incorrect answers are pointed out by the text and the trainee is directed to review the portion of the text where the correct answer is given. Good programming is a highly specialized art, however; there are sources available who offer programming expertise or preprogrammed courses.

4. *Social interaction.* While this is the least effectively measured area, it probably is the most important one for a salesperson. As we have said, *interpersonal effectiveness* is what selling skills are all about. Each salesperson brings to the customer point of contact a certain "impact" of personality, organization sensitivity, sincerity, logic, and relevance. This impact creates an impression that is either negative or positive to some degree.

The capability of socially interacting positively as well as technically with people has to be instructive. This can be measured informally by instructors and coordinates of the program. Judgments must be made! Since they will be made by our customers, it is critical that we make them first. Three or four judgments that agree are highly indicative of the input of the trainee.

PERFORMANCE EVALUATION FOLLOW-UP

It should be quite clear that all this evaluation will not be productive unless it is used effectively. The purpose of such evaluations should be developmental: that is, once areas of improvement are uncovered programs of action to help improve those areas should be followed through as soon as possible.

It is true that sometimes such evaluations uncover such an amount of needed improvement that ultimate satisfactory performance seems questionable. If this does happen, it should be confronted directly for the good of the individual as well as the job. The trainee's manager is the critical factor here. The manager should immediately follow up any training exposure with discussions about the experience and at that time implement the plan of action.

Table 5
PRODUCT INTENSIVE TRAINING COURSE

QUIZ GRADES

| | First Day | | | Second Day | | | Second Day Average | Third Day | | Third Day Average | OVERALL FINAL AVERAGE |
	Case Sealing	Carton Sealing	Paper Box Trade	Labeling	Tube Winding	Bag Making		Laminating	Envelopes		
F	100			100	100	100	100	80	100	90	97
E	100			100	100	100	100	80	80	80	93
R	100			90	75	100	88	80	100	90	93
D	95			100	100	100	100	80	85	83	93
E	95			100	100	88	96	100	70	85	92
G	100			75	100	100	92	60	100	80	91
B	100			70	75	100	82	80	100	90	91
D	80			100	100	63	88	80	85	83	84
B	60			70	100	100	90	100	100	100	83
R	95			70	100	62	77	60	80	70	81
J	85			70	75	63	69	60	100	80	78
R	70			65	75	82	74	70	85	78	74
O	85			25	100	50	58	20	75	48	64
GROUP AVERAGE	89.6						85.7				85.7

Evaluation of sales trainees is a very important part of your job. Field sales managers expect the training department to provide them with guidance in further developing their salespeople. If you are able to establish a creditable evaluation system, you will be providing a valuable service to your field sales managers.

One word of caution is necessary, though, in presenting your evaluations to field managers. Remember that you are measuring the trainees in an artificial training environment which differs considerably from their normal field assignments. Some trainees, particularly those academically inclined, flourish in a training situation but fail in the field. This is due to a large extent to the differing conditions, leadership style of their manager, and peer pressures within their own office. Thus your findings, if discussed at all with field-sales managers, should be presented as those observed and measured in a training environment. Then the sales manager can judge if the same behavior exists in the field.

CHAPTER 8

COORDINATING AND INTEGRATING SALES TRAINING

THOMAS R. CURRIE

Thomas R. Currie is General Director, Human Resource Development, for the Reynolds Metals Company of Richmond, Virginia. Mr. Currie joined the Reynolds organization in 1965 as Assistant Director of Sales Training, and has since been successively named to the position of Director of Sales Training, General Director of Training and Development, and to his present position in 1974. In addition to all training, he is responsible for manpower planning, career planning, and performance evaluation.

Mr. Currie has been a member of NSSTE since 1968. He has served as a committee chairman, program chairman, parliamentarian, member of the Board of Directors and 1977 President of NSSTE. He has twice been the recipient of coveted NSSTE awards for Editorial Excellence.

One of the most perplexing, frustrating, and difficult challenges you are likely to face as a manager of the sales-training function is how to mesh and harmonize your efforts with those of others in your organization. Yet it must be done. If you are to achieve maximum success and if sales training is to contribute all that it can and should contribute to the accomplishment of organizational objectives, you will need to establish those kinds of working relationships with your associates that promote and maintain cooperative and coordinated effort.

In this chapter we will discuss coordinating sales training with other training functions and with other key departments of the organization. In addition, we will present some thoughts on how to build productive relationships that will help you do your job better.

COORDINATION DEFINED

Your organization and mine have at least three things in common: a purpose, a hierarchical structure, and people. The purpose of an organization is usually stated in terms of its goals or objectives. Sometimes these are clearly defined and articulated in a precise way. In other instances the objectives are somewhat obscure and less well known. Whatever the case in your organization, you and your associates are expected to work together in such a way that the sum of your individual contributions produces the desired result—the achievement of the organization's purpose.

The hierarchical structure or organization chart is the main instrument through which working and reporting relationships are established. Together with position or job descriptions, organization charts can help to insure the integration and coordination of individual effort.

In the final analysis, however, it is people who must interpret and translate the charts and descriptions into meaningful action. It is people who must bring a common focus to their work so that a unified movement toward a common goal is the result. You can make a major contribution to your organization by taking whatever steps are necessary to make certain your work is in concert with others' and that it is directed toward the overall organizational purpose. Coordination of effort, then, is people working together within a hierarchical structure in harmonious, productive ways to achieve a common purpose. In short, it is teamwork, without which important objectives are not likely to be accomplished.

WHY COORDINATION IS IMPORTANT TO YOU

Too many of us in sales training make the costly mistake of viewing ourselves as separate entities concerned only with the achievement of training objectives which will help the sales department accomplish its goals. We occasionally lose sight of the fact that we are a part of the total organization and that our obligation extends beyond the boundaries of a single organizational unit. This might explain, in part, why managers of the sales-training function sometimes have difficulty justifying their programs, their budgets, or their very existence to "top" management.

When you and I allow ourselves to develop a narrow perspective concerning our jobs, we place unnecessary constraints on ourselves and on the contribution we can make. It is important, then, to your success as a sales-training manager that you see yourself as a member of the larger entity with an opportunity to contribute in a significant way to the achievement of organizational objectives. Major progress can be made in that direction through a continuous, conscious effort to integrate and coordinate your work with that of your associates.

REASONS FOR COORDINATION

1. *To accomplish sales-training objectives.* To realize maximum success you will need to establish sound goals and achieve tangible, measurable results. No longer can training managers justify their existence simply on the premise that "training makes people more productive." Today's corporate management rightfully expects your work to result in improved human performance that translates into hard bottom-line figures. That is a tall order. You are going to need help. But don't despair! Help is available right there in your own organization if you will but seek it out.

Never be reluctant to ask for assistance from whatever resources can be found within your company. Above all, don't let personal feelings get in the way if you honestly think someone else can teach a sales-training subject better than you. If someone from advertising or market research is the expert in determining customer buying habits and motives, utilize that expertise. If there is a trainer from another area of the organization (manufacturing, for instance), who does a creditable job of teaching communication skills, solicit that person's help. They will be flattered, you will have furthered your own cause, and a mutually beneficial working relationship will have been started.

Are you having trouble putting together a program to teach your sales personnel how to set precise, measurable objectives? Talk to your corporate or division long-range planning people. Setting objectives, after all, is their business. In addition, they can help you to understand the organization's goals better. You will need to know that if you are going to teach others how to use the Management by Objectives concept.

The point is, none of us are or can be all things. We just are not that good. We simply cannot afford to let pride or prejudice or ignorance stand between us and the realization of our worthwhile goals. The stakes are too high. So, look around you. Where are the best resources to help you get the job done? Coordinate with them. Use them. It will pay dividends.

2. *To accomplish organizational objectives.* To restate a point made earlier, meeting the objectives of an organization requires the concerted movement of a lot of people and functions toward a common purpose. When its combined training objectives are achieved, the organization should be much closer to attaining its overall objectives. It is far more likely that the training objectives will be reached when there is coordination of the various training interests.

If your organization has a corporate or division training manager with training specialists (sales, manufacturing research, etc.) reporting to that manager, coordination should not be a problem. If, on the other hand, you report to a sales marketing executive and the manufacturing trainer reports to an operations manager, there can be a very real problem.

Oftentimes under such circumstances there is a costly duplication of effort and expense. Without coordination, training managers sometimes work at cross-purposes even to the extent of teaching different organizational philosophies or goals. The attainment of the organization's objectives is hardly well served under those conditions.

You can do something about that. You can take the initiative to coordinate when no coordination exists. Talk to your training counterparts. Find out what they are doing and how they are doing it. Research and adapt their successful methods and share yours with them. Offer your assistance and don't hesitate to ask for theirs. Determine when, where, and how you can share facilities, instructors, audiovisual aids, or whatever will benefit both you and the organization. Make it your business to learn what your training peers are trying to accomplish— what their objectives are. Are yours and theirs mutually supportive? If not, is it feasible and desirable to make them so? When you add them together, will the attainment of all the training objectives help the organization achieve its objectives in the most efficient and economical way possible? That, after all, is why you and other trainers are in business. There is no other reason.

If you are in a division of a multi-division corporation or conglomerate, which may be spread out all over the country (and which may sell a wide spectrum of products to a variety of markets), you would still be well advised to make an effort to meet, learn, and work with as many of your counterparts as possible. Trade ideas, swap presentations (one of them may have a great slide presentation on "motivation," and you can share yours on "closing"), and learn from each other.

The Johnson and Johnson Corporation feels so strongly about the importance of such an exchange that it sponsors one-day meetings on a quarterly basis for all of its sales trainers. The group is known as the "J&J Training Council" (and consists of trainers from textiles, consumer products, instruments, pharmaceuticals, etc.). It reviews common problems, common solutions, and training methodology. They have learned that the fundamentals of sales training are pretty much the same, regardless of product, and all look forward to these sessions. It is a sure-fire way of compounding one's effectiveness. Perhaps a similar group in your corporation could be initiated.

3. *To establish a proper image of the sales-training function.* It is important that sales training have a "place in the sun" within the organizational structure if it is to make its best contribution. That is possible only if key people know who you are, what you do, and why you do it. Of critical importance is that they fully understand how your work helps them to attain their goals. It is unlikely that everyone who needs to know has the answers to those questions and even more unlikely that they will come to you in search of them. In any event, don't assume that they have the answers or that they will seek you out.

Take the initiative. Identify those people and functions upon whom your work has direct or indirect impact. Determine as best you can what the nature of that impact is. Once you have done that, establish contact and explain how your work affects them and, most particularly, how it can help them.

For example, if you train your salespeople to sell the most desirable product mix, you would be wise to let manufacturing know that. Chances are they will see to it that you are kept current on the best product mix. Also, they will appreciate your effort, and you will have helped to reduce the friction and misunderstanding that so often exists between sales and production.

Remember, by communicating with key people you not only coordinate your effort with theirs, you also build a stronger working relationship and, thus, a better image for sales training.

4. *To enhance your own development and career opportunities.* Your organization undoubtedly offers many excellent career opportunities. Perhaps you have already decided that sales training represents a challenge that is just right for you. Maybe you want to move in a related or even totally different direction. Whatever your choice, future opportunities will be yours largely as a result of what you do now.

Your performance as a manager of sales training will be measured chiefly against your accomplishment of sales-training objectives. And that is as it should be. But, if you allow yourself to become altogether concerned with sales training, you could impose self-limiting restrictions. This is true even if you choose to remain in sales training. Anytime you permit your vision to become "tunnelized," you will be less effective than you can be.

Learn all you can about your organization. What are its objectives? How is it structured? What is its philosophy of management and leadership? How does the organization evaluate and reward performance? Who are its people and what are their personal goals? You need to know those things to be an effective sales-training manager. You especially need to know if you aspire to other responsibilities in the organization. How do you get the answers? One of the best ways is to begin now to talk to people. Explain your role and ask about theirs. Find out how you can be mutually supportive. Communicate. Coordinate. Integrate. It is good for you and your career.

COORDINATING WITH OTHER KEY FUNCTIONS AND DEPARTMENTS

Thus far, we have discussed what coordination is, why it is important to you, and some of the main reasons for coordinating. Earlier, we talked specifically about coordination with other training interests and generally about coordination with nontraining functions. In the final part of this chapter we will take a more detailed look at some of the key functions and departments whose primary responsibility is normally something other than training but with whom the sales-training manager needs to coordinate.

1. *Personnel.* In some organizations, sales training reports to a corporate training executive who in turn reports to Personnel. When such is the case, coordination is usually assured. In those instances where sales training reports to a sales or marketing executive, coordination with Personnel is usually more difficult but nonetheless important. Many times Personnel is the source of the raw material we work with since they often actually recruit the sales trainees for the organization. If so, the sales-training manager has a responsibility to assess the caliber of trainee being recruited and to offer feedback and guidance to Personnel for future use.

Even if they take no active role in the recruitment of sales people, Personnel will normally have a direct administrative relationship to all people in the organization. They usually will be involved in setting compensation policy and practices, employee benefits, personnel-records, maintenance, performance evaluation, manpower planning, and so on.

You will be well advised to coordinate closely with Personnel and to develop a sound working relationship with them. Not only can they provide expert instructors on matters of personnel policy and procedures, but their records can be a valuable source of information for you.

For example, wouldn't it be helpful to your planning to know how many new salespersons your division or company expects to hire over the next two or three years? Personnel's manpower-planning specialist should be able to give you a fair estimate. Are your sales-personnel turnover rates excessive? Many personnel departments are equipped to analyze the reasons for high turnover. Sometimes the causes can be traced directly to their initial training and to the quality of field sales supervision. Such studies can help you identify some of the critical training needs of your people. Don't overlook the potential of the personnel department as a source for helping you do your job better.

2. *Management development.* Unfortunately, there are almost as many definitions of management development as there are organizations. For the purposes of this discussion we will consider it as a function separate and apart from sales training and concerned primarily with specialized in-house management training, internal job rotation aimed at individual manager development, and external executive-development programs.

Specialized in-house training such as financial management for nonfinancial managers is normally done at the corporate level, and extends across all functions within the management ranks. Sales and marketing managers can benefit greatly from this kind of training. Though you may not be directly involved in planning or conducting it, you have a responsibility to see that all managers in sales and marketing have the opportunity to take advantage of whatever programs will benefit them and the organization. Moreover, it will not hurt your image or career development to offer to serve as an instructor in specialized management-training programs when you are qualified or can become qualified to do so.

A well-conceived plan for the internal rotation of high-talent people can be a most effective way of developing managers for top responsibilities. You should be thoroughly familiar with your organization's policies and practices with respect to this approach to career development. You will want to be sure your training programs are in harmony with the total career-development scheme, and that you are prepared to recommend specific job experiences for sales personnel to help develop them for larger responsibilities. One of the people you should definitely coordinate with is your management-development specialist or whoever handles career planning.

An examination of any training manager's daily mail will tell you that an abundance of external executive-development programs exists. Almost every university has one. The trick is to find the ones that will best serve the needs of your managers. Few sales-training managers have the time or budget to audit even a representative sampling of these programs. If your company has a management-development group, it is entirely possible that they will have information on the executive-development programs most appropriate to your needs.

3. *Organization development.* Here again we encounter the problem of definition. Just what is organization development? Some say it is a total strategy developed for the purpose of bringing about organizational change and improvement. That is an extremely broad definition which most certainly would include sales training. Others maintain that it is nothing more or less than seeking to find solutions to organizational problems through team building and team action.

However it is defined and practiced in your company, you are a part of it. Find out, if you don't already know, what organization development means in your organization. Then determine what role sales training plays or should play in the overall strategy for organization development. Since, in most companies, organization development involves so many different functions, your investigation could serve the useful purpose of providing you with a master blueprint for all your coordination efforts.

SUMMARY

If complex organizations are to accomplish their objectives, there has to be a close coordination and integration of individual efforts and functions. The charts and job descriptions which establish working relationships and define position responsibilities are important instruments for achieving coordination. Ultimately, however, it is the people in an organization who determine whether they will work together in harmonious, productive ways.

You, as manager of sales training, have a responsibility to coordinate with those people on whom your sales-training function has direct or indirect impact. Failure to do so will likely result in costly duplication of effort and expense. In the absence of coordination, it is improbable that sales training will accomplish its objectives in the most efficient and economical way or that it will contribute all that it might to the achievement of organizational goals.

SECTION IV

MEASURING AND EVALUATING
TRAINING

CHAPTER 1

ASSESSMENT AND MEASUREMENT OF TRAINING EFFECTIVENESS

JAMES F. EVERED

James F. Evered is Manager of Marketing Education and Development for Redman Industries, Inc., of Dallas, Texas. Mr. Evered has been a training professional of national standing for twenty years. An accomplished speaker, he has addressed many training groups throughout the country and has conducted both sales training and management seminars in this country and abroad. Mr. Evered is the author of many articles on training and development, and has been a member of NSSTE since 1965. He is the recipient of several awards for the excellence of his Editorial Contributions, including the Society's Gold Medal, the highest honor that can be bestowed upon a member.

The best job-insurance policy you will ever buy is your investment in a system to prove your worth. The importance of proving to top management the profitability of your training program cannot be stressed enough. This important point was overlooked by a lot of former trainers. And I say *former,* because they were the first to go when times got rough.

During times of economic uncertainty, corporate axes are brought out of mothballs and heads begin to roll. Production cutbacks, austerity drives, budget cuts, and manpower reductions are certain to blossom. Historically, the sales-training department becomes one of the first targets for reduction—an unfortunate situation, indeed—not only for the sales trainer, but for the entire corporate structure. Companies which make such reductions fail to recognize that selling is the only thing which contributes to earnings—everything else contributes to cost. During uncertain periods, every effort which can contribute to greater selling activity should be *intensified.* That certainly includes sales-training efforts. It is unfortunate when a company's management can't see the need for intensifying training efforts during difficult times.

Why, then, does the sales-training department become a prime target for the corporate axe? Simply because management does not see enough value to the function to retain and intensify it. They probably have a "gut-feeling" that it's doing some good—but how much good? Therein lies the problem. When management looks around for some excess weight to throw overboard, they look at it in terms of cold, hard dollar figures. Unfortunately, the only figures they usually have regarding sales training reflect the "cost" of the program (salaries, facilities, materials, equipment, and the fortune they have spent on meeting rooms, meals, and travel). Sadly enough, these people are looking at only *half* an operating statement. It's like judging the health of a business by considering only the operating expenses.

Why, then, don't they analyze the other side of the statement? They don't have the other half—that's why. And it is the sales-training department that failed to set up a system of measuring its own worth. When you question the sales trainer about failing to establish a measuring system, you hear a host of old familiar copouts like, "There are just too many variables to . . . ," or "We're dealing with personalities," or "No matter how well I teach, if field management doesn't support it, you can't. . . ." Hogwash! If you can't measure your results, you better get out of the business of training sales personnel.

Of course, one can find some measurable results in almost any sales-training program, results against established goals or objectives. But these are usually *second*-level evaluations:

Level 1: Setting training objectives (performance standard)

Level 2: Evaluation of whether the above objectives were reached (did they learn it?)

The objectives set by the sales trainer usually consist of the number of meetings to hold, number of people to be trained, new programs to be developed, budgetary controls, etc. These objectives are most commendable, and we all have them (or should). But they are not enough to establish and protect your position as a sales trainer.

The third level of evaluation must be established if we are to justify our position beyond a "gut-feeling" that we're doing some good. You must establish:

Level 3: Measuring the *results* of what was taught (or measuring the *results* of our *results*).

To clarify, this does not refer to any tests you might give or demonstrations your trainees might make at the end of the course to see whether you achieve your *instructional objectives.* Such measurements are still a part of level 2. What I'm referring to here are the results achieved back in the field *because* of your teaching. This is where you prove your worth as a sales trainer; and this is where you strengthen your position against a corporate layoff. It is also your justification for budgetary increases. If you are producing good, solid measurable results, and management knows about those results, they can't afford to lose you.

Why, then, don't many sales-training managers have a system of measurement set up? Often, perhaps, they are sincerely afraid to get themselves into a measurable situation because of the inherent threat factor that goes along with it. They are surviving by "gut-feeling," a few testimonials, and an impressive platform performance. I wonder whether they have enough faith in their own competence to stake their reputation on it. Will they lay their job on the line, protected only by professional ability? I don't know. Perhaps they just don't know how to set up a measuring system. Or perhaps they haven't really thought about it!

Start right now: set up a system of third-level evaluation, and prove to the world that you are getting measurable results where it counts—in the field.

You should set up a measurement system for two reasons. First (and most important), you want to *know* what you are or are not accomplishing. You want to know where you're missing targets, so corrective action can be taken. You need to know where adjustments are needed in programs, techniques, materials, and methods. These can be achieved only through an objective measuring system. Second, you want to establish your function in the company as *vital,* and you want your management to *know* that it is vital to the corporation. If you have a good program, you should protect it against reduction or elimination.

How can you measure the results? You should determine as many measurable items as possible, and select those most appropriate for a short-run and/or long-run evaluation period. I am going to suggest as wide a spectrum of items as possible. You will find numerous criteria which are applicable to your particular sales force. Implement them as soon as possible, and begin establishing your track record.

Let's approach our measurements from two standpoints:

1. *systems* used to gather measurable items, and
2. *specifics* to measure.

By considering several systems of gathering data, and several of the specific items to go after, you will see countless possibilities for determining the results of your training efforts. Many of the possibilities will be pertinent to your particular company. These, too, will remind you of even further possibilities within your own organization.

SYSTEMS

• *System 1:* Current year versus previous year comparisons provide "fresh" information, and allow corrections to be made in current training programs. Current figures are, of course, always available, and last year's figures are still on file. In comparing results, it may be wise to compare shorter periods, such as quarterly, monthly, etc., but a word of caution: Be sure to compare the same period each year to avoid seasonal fluctuations. Don't, for example, compare winter sales of antifreeze with summer sales of antifreeze. Keep the comparative periods identical, as far as possible. Also, be sure last year's period didn't include a special promotional effort not found in this year's activities, or vice versa.

• *System 2:* Controlled group comparisons. Improvements are easily measured with a group receiving training versus a group untrained. This does not imply that you should deny any group the training. But comparisons can be made between groups A and B, *prior* to B receiving the training. There should be a measurable difference in performance between the two groups. At least, you better hope there is.

• *System 3:* Deliberately controlled group comparisons. To prove or validate a program, you may wish to conduct the training for one sales group only and compare their activity for 90 days with an untrained group. During the 90-day test period, you may wish to make adjustments in the program prior to presenting it to other groups.

• *System 4:* Trial, or pilot-run. This system would be comparable to System 3, with smaller groups. You might present your program to half your sales force in a given city (like Chicago), and compare their results for a 30-, 60- or 90-day period with the untrained half. This would eliminate geographic variables, presumably each group having the same promotion, advertising, incentives, seasonal activities, etc. Again, the test period could be used to make adjustments based on feedback from the first group.

• *System 5:* Pre/posttesting. This is especially easy with newly hired salespeople, but can be used effectively on existing personnel. The testing should be a combination of (1) knowledge, and (2) skill demonstration, with an equitable grading system established.

• *System 6:* Six months before/six months after. Where groups cannot be isolated, the sales performance can be measured by comparing results during the six-months prior to training with the six-months following. Again, watch out for seasonal variations and differences in promotional activities.

• *System 7:* Profit and loss system (see sample statement Table 1). Establish an actual territorial profit and loss statement for sales per-

Table 1
TERRITORIAL
PROFIT AND LOSS STATEMENT

Salesperson: _____   Territory: _____

Period covered by statement: _____ To _____

	Sales volume	×	Product gross profit	=	Gross profit generated
Product A	$_____	×	_____%	=	$_____
Product B	$_____	×	_____%	=	$_____
Product C	$_____	×	_____%	=	$_____
Total sales:	$_____		Total gross profit:		$_____

Percent of gross profit (Gross profit ÷ sales)   _____%

Less operating expenses:
Salary $_____
Bonus or commission $_____
____% Employee benefits $_____
Traveling expense $_____
Returned merchandise $_____
_____ $_____
_____ $_____
Total operating expenses: (Subtract from G/P) $_____

Profit contribution before allocated expenses = $_____

Percent profit contribution (Contribution ÷ total sales)   _____%

Less allocated expenses:
Allocated overhead $_____
Interest $_____
Depreciation $_____
Taxes $_____
Advertising and Promotion
  Costs $_____
_____ $_____
_____ $_____
Total allocated expenses (Subtract from profit contribution) $_____

Profit contribution total: = $_____

Percent profit contribution (Profit ÷ total sales):   _____%

sonnel, and compare their bottom-line profit contribution before and after training. Be certain that "allocated expenses" are equitable for both periods.

• *System 8:* Company versus industry averages. Although this measurement will encompass every known variable, it can still provide information relative to your training efforts. You may be happy to learn that your company increased considerably more than the average of your competitors. If so, consider the impact your efforts had on it.

• *System 9:* Customer purchase comparison. If you are directly involved in training either retail or wholesale customers, compare their purchases (from your company) for the period prior to training with the period following. I would suggest a short-period comparison with customers because of residual decline in applying the training. The reason for the decline is the absence of regular follow-up on the customer to keep selling skills in practice. You just can't manage the customer that closely, and it's not likely your sales force will do it with any degree of diligence.

• *System 10:* Feedback from trainees, sales representatives, sales managers, and customers. Although not as objective as dollar sales figures, you can learn a lot about your training effectiveness from these sources. It can also help you "build a file" of your successes. By this system, I'm not referring to the "program evaluation" the participants might fill out at the end of the course. This evaluation should be sought 30, 60, or 90 days after the training is over and the residual depletion has taken place. You may wish to prepare a questionnaire for this purpose. If so, be sure to include key questions like:

1. What particular selling skills were improved by the training program? To what degree?
2. Specifically, which part (or parts) of your selling activity has improved?
3. What evidence do you have to the above?
4. What are you now doing that you were not doing prior to the training?
5. Approximately how many *additional* sales have you made as a direct result of the training?

• *System 11:* Pre/posttaping of sales presentations. Again, not completely objective, but very helpful. It may help you see where you really met your instructional objectives. You may even want to alter those objectives before the next session. It may not give you a readout of results, but it could point out the *reason* for the results (or lack of results).

SPECIFICS TO MEASURE

Following are several specific items you can measure to prove your effectiveness. Most of these can be translated directly into corporate earnings, and you should certainly do this with a high degree of regularity. Again, keep your management informed constantly of your results. "Bottom-line" figures is one thing they understand, and will always read.

You should find several of the following appropriate to your sales organization:

1. *Expense/sales ratio:* Sales figures can be rather academic if the cost of selling overrides them. All salespersons should be concerned with reducing operating costs as well as generating revenue. Naturally, part of their training should concentrate in this area. A substantial improvement in the expense/sales ratio, coupled with a sales-volume increase, is excellent evidence of training value. And it can be translated right to the bottom-line.

2. *Employee turnover:* Sales personnel who are well trained earn well and seem to stay with us. Low sales and low income can contribute to turnover. This is another area where training can make a big contribution.

3. *Absenteeism:* Training can correct many problems which contribute to absenteeism (morale, attitude, lack of skills, etc.). Don't overlook your impact here.

4. *Sales volume:* Unfortunately, sales volume is usually the sole criterion used for comparison. As a result, the salesperson is frequently the victim of variables over which he or she has no control. When sales volume is used for comparative purposes, it should be in percentages; for instance, percent of increase, percent of product mix, percent of gross profit, percent of net profit, etc. Using percentages often compensates for some of the variables.

5. *Average commission per sale:* This will provide a qualitative measurement of selling ability, as well as a quantitative measurement of results.

6. *Product mix:* Is the selling balanced? Are sales being pushed in the

easy low-line, low-profit items? Or are you gaining sales in high-return items which may be more difficult to sell?

7. *Average size of sale:* Again, this could give you both qualitative and quantitative information. It could indicate better use of face-to-face selling time. Written orders (especially if computerized) provide easily gathered information.

8. *Number of sales calls per week/month, etc.:* If selling time is utilized to greater advantage, more productive calls per week can be made. Training, of course, is aimed at helping gain active selling time. Measure it!

9. *Calls/sales ratio:* This ratio is, for the most part, a combination of (7) and (8).

10. *Number of customer complaints:* Complaints can serve as an excellent barometer of sales activity. They may indicate neglect, overselling, misinformation, or a host of other problems training is designed to preclude.

11. *Reduced training time:* If you are able to maintain the productivity of your newly hired sales personnel and shorten the training time, you have made a very substantial cost reduction. At the same time, your trainees will become productive sooner. This is a double contribution made by training which can be translated directly to the bottom-line. Translate it!

12. *Implementation of promotional programs:* This will provide a measure of whether a trained salesperson is taking advantage of all support facilities and programs. The effect of promotional programs on sales volume is obvious. You may also want to measure how many promotional programs are actually developed by the salesperson.

13. *New customers per week/month:* A strong measurement of prospecting ability. Are they drifting with old comfortable accounts, or aggressively going after new business?

14. *Sales forecasting accuracy:* Has ability to make accurate forecast of sales, expenses, etc., improved as a result of training? (Or was it even included in training?)

15. *Percent of objectives met regularly:* A readout from performance appraisals will provide the information. Are they achieving a higher percentage of objectives than prior to the training?

16. *Volume increase through existing accounts:* Are present customers growing? How much? What percent of the customer's inventory is being maintained?

17. *Volume of returned merchandise (or repossessions):* Poor selling ability can cause a problem here. Is the situation improving?

18. *Qualitative call improvement:* Are more customer benefits, demonstrations, trial closes, etc., being used? If so, how many more?

19. *Improvement in sales-rank position:* Are they "moving up the ladder" when ranked (and I hate these systems) against the entire sales force?

20. *Sales/travel ratio:* What are the average dollar-volume sales per 100 miles traveled? It's an interesting comparison, but the ratio improves as selling improves, or as travel planning improves. Both are important.

21. *New customer/old customer ratio:* Are they concentrating on new business only? Are they failing to get enough new business? Are they maintaining a good balance with volume increases in both? Are they "drifting" with old, familiar, comfortable accounts? Check it out!

22. *Ratio of CL to LCL sales:* Are they selling an increased number of Carload orders, as opposed to Less-Than-Carload? (Tank Car, Truck Load, etc.)?

23. *Competitive investigations:* Are they becoming more diligent in investigating, reporting, and reacting to competitive activities in the territory? Have they successfully "scooped" their competition in time to develop and implement offsetting promotional activities?

24. *Sales/phone-call ratio:* Telephone selling is becoming more and more prominent. Are the batting averages improving in calls per sale? How much?

25. *Complimentary letters from customers:* Although this category could easily be "padded," feedback from customers on a voluntary basis serves as a pretty good barometer of a salesperson's value to the customer. It can be very subjective unless the customer can be specific about *how* the salesperson has improved his or her operation. Verbal feedback is also important.

26. *Developing new product demands:* Are they developing a demand for new, allied product lines to complement the regular line?

General comments about measuring training results

1. Select as many of the measuring systems as are appropriate to your corporate operations. Apply those systems to as many of the specific items as possible. Any trainer should be able to apply scores of the combinations to learn what results the training program is producing.

2. Avoid as many variables, or compensate for them whenever possible to improve the accuracy of your measurements. These variables might include price increases, seasonal trends, economic conditions of the area, materials shortages, etc. Try to measure those specific improvements which resulted from obvious application of management and selling skills.

3. As difficult as it is, try to keep the subjective out of it, as much as possible. Avoid "gut-feeling" reports and stick to the objective, measurable items.

4. Convert as many of the measurables as possible into terms of corporate earnings or gross profit. This should be done in your report to management. For example, if sales increased by $125,000 and the departmental gross profit percentage is (if you know it) 12 percent, $15,000 extra profits were generated on sales alone. This increased earning should be reported. If the salesperson reduces operating expenses by $3,000, it should be reported as $3,000 additional earnings for the territory (dollar-for-dollar). You might note, also, that a reduction of $3,000 in expenses will generate the same profit as a $25,000 sale (at 12 percent gross profit). Both the sales increases and cost reductions should be reported. They are the two most significant contributions to the organization.

5. Be sure you report all results to your management, even areas where little or no improvement was noticed. This is what provides the "other half" of the operating statement when management is analyzing the contribution the sales-training department is making.

6. The analyses listed will provide three very important tools for you:

a) A measure of your contribution to the company.

b) Specific performance objectives for use by the sales manager and/or sales personnel.

c) Targets where additional or intensified training is needed.

RESULTS

Following are some specific examples of measurable results of sales training within my own company. These results, when translated into corporate earnings and reported to management, greatly strengthened the training function and established it as vital to the organization. There were other results I am unable to include because of the confidential nature of the information, including *substantial* reductions in turnover of both salespersons and sales managers.

Incidentally, our most productive method is System 1 (current year or quarter versus the same period last year, where training has been conducted in the interim). We often use controlled groups and measure results before and after the training, for shorter periods of time.

Result 1: To gain a qualitative and quantitative analysis of results in telephone sales, we measured the "Sales Batting Averages" (the ratio of units sold to calls made) for a period of one month prior to a training program on telephone-selling techniques. We then measured the average for one month following the program. The average increased from .105 (batting average) to .150 percentage points. This translated, roughly, into $2,700 additional gross sales per man *per day*.

Result 2: At the same time we measured the sales batting average, we measured the "Prospecting Batting Average" (the ratio of calls made to dealers signed up). Here the percentage went from .040 to .053, a reduction of eight calls per prospect signed.

Result 3: Although somewhat subjective, the following quote from our Annual Report for the company appears significant for our purpose here. It indicates the attitude of corporate management toward a program which produces (and reports) measurable results:

> During the last fiscal year, we conducted 69 retail sales seminars for more than 1,400 of our dealer personnel. We believe in serving our dealers and have on our home-office staff two experts in sales training. Their sole job is to continually support and upgrade the dealer by helping him recruit, train and motivate salespeople.
>
> This program—which has been operating for nearly four years —has played a major role in the strong performance of the company's largest and most profitable operating unit.

Result 4: In four years, our salesperson's average compensation per year increased by $4,500. There was no substantial change in base salary and no cost-of-living increase. The increase was earned through greater sales-volume commissions.

Result 5: During the time we were enjoying the indicated sales increases, our training costs were being reduced. We shortened the training program by 50 percent, with no noticeable reduction in performance. This, of course, also produced a 50-percent reduction in cost per individual trained.

Result 6: One-day retail-sales seminars held for our retailer (see Result 3) have generated a lot of extra business. By training retailers to sell more, their purchases from us have increased. We average 20.3

attendees per seminar. Statistics provided by the retailers attending re-ported 78.5 *additional* units sold (at retail) per seminar held, within 120 days following the seminar. The increase represented approximately $78,000 *additional* sales (to us) per seminar held.

Result 7: This is subjective to a degree, but one retail dealer re-ported that as a direct result of the training his sales increased 180 per-cent over the previous year. During the same period, our share of his business increased from 25 percent to 45 percent. We were receiving a larger volume of a larger percentage. That translated into corporate earnings in a hurry.

SUMMARY

Using as many combinations as possible of the "systems" and "spe-cifics" should enable any sales trainer to establish a track record. If you find the results favorable, it will help establish your position as vital to your company. If, however, you find the results unfavorable, all is not lost. This should establish firm objectives for alterations in your training program (or in your personal skills). In either case, you have gained.

Don't measure your training results on a one-shot basis. Establish a system of measurement, and keep it on a perpetual basis. It is an im-portant part of an important job. The enormous influence you have on corporate sales, earnings, and image should be appreciated—*and pro-tected*—by your management. It will be, too, if you get the results, measure the results, and give the facts to your management. It's your job to see that they get the facts. It is the greatest job security you can have.

CHAPTER 2

THE TRAINING DEPARTMENT: STEPPING STONE OR CAREER?

IAN E. McLAUGHLIN

Ian E. McLaughlin has been responsible for Corporate training of the Del Monte Corporation and its subsidiaries. An experienced professional, Mr. McLaughlin has conducted training programs throughout most of the free world.

The author of many books and articles on sales training, Mr. McLaughlin lectures on training at Golden State College. He is a member of the Air Force Reserve and Chairman of the Board of Training and Educational Consultants, Inc. Mr. McLaughlin is a member of NSSTE, a past President, and winner of five awards for the excellence of his Editorial Contributions. On two of these occasions, he was awarded the Society's Gold Medal, its highest honor.

"To be or not to be—that is the question." Shakespeare wasn't referring to the organization and staffing of a training department, but he could have been.

In many companies there is considerable indecision as to whether the sales-training department should be used as a stepping stone for development of many individuals, or whether it should be considered a career position. We'll discuss the pros and cons of several approaches to this problem of organization and staffing.

THE TRAINING DEPARTMENT AS A STEPPING STONE

In organizations where the training department serves as a stepping stone potential top-management people are brought into the training department for a scheduled period of time and then moved out. The advantages to this procedure include the following.

1. If you want someone to learn a subject in depth, have them teach it. The "teacher" learns a great deal through performing the research

needed to design a good training unit and then teaching it and fielding the questions of the trainees.

2. A properly positioned training department will be in continuous contact with many other departments at headquarters. This interaction allows the new trainer to learn about the various functions in much greater depth than any overview program could. The trainer, when moved back to the line or to some other staff job, should have a better understanding of the strengths and weaknesses of many departments in the company.

3. It allows management a chance to evaluate the trainer's management skills. In the performance of many jobs in a company the person's ability to plan, organize, direct, and control is displayed. Most such positions, however, don't have a lot of leeway in all four areas. In some jobs, directing and controlling are important; in others, they are minor. In some positions, planning and organizing are paramount. In the training spot, every one of these management functions is important and is performed in full view of management.

4. It develops, or offers the opportunity to develop, each of the trainer's management talents to the fullest. The new trainer is soon on his or her own, and had better learn to develop and use his or her talents to the fullest.

The disadvantages to using the training department as a stepping stone include:

1. Each new person assigned to the job must spend time learning about training. This learning period is wasteful from the point of view of the department's function of training others, since it may be several months before the new trainer can assume much responsibility.

2. Some people assigned to this work might be excellent managers but poor trainers. Since their impact is greatly magnified in a training role, this developmental step for one individual could impede the development of many.

3. It reduces research time. The new person must spend so much time learning what's already going on with the company that he or she seldom has time to learn what's going on in the outside world. New ideas, new techniques, and new findings in the behavioral sciences could easily be overlooked. That's not good, since a truly creative trainer has to know what's going on.

4. The credibility gap is widened. A prophet in his own home is seldom heard. A career trainer sometimes hears from the field people

that "That's ivory tower stuff," or "That won't work in my territory." Over the course of years, however, most professional trainers are able to establish a solid base of success for their ideas. Imagine the handicap of the new trainer trying to sell an idea or program to former peers: "How come you know so much more now than when we worked together in Oshkosh last year?"

5. The normal work flow is reduced. If there is a training staff, much of their work has to be explained to the new staff trainer. This takes time. If there is a minimum staff, many of the short cuts that get fast action are unknown to the beginner. These take time and experience to learn (such as, when's the best time to see the boss for a discussion on a concept; how can you get duplicating to give you a break on a rush job?, etc.).

THE TRAINING DEPARTMENT AS A CAREER SPOT

This type of organization calls for a career-minded trainer. But it should never be considered a dead end. A good career-minded person will undoubtedly have offers to move ahead into other positions within the company. But usually a person who enjoys this work of developing people will wish to stay in this field.

Many companies have begun to recognize the value of having a successful trainer remain in this position. They find ways to promote and recognize the worth of the individual's contributions to the company, such as promotion to an executive position with an officer's title.

There are advantages and, obviously, disadvantages in this approach to staffing a training department. The advantages include the following:

1. A dedicated person puts more effort and more enthusiasm into his or her work. We all know that when people are committed on a long-term basis to a task or job, their work tends to be more interesting to them. The more the personal interest, the better the result should be.

2. The continuity of programming is better. When department heads are changed often, particularly in the training field, the approaches and concepts are frequently changed. This means that the line people receiving the training could have a new way of doing things handed to them just as they were beginning to master the old way. Change is good, sometimes. New ideas are good, sometimes. But constant change could cause frustration and lead to an attitude of "They don't know what they're doing at headquarters, so we'll do it our way."

3. Acceptance of ideas tends to grow as the field's confidence in the manager grows. This takes time: time for the training manager's ideas to be tested, then accepted; time for the experienced "pro's" to acknowledge that even they can learn from these programs.

4. Company management tends to give better support, both in money and backing, to ideas from someone they have tested, tried, and found sound. This, too, takes time—time that would not be available in a developmental type position.

5. Support from other departments can be better, faster, and more willingly given. Good career training managers are always good salespeople. They have to be. They are constantly selling ideas. In the course of work, a training manager will be developing rapport with many departments. This all helps in giving better training to more people.

6. Influence with the trainer's peers throughout industry increases in the course of time. This is a valuable aid to the career trainer and to the company. The biggest single cry from newly-appointed sales-training managers is "Where can I get my answers?" An experienced, well-known trainer can pick up the phone, or write a letter and get some usable answers immediately.

7. As the career person gains more credibility for the department's programs, the scope of assignments given to the department tends to expand. This enhances not only the manager's position, but the department's reputation. As its reputation for accomplishment increases, its staff positions become more sought after as jobs. Better people are attracted and, consequently, better results are generally the outcome.

The disadvantages to organizing the training department as a career position include:

1. A career person can get into a rut. Someone once said that the only difference between a rut and a grave is six feet. A trainer who is in a rut is digging his or her own grave.

2. Sometimes, when trainers have been successful for a long time, they begin to get delusions of perfection. They "can do no wrong." Their dogmatic statements begin to offend their peers in the line organization; then they lose their value to the company. Generally, when this happens the trainer is too old to move; and the remedy, replacing the training manager, becomes a painful operation for the company.

EITHER, OR, OR WHAT?

In case this chapter has made it sound like the trainer's position must be either a career spot or a developmental spot, this need not necessarily be the case. First, a combination of career positions and developmental ones seems to many to be the best of all possible worlds. Even a small department consisting of a manager, an assistant, and a secretary can have both types of positions. The best of both paths can be utilized.

The career person can provide stability and continuity. The developmental person can bring new ideas and a new way of looking at things. The career person can lend experience and open doors within the training field. The developmental person can gain by using these doors. The company can have its cake and eat it too—good continuing programs and an excellent developmental spot.

It is perhaps most logical for the boss's position to be the career one. It doesn't have to be this way, however. A good assistant, dedicated and turned on by the work, might well desire to stay put, enjoy the work, and sacrifice moving around, or up, or doing other types of work. The assistant trainer could be all the things a boss in a developmental position couldn't be: He or she could provide continuity, act as the department liaison, and bring to the department the company inside knowledge.

If the career spot is the boss's spot, great care should be given to selecting the right type. He or she should:

1. be open-minded, receptive to new ideas, have a proven reputation for these qualities;
2. be genuinely interested in helping others—that's what training is all about;
3. get job satisfaction from the development and success of others; and
4. be enthusiastic—he or she had better be able to demonstrate this when selling program ideas.

When the developmental spot is that of an assistant, one word of caution is in order. It should be company policy that if the person turns out not to be suited for training others, he or she will be moved out immediately. Conversely, when a person is brought in for a two-year assignment and is satisfactory, only an emergency should cut down the time. Two years is about the minimum span of time in which to benefit both the individual and the department's work.

CONCLUSIONS

There appear to be more advantages than disadvantages to designing the staffing of a training department with two types of persons. One type could be a career trainer. Others could be in developmental positions.

The manager of the department is the most logical position to serve as the career trainer. Staff positions are ideal as developmental ones. If the staff positions are used as developmental ones, then a good manager will give these assistants major and almost complete responsibility for some programs. This will give these individuals the opportunity to develop faster and to a greater degree than if they are given only limited parts of jobs as their responsibility.

When assistants are brought into a department in a developmental position, a two-year assignment is probably a minimum period of time; three to four should be maximum.

CHAPTER 3

ASSESSING TRAINING STAFF PERFORMANCE/SELF-ASSESSMENT
ANTONIO J. PEREZ

Antonio J. Perez is Manager of Sales and Service Training of the Airtemp Division of the Chrysler Corporation in Dayton, Ohio. He is responsible for all dealer and service training in the organization.

Mr. Perez is a graduate of the Milwaukee School of Engineering (B.S. in Mechanical Engineering) and has been with Airtemp for 29 years. During this period he has held a series of key positions, including field-service engineer, district sales manager, manager of builder sales, and product engineer. He has been in charge of Sales and Service Training for six years.

Trainers spend much of their time assessing and evaluating the performance of others, but sometimes forget to take a good look at themselves. This is very important to do if the department is to grow—and to fulfill its critical role.

One of the most difficult tasks for a person in charge of a training department is to assess without bias or prejudice the staff and himself or herself. Self-assessment is not a particularly glamorous training activity; and it requires a training director with time to gather the facts, measure the facts, and willingness to say, "The last program was a dog!"

This "self-assessment" task can be accomplished and should be done periodically, at least once a year. (Budget-submission time might be the best time).

Assessing training staff performance by self-assessment can be undertaken in four ways:

1. assessment of the individuals on the training staff by the training director,

2. assessment of the training staff by the training director,

3. assessment of a one-person training department, or

4. summary of self-assessments.

1. *Assessment of the individuals in a training staff by the training director.* It is surprising how many training directors do not have a written set of standards with which to assess the individuals in the training department.

   In fact, a recent survey of various training directors (having from two to more than fifty trainers on their staff) listed the following ways in which they assessed their trainers.

   a. Gut Feeling. Training directors observe the trainer in front of an audience for a period of time which can be an hour, half a day, a full day, or a week, depending upon the subject taught. The training director comes away with a feeling as to:

      1) audience reaction to the trainer as a person,

      2) interest in the subject presented, and

      3) reaction to the trainer as their instructor.

      Responses from the audience are both verbal and nonverbal. The training director has to be an exceptional person to be able to assess fairly and accurately by this method. Personal opinion sometimes affects the assessment.

   b. Evaluation by Written Forms. The training director evaluates the trainer by filling out an evaluation sheet. Evaluation sheet number TE–1 (see Table 1) has been used by a leading training director to evaluate his trainers. Evaluation sheet TE–2 (see Table 2) is another method of evaluating the trainer, but it is not as complete as TE–1. Evaluation Forms CE–1 through CE–5 (Tables 3 through 7) are being used to evaluate the trainer and course by either the training director and/or the trainees.

   Many training directors feel that one of the most valuable assessment tools they possess is the evaluations done of staff members by the trainees. You tend to get a more candid response if the trainee is told not to sign it. As these are received and reviewed over a period of months, a clear pattern of response develops. It is generally fair and accurate—provided you have sincerely urged candor and there is a trust relationship between the department and the trainees. How staff members re-

Table 1
TRAINER EVALUATION SHEET

Trainer's
Name _____

VOICE

Volume	Low	Good	High
Rate	Slow	Good	Fast
Pauses	Few	Good	Many
Bridges	(Use of ands, ah's, etc.)		

Repeat words used

PERSONALITY

Enthusiasm	No	Ave.	Yes
Sincerity	No	Ave.	Yes
Confidence	No	Ave.	Yes

DELIVERY

Poise	No	Ave.	Yes
Eye contact	Fair	Ave.	Good
Gestures	Fair	Ave.	Good
Use of props	Fair	Ave.	Good

DISTRACTIONS   (Jingles coins, etc.)

List here

FEATURE BENEFIT

FAIR	AVE.	GOOD

COMMENTS:_____

_____

_____

_____

Table 2
BASIC SALES-TRAINING PROGRAM

Page: _____

Day No. _____ Date _____

Location

General subject:	Specific topic:	Code:

Scheduled time	Scheduled speaker(s)
Start: _____	Primary: _____
Finish: _____	Back-up: _____

Department responsible for this session:

Prereading
Required or recommended:

Brief outline of
this session:

Reaction by participant—basic

Date: _____   Topic: _____   Code: _____

Speaker(s)

Time started: _____   Time ended: _____

	Rating		
	Excellent	Good	Fair
Was this session well prepared?			
Was the presentation well organized?			
Were you involved?			
Were your questions adequately answered?			
Were the tests or feedback effective?			
Was the session relevant to the selling task?			

Specific comments on how this session might be improved:

Table 3
APPRAISAL

(We welcome your constructive comments)

Name of course——————————————————Location——————————

Length of course (Circle one)   *Too Long   Too Short   Satisfactory*

   Comments:——————————————————————————

————————————————————————————————————

Subjects that should be deleted and why:———————————————

————————————————————————————————————

Subjects that should be added and why:——————————————

————————————————————————————————————

Present subjects that should be expanded or shortened and why:———————

————————————————————————————————————

Quality of instruction (Circle one)   *Poor   Fair   Good   Excellent*

   Comments:——————————————————————————

Motel accommodations (Circle one)   *Poor   Fair   Good   Excellent*

   If Fair or Poor—Why?——————————————————————

————————————————————————————————————

Additional overall comments:——————————————————————

————————————————————————————————————

————————————————————————————————————

————————————————————————————————————

————————————————————————————————————

— DO NOT SIGN —

Table 4
ADVANCED PRODUCT SEMINAR

APPRAISAL SHEET

To help us refine and improve our future seminars, would you please give us your impressions and reactions.

Be specific and frank, and give honest opinions—*no signatures.*

My objective in coming to the Advanced Product Seminar was:

_____

_____

_____

Was this objective achieved:

Well Achieved ( )   Moderately Achieved ( )   Not Achieved ( )

I feel the following additions or changes should be made in future seminars (Product area, Organization, Procedure, etc.)

1. _____

2. _____

3. _____

In general, how do you rate the seminar?

Excellent ( )   Good ( )   Fair ( )   Poor ( )

Comments:_____

_____

_____

_____

_____

Table 5
TRAINING

Date_____Trainer_____

Topic of seminar_____

Location_____

_____

ATTENDANCE

Please print

	Name	Title	Representing
1			
2			
3			
4			
5			
6			
7			
8			
9			
10			
11			
12			
13			
14			
15			

Training material used _____

Material distributed _____

Comments and recommendations:_____

Table 6
MEETING EVALUATION REPORT

A.   TYPE OF MEETING

[ ] Sales orientation   [ ] Product manager   [ ] Regional sales
                               workshop

[ ] Basic sales training [ ] Sales operation   [ ] Department
                               workshop

[ ] Selling skills   [ ] Field sales man-   [ ] Outside _____
                               agement workshop

Meeting   Meeting
dates   location

B.   CONSOLIDATED EVALUATION

---

1. Considering the length of time it has taken you away from your regular duties, did you find this meeting worthwhile? [ ] Yes [ ] No. Why?

2. Do you feel that your experience in this meeting will be practical and useful to you in your working situation? [ ] Yes [ ] No. How?

3. In your judgment, was the length of the meeting [ ] About Right, [ ] Too Long, [ ] Too Short? Why?

4. Would you recommend that such meetings be conducted periodically for others with similar responsibilities? [ ] Yes [ ] No. Why?

5. What changes do you recommend for any future program?

6. What was the most significant concept of the *program* which you feel might modify your future actions in any way?

Signature	Marketing group	Region and territory	Date

Table 7
CONFEREE COMMENTS AND SUGGESTIONS

_____
Conference name
_____
Date

PLEASE NOTE: The clinic you have completed was designed to assist you in getting your job done. We are very interested in your opinion. What you tell us is one method of determining the effectiveness of the training. To help us keep the clinic up to date, and make future clinics better, please answer these few questions completely and candidly.

1. Were these sessions all you expected?

_____

_____

2. Which subject covered will do you the most good?

_____

_____

3. Would you recommend this training to someone else?

_____

_____

4. Would you be interested in attending future training sessions?

_____

_____

5. General comments:

_____

_____

_____

_____

spond to negative criticisms will tell you a great deal about them.
  c. Evaluation by Comparison. Comparing one trainer with other trainers. This comparison can be accomplished by:
    1) pretest and posttest versus class average,

   2) comparing evaluation forms of one trainer to another, and

   3) number of complaints or compliments of one trainer to another.

   d. Evaluation by Complaints. All too often the only time a trainer is evaluated is when the training director receives a complaint that a trainer isn't performing.

2. *Assessment of the training staff by the training director.* The training director evaluates the training staff as a whole unit. The assessment analysis should have the following parameters:

   a. Has the department met the overall objectives set forth by management? Did the staff members know the objectives? Each objective should be:

   • challenging,

   • measurable,

   • time-phased, and

   • achievable.

   Objectives must be periodically checked due to changes in product, management personnel, policy, and budget.

   b. Could the training objective have been met with more trainers? Fewer trainers?

   c. Could the training objective have been met with an increase in budget? Decrease in budget?

   d. Was the allocation of budget funds realistic?

   e. Does firing the less qualified trainers mean that they can't be replaced because of a current "no hiring policy"?

   f. Are the programs being produced just getting your department by?

   g. Is there a great demand for your staff members by field managers? By other departments?

   h. Do you know which staff members are good at:

   1) competitive product knowledge?

   2) product knowledge?

   3) subject knowledge?

   4) customer knowledge?

   5) impromptu discussion?

      6) extemporaneous leadership?

      7) memorized speech making?

      8) manuscript lecture?

      9) new-trainee instruction?

    10) in-basket exercise?

    11) role playing?

    12) case study?

    13) seminar leadership?

    14) management games?

    15) group discussion?

    16) programmed instruction?

    17) script writing?

    18) on-the-job training?

    19) audio-video programming?

i. Are trainee assessments carefully reviewed and discussed with each trainer?

j. Do staff members react defensively to criticisms in trainee evaluation—or try to benefit from them?

k. Supervision

    1) Is staff too loosely run?

    2) Is staff too confined in creativity?

l. Reward

    1) Is the staff recognized and rewarded for outstanding performance?

The purpose of a staff assessment is to discover any weak areas that can be brought up to a standard level, or strong points which can be used to the trainers' benefit. An evaluation form designed by the trainers on the staff being assessed makes it more realistic and acceptable.

Remember than an assessment program is often perceived as a threat to the position, status, and opportunities of every person on the training staff being assessed.

Another method in finding out about the direction of your staff is to have each trainer write up his or her own individual job description. Compare it to your idea of the job. A good philosophy is to build on strengths, thus reducing weaknesses.

3. *Assessment of a "one-person training department."* True assessment can be next to impossible without stringent guidelines for the trainer who is a "one-person department." How many individuals can give an accurate accounting of themselves when it concerns their job performance and may dictate their livelihood? Not many. Nevertheless, this self-assessment must be accomplished if the objectives set by management are to be met. This self-assessment should include the following:

   a. Has the department met the overall objectives set forth by management?

   b. Could the training objective have been met with more trainers?

   c. Could the training objective have been met with an increase in budget? Decrease in budget?

   d. Was the allocation of budget funds realistic?

   e. Are my programs being used?

   f. Is my advice sought by management concerning new programs being introduced to the field?

   g. Is my assistance and/or personal presence sought by new and experienced salespeople?

4. *Summary of self-assessment.* One can say that the results of self-assessment can be determined by the guidelines used in the assessment. If the guidelines are such that only positive results would be secured, then you really haven't made a true self-assessment of the training staff.

   How long should an evaluation form be, for true assessment? The evaluation form should contain as many items as you feel are necessary to give you the facts in order to secure a true assessment of your staff and programs. The more items on the evaluation form, the more time it takes to fill it out, the harder it is to remember what was filled out, and it is even harder to compare it with the standard. One training director had a form more than 20 pages long for evaluating his staff!

   The guidelines of self-assessment of the training-staff performance will vary from company to company due to product or service sold. Also taken into consideration is the person to whom the training director reports.

   A simple to use, but effective, set of guidelines that can be expanded for use by any training director is shown below:

	COMPARED TO LAST YEAR	
TOPIC	*Increase*	*Decrease*
a. Budget-dollars		
b. Trainers hired		
c. Programs produced		
d. New programs produced		
e. Current programs being used		
f. Demand for new programs		
g. Demand for training held by field personnel		
h. Demand for training input by top management during new program formation		
i. Demand for training input by other departments		

In summary, it is only fitting to say that a self-assessment program is worth only what happens as a result. And it's well to keep in mind that a favorable response to a program or trainer by the trainee doesn't assure learning or a behavior change. Thus, it's important to evaluate the right things.

SECTION V

CONTINUOUS SELF-DEVELOPMENT
OF THE TRAINER

CHAPTER 1

FORMULATING A SALES-TRAINING PHILOSOPHY

KEYTE L. HANSON

Keyte L. Hanson, CLU, is Superintendent of Education and Field Training of the Agency Department of the Northwestern Mutual Life Insurance Company of Milwaukee, Wisconsin. A graduate of Brigham Young University of Provo, Utah, Mr. Hanson joined Northwestern Mutual in 1960, and was promoted to the home office after a successful career in Agency sales and management. He was awarded the C.L.U designation in 1966.

Mr. Hanson is a member of the American Society of Chartered Life Underwriters and serves on the LIMRA Education and Training Committee, as well as the LUTC Content and Curriculum Committee.

BE NOT THE FIRST NOR THE LAST

One of the challenging opportunities facing the sales-training executive is the responsibility for formulating a philosophy of sales training that can keep pace with changing needs. The challenge comes in maintaining a balance between the desire to be innovative, yet, at the same time, retaining the proven methods and principles of sound basic training.

It is well to remember the words of Alexander Pope, who advised, "Be not the first by whom the new are tried, nor yet the last to lay the old aside." Maintaining the delicate balance between the old and the new will make your job exciting and fulfilling.

THE WISE LEARN FROM EXPERIENCE

The successful training director knows the importance of sticking to the basics. In the past, selling was simple, and sales training (if it existed at all) was pretty fundamental. Even though selling has developed into a sophisticated art and sales training has progressed to a highly scientific level, there is still great value in the tried and true. As a training director, it is important to concentrate on the factors involved in learning. Also, you need to gain an understanding of the process of individual development.

It is essential that you be aware of the psychological influences of all elements in the learning environment. Above all, the individual needs of each person involved in training must be considered. Furthermore, the appropriate use of techniques, equipment, methods, and procedures will have decided impact on your sales-training program. Therefore, you will first want to be well versed in what has worked well in the past and what is working well now (and why) before you endeavor to be too innovative or creative in developing your own sales-training philosophy. The wise learn from experience, but the super-wise learn from the experience of others.

THIS THING CALLED CHANGE

Things are never the same, or so it seems. Occurring in many forms and with greater speed than ever before, change is one of the few constants in our world today. As a sales-training director, you must recognize and welcome change. You must also be mindful of a natural resistance to change; at the same time, be ready and able to adjust and grow.

Here are some guidelines that can be helpful to you in considering and coping with change:

1. *Expect* changes to happen and welcome them.
2. *Recognize* when changes occur.
3. *Evaluate* the effect of change.
4. *Adjust* to the new circumstances.
5. *Respond* to the changes.
6. *Prepare* the course of action.
7. *Plan* the steps to be taken.
8. *Gain acceptance* of the changes to be implemented.
9. *Put into action* the changes.
10. *Support* the action taken.

As you go through this process, it is also important to reduce your thinking to concise, specific terms—in writing.

HERE WE GO AGAIN

The role of the salesperson has changed considerably, and this brings about the need to change your approach to training. The salesperson must, of course, have a sound knowledge of the product or service being sold and the many things necessary to market it successfully. Additionally, the salesperson must develop skills in dealing with people and learning to solve the buyer's problems effectively. This usually calls for changes in the way we have traditionally trained salespersons.

Innovation brings about change. New products or services, new methods of distribution, or new markets frequently require changes in training programs. Outside influences due to changes in the economy, taxes, unemployment, and other factors can also have substantial effect on training methodology—and even on the department's continued existence. Sometimes, it is worthwhile to evaluate a program that has not changed for some time to determine if the lack of change itself may be an indication that a change is needed. On the other hand, today there are likely to be pressures from so many directions that change will be a constant (whether we like it or not). The byword in many training departments today seems to be: "You mean you want the original revised revision of the original revised revision revised?"

PRINCIPLES VERSUS PREFERENCE

It is worth mentioning again that there is great value in basic and fundamental training principles which have stood the test of time. One cannot readily make a break from the basic foundations of proven principles and be assured of success. With the pressure to change so great, it is easy to tear down, reject, or discard that which is old. Remember, however, there are some things that don't go out of force even if they seem to go out of fashion.

Many training directors feel the need to "reinvent the wheel," rather than continue to rely on something that is already available and working well. A word to the wise: don't discard time-honored safeguards and principles for the unknown. Leaving a sound principle behind purely for personal preference or mood of the moment can lead to chaos.

One of the most important decisions you can make is to define clearly the difference between what is a principle and what is merely a preference. Weigh carefully the advantages and the consequences before leaving a firmly fixed foundation or principle for something that seems progressive, exciting, or innovative which may turn out to be only a preference.

THE TRAINING FAD SYNDROME

With all the changes that are occurring, it is only natural that training directors feel the need to update their training programs and incorporate new techniques from time to time. You will want to use the old but be on the lookout for the new as well. This is part of the reason you will find your job exciting. You have a responsibility to keep on top of new developments, and it is often lots of fun to evaluate what's new even though you surely won't want to use everything that comes along.

There are many new techniques and procedures on the training scene, and it is important that you consider how they may add to your program or complement what you are trying to do. Some can add a dimension that may be very valuable while others will be detrimental.

Variations of on-the-job training and call-coaching have been used successfully in some organizations. "Job enrichment" became the by-word for a time, and many training programs were built around the concept. Sensitivity training, perceptive-listening sessions, encounter groups, and group learning sessions also became fads which attracted much attention for a while, but there were disastrous results in some instances. Some of these have passed into oblivion, and some have held up well. Others, such as paired tutoring, team teaching, and similar innovations, have had measurable impact.

Programmed learning, case-study exercises, role-play workshops, and buzz groups are among the many techniques that should definitely be considered. Business games and simulation exercises have also proven to be effective for some organizations.

More recently, transactional analysis and behavior modification programs have also come on the scene, including innumerable audio-cassette tape programs, videotape, closed-circuit TV, and a wide range of training films. The audiovisual age is here, and new equipment and techniques are emerging faster than one can imagine.

There are many ways to update your training program. The important thing is to remember to weigh carefully the advantages and consequences of each new idea. Don't jump on a fad bandwagon. It can be a very expensive mistake if you get involved in a fad that doesn't last, or with one whose time has not yet come.

DECISIONS—DECISIONS

The choices are vast and complex. Training directors have dozens of methods and hundreds of combinations of training programs from which to choose. There is no easy answer to help you in your decision regarding which training method is best for you.

It is your responsibility as a training director to make decisions that affect the human-resource growth and development of your organization. There is no one best way for everyone. So how do you decide what will work best for you? Here are some guidelines that may help:

1. Clearly define your objectives (consistent with corporate goals and marketing philosophy). Communicate them to the members of the sales team and management personnel.
2. Evaluate the results of current training efforts.
3. Determine training needs that exist in the organization.
4. Identify the trainees and their particular needs (collectively and individually).
5. Consider cost limitations and budget availability (both direct and indirect costs).
6. Weigh the constraints of time and location, including the corporate environment and training climate.
7. Study the implications of mechanical implementation and administration, as well as other possible limitations and constraints.
8. Formulate your program incorporating sound learning principles (involvement of trainee, reinforcement, review, feedback, validation, etc.).
9. Check with other trainers from noncompetitive companies who have used the new approach or evaluated a new program.
10. Implement your program following an enthusiastic plan of action. Delegate responsibility, and get support of the other members of the training team.

Consider each point in the formulation of your training program, and remember to use Rudyard Kipling's six honest serving men: *What? Why? When? Where? How? Who?*

DOING YOUR THING

It is essential that you personalize your training philosophy to ensure that it fits your particular needs and circumstances as well as those of the organization. Keep in mind that your decision should clearly identify the training objective—whether it be to change the level of knowledge, develop skill proficiency, modify attitude and outlook, or establish organization and time-control procedures.

Focus a great deal of attention on behavior rather than personality. Also, design your training for results rather than the process. I find it helpful to remember that probably the third most important thing in your training program is what you say. The second most important thing is how your trainees feel about what you say. But the most important thing is what they do about how they feel about what you say.

In formulating a sales-training philosophy, remember the old principles of sound training. Stay on top of new developments. Try new things, but don't try to do everything. Be bold but be cautious, and don't be surprised if your own training philosophy turns out to be the best of all!

CHAPTER 2

EDUCATIONAL CAREER PATHS FOR PROFESSIONAL TRAINERS

JAMES RAPP

James Rapp was Director of Education for Berol Corporation, Danbury, Connecticut. He is also President and founder of Outlook Associates, a sales-consulting organization. Previously, he held sales, sales-management, and sales-training positions with the General Foods Corporation. Mr. Rapp is a specialist in sales force organization, training, and compensation.

Mr. Rapp developed one of the first programs in the food industry for the selection and training of minorities and women as sales representatives. He also authored the book *Retail Food Store Operations,* used to train sales personnel.

What does the future hold for the trainer who finds the assignment to be challenging and exciting, who does it well, and who wants nothing more than to be allowed to grow in the job, and to increase the scope and contribution of the training activity? In short, what does the future hold for the individual who wants to be a career trainer rather than simply use the job as a short-term stepping stone?

This chapter is directed primarily to those individuals who honestly want to *stay* in training and education. They enjoy their work. They want to develop themselves not only for the purpose of performing at top level in their current job, but also want to prepare themselves for positions of increased responsibility in training and education throughout the organization. In some instances, of course, the sales trainer wants nothing more than to stay in the current job until retirement.

The thoughts presented in this chapter apply equally to both individuals because to continue to be effective in the same or a similar position over an extended period of time requires:

1. keeping up with new training techniques and technology,
2. being seen by top management as effective,
3. meeting the changing needs of a changing sales force, and
4. having a realistic awareness of the politics of the organization.

It is difficult to lay out specific career paths for sales trainers. Each company, each individual, and each situation is different; there are no hard-and-fast rules. But there are several questions that should initially be asked:

1. Where do sales-training managers come from?
2. Who decides the future of trainers?
3. What career choices are available to the trainer?

ORIGIN OF THE SPECIES

Most sales-training managers come from the sales ranks. This has been true from the beginning, and continues to be so today.

A recent survey conducted by the Department of Marketing of the University of Oklahoma shows that 61 percent of the sales-training managers responding came to the function directly from field sales or field sales management. In previous years this percentage was probably higher. There is no denying that sales-oriented people are primarily in control of sales training. Still, this is not a hard-and-fast rule everywhere. Some great sales trainers have had academic or other backgrounds.

WHO DECIDES THE TRAINER'S FUTURE?

Each of us should be taking an active role in deciding what our future will be. It's reassuring to note how many more companies and individuals are becoming more interested in career planning.

The reality of the situation today in most companies is that the sales manager is usually the person who decides who will be chosen as sales-training manager. This same person also decides when the sales-training person will leave this position and move on. That's why the majority of sales trainers come from the sales ranks and eventually move on to sales or marketing-management jobs or line-management positions. The same University of Oklahoma Study shows that 46 percent of the sales-training managers stated that they expected to serve in sales training for their present employer "no more than five years."

Designing a career path within the training function is difficult in any organization where it isn't really viewed as a career job. The position of sales-training manager in many organizations today is simply a "pass-through" job, a place to give someone experience for another job. Other training positions in the same company often report to the personnel department.

In fairness to sales managers, it must be said that most individuals who pass through the sales-training job are not particularly upset at the thought of leaving. This was the original plan, and they are richer for having had the experience. They are also eager for the "greener pastures" anticipated after their tour of duty in sales training. Nevertheless, this system can be highly frustrating to those individuals who want to remain in sales training but feel they must "bow to the system." By exercising some self-determination and with a little planning (and some luck!), it is possible to stay in the training field, even if it means "bucking the system."

WHAT CAREER CHOICES ARE AVAILABLE?

Assuming you are now in a position that involves sales training, or are about to enter the field, you should consider each of these possibilities:

1. Moving through the various positions within the sales-training department of your organization.

2. Moving into other training positions within your organization, such as plant training, supervisory and management training, organization development, etc.

3. Continuing to be responsible for sales training, but expanding the job to include the training and development of all sales *and* marketing personnel.

4. Moving from a division-training position to a corporate-training position (or the reverse).

5. Moving from your current training position to a higher level position in another organization. This may be necessary when you have advanced as far as you can within the training department of your present employer, or the job you really want in your company is blocked—or it doesn't exist and isn't likely to be created.

Consider the idea of modifying the structure of your company's training function to fit your own capabilities. Of course, the change should also benefit the organization. This occurs most frequently when the training job is broadened as the incumbent becomes more experienced. A common example is the sales-training manager who is initially responsible for designing field sales representative training and is then asked to work on sales supervisor training, followed by development of special programs for the sales manager, and so forth.

If these tasks have been done well, the trainer may then be asked to work with others in the marketing department. At this point, his or her title may be changed to "Director of Marketing Training" or "Training Manager—Sales and Marketing."

Getting such changes effected will be gradual and, probably, difficult. Many companies are set up so that each functional area has full responsibility for training its own people. The top manager in the department will often be reluctant to give up any responsibility and authority for the training of his or her people.

There is also the problem of the sales department versus the personnel or industrial relations department when training is involved. Sometimes this is a split responsibility. Often the responsibility is not clearly defined. When it isn't, a struggle is usually inevitable.

A typical example is a large manufacturer of consumer durables that maintains two large and completely separate training departments. One department reports to the Vice-President-Sales and the other to the Vice-President-Personnel. There is little communication between the two departments and, consequently, duplication of services exists, particularly in employee communication and distributor development. Managers in the sales department have been excluded from certain training programs developed by the personnel department. Not to be outdone, the sales department developed a similar program for their own people, along with thicker binders, more expensive speakers, and longer meetings!

When one is involved in a situation such as this the chances of pulling things together into one super-department are not very good. Trainers have historically bargained from a position of weakness in their organizations, compared to the level of those they must convince, such as sales managers, marketing managers, personnel managers, and assorted vice-presidents.

This does not mean that one should give up. It only means that a change of this type is difficult to accomplish, and serious thought has to be given about the risks involved. One of the risks could be losing your job or being transferred to another job, possibly outside the training field!

CHANGING COMPANIES

When all else fails, one can always consider going elsewhere. This is common practice, because many organizations are looking for experienced trainers, and do not have anyone in their company who is qualified—or who wants the position.

If you do not see a career path in your present company that appeals to you and do not see one opening up soon, you should give thought to changing organizations. This is a necessary step for many sales trainers who really want to stay in the profession, who have gone as far as they can go with their present employer, and perhaps have outgrown the job.

There are all sorts of possibilities. You could move from a small to a large organization, doing the same type of work. This might be a situation where you are going from the number 2 position to the number 1 job. Or you could move to a slightly different but more responsible position. For example, you could move from sales-training manager in one company to manager of *all* training in another firm. Sometimes you will need to make a lateral move, just for the opportunity of joining a company with promotional possibilities.

How best to go about looking for the "right" position in another company is beyond the scope of this chapter. Suffice it to say that training people now move quite freely from company to company. If done with care, planning, and a little luck, you should be on the way to realizing your full potential in a field that has many rewards.

SUMMARY

There is a place in today's and tomorrow's organization for the professional career-minded trainer. Remaining an effective member of your organization over many years requires a combination of interests and skills found in few people.

Perhaps you can get by with only a few of them. Such technical skills as understanding program design and being a good conference leader are important, but they are not critical. In fact, you can get so immersed in the finer points of training technology that you fail to observe or respond to the day-to-day situations and problems that have a much greater impact on you and your department.

You *must* do what is necessary to be seen as an effective, competent staff person by those individuals who count: the sales manager, marketing manager, and staff vice-president; perhaps even the president of the company. One of the best ways to do this is to measure the results and effectiveness of your function on a regular basis, then feed the information to those persons. Be sure to tell your boss first! Do it in person whenever you can.

The measurements should be as honest and accurate as you can make them. If they occasionally sound too good to be true, tone them down. Better to retain your credibility than raise doubts.

Pay close attention to the makeup of the sales force and all others for whom you have training responsibility. Their attitudes about work and training are changing rapidly and surely will continue to change. You must be responsive to these changes. As a general rule, most new employees today (particularly younger persons) are uninterested in learning "everything" about the job and the company. Mostly they want to understand the "output" or end result of their jobs and how they will be measured. They would like to have the freedom of figuring out for themselves how to go about doing the work, even though they will make mistakes. They dislike mass training. They prefer to study things on their own. They like condensed materials, short training sessions, and lots of participation and involvement. It may not always be the most efficient way to learn, but it's "their" way.

Never forget that corporate politics and internal power struggles are always with us. Like it or not, our careers are affected at one time or another by corporate politics. We should try to understand this harsh reality and manage our work in such a way that we can use it or react to it in a positive manner. To do otherwise is to play "Russian Roulette" with our careers.

Always keep in mind that you need to acquire more management skills and nontraining type skills as you move up in the organization. Many training specialists forget this important point.

A few years ago, true career trainers were almost nonexistent. Fortunately, however, more and more organizations appear to have realized the importance of sales training—and the need to provide real continuity in their training. Consequently, we are seeing more and more career positions emerging. So—if you like training and want to stay in it, there is hope!

TRENDS, CHANGES, AND EVOLUTION
IN TRAINER SELF-DEVELOPMENT

Chances are you would not be reading this book if you were not interested in self-development. Training people seem to have an above-average desire to learn more about their work and to acquire new knowledge about their particular field. This is probably true because each of us is so keenly aware of the need to help others develop, for this is what we do each day. Also, we understand how people learn, and we know how and where to find the tools of learning—books, periodicals, seminars, films, etc.

RAPID CHANGES

The training field is changing so rapidly it's difficult to keep up. It's also difficult to know where we are at any given time relative to the state-of-the-art. For example, we may know all about the latest audio-visual equipment because we are using it in our classroom training sessions, yet we may be totally unaware of the latest uses of transactional analysis relative to the buyer-seller relationship. The latter may reflect a lack of interest on our part, or lack of involvement in a particular training area that uses this new knowledge. It's one of many holes that have to be filled if we are to become and be treated as professional trainers.

IT'S UP TO YOU

Let's look at the trends that are now taking place in trainer development and those that are appearing on the horizon. At the same time, it must be stated that the burden for "keeping up" rests squarely on your shoulders. Only *you* know exactly what you *know* about any particular subject. It's your task to scan the training field constantly to determine what new research has taken place, what others are doing, what's been successful, and what hasn't worked.

The old adage "A doctor who treats himself has a fool for a patient" is certainly not true in this case. A good rule of thumb for sales trainers might be "You had better diagnose and treat yourself, because no one else is going to do it for you!"

SKILLS OF THE PAST

It is helpful to understand something about the skills sales trainers needed in the past, because many are still needed today. It also tells us the evolution that has taken place in the field and suggests what is likely to evolve in the years to come.

Sales training started when salespeople and sales managers began to wonder why some sales presentations were more successful than others. They began to investigate why one person was more successful than another; why enthusiasm, for example, seemed to have such a positive influence on the buyer.

As products, services, and sales organizations became more complex, it became apparent that some training of new sales representatives was not only profitable but necessary. By getting the new person productive in three months instead of six months or a year, more sales could be made, resulting in a profitable territory much more quickly.

Early sales training was concerned primarily with teaching product knowledge, and a standard "pitch" or "spiel" was usually developed for each product. There was no formal classroom training. The new salesperson generally worked alongside an experienced one in the field. Many times it was the person leaving the territory or an experienced salesperson in an adjoining territory. The trainee would spend from a few days to a few weeks with the experienced person and was then left alone. Sometimes it worked. Often it didn't. This is sometimes referred to as "sink-or-swim" training.

The quality of such training depended on the interest as well as the skill of the senior person. If the trainer was willing to take extra time to explain things to the new representative as they went along, the results were likely to be positive. If the trainer was more interested in "getting the order" and ignored the new person, little was learned.

One of the biggest problems with this arrangement was that the senior person usually insisted that the new salesperson do everything "just like me." Unfortunately, this approach ignored the personality and the natural style of the sales trainee. This often turned the new member of the sales team into what appeared to be a "bumbling idiot." This was especially true when he or she was required to memorize, word-for-word, long sales presentations.

For example, one large cigarette manufacturer required all their salespeople to memorize a long product story, which had to be given on every store call, regardless of whether the particular brand was stocked. Some retailers delighted in stopping the salesperson before they finished, figuring they would forget where they left off, thereby forcing them to tell the whole story over again! A sad commentary, but true.

Much of the sales training of days gone by was a reflection of the selling styles of that particular era. Prior to World War II, "personal selling" was the accepted standard. By "personal selling," I mean that buyers paid more attention to the salesperson than they did to the product or service. If they liked "good old Charlie," they would buy from him and turn down his competitors. Good old Charlie was very friendly, always had a good story to tell, inquired solicitously about the health of the customer and the customer's family, and tended to sell the customer "what I think you need," which was often a quantity large enough to discourage the customer from stocking or switching to competitive products!

CHANGES CAME SLOWLY

Genuine sales training was slow to develop. When post-World War II shortages ended, many companies began to realize that their sales people needed more training than their field suprvisors could give them. Competitors were becoming stronger and more numerous. Products were getting more complex. Customers were smarter, and began demanding more of the salespeople who called on them.

This was the beginning of the centralized, headquarter-controlled sales-training function. It usually started with the appointment of a sales-training manager, a staff position reporting to the sales manager.

The person picked for the sales-training job was *usually* a salesperson or sales supervisor who had demonstrated an interest in or a talent for training others. In the company I worked with as a salesman, they promoted a district sales manager who had previously been a school teacher.

Depending on the size of the sales force, the new sales-training manager either trained all the new representatives, one by one; or if it was a large organization, the training person most likely prepared a sales manual, which was distributed to each person in the field. This manual consisted mostly of product information, such as:

- ingredients,
- how it was manufactured,
- history of the product,
- stories about satisfied users, and
- technical information.

In short, it told you what to say about your product, *but not how to say it*—and not how to get the prospect involved.

It wasn't until the late 1950s and early 1960s that sales-training managers began to pay attention to the needs of *individuals* in their organizations or to take notice of the *differences* in their salespeople *and* their customers.

By this time formal classroom sales training began to be used more and more. The professional sales trainer began to interact with large numbers of salespeople in a face-to-face situation. Both learned much in these encounters.

THE RECENT PAST

The demands placed on us by those we train have a significant impact on our own self-development. As classroom training increased, we have needed to learn a whole range of new skills. We could no longer simply prepare manuals and send instructions to the field.

We have learned to do many things which, incidentally, are still needed today. In addition to writing ability, we have learned:

- How to design a training course or seminar.
- How to evaluate its effectiveness.
- How to handle meeting arrangements.
- How to develop interesting lectures.
- How to make and use meeting visuals.
- How to prepare and deliver speeches.
- How to use audiovisual equipment.
- How to be a discussion leader.
- How to handle role playing well.
- How to prepare budgets—and live within them.

How did we learn all these things? How did we acquire the skills? For the most part, we acquired the knowledge and skills *outside* our own organizations. The reason is simple. They were usually not available on the inside. This is still true today. We read periodicals and trade publications. We attended courses and seminars, such as those sponsored by the American Management Association. We probably learned as much by talking with other trainers as we did from the courses themselves. We compared notes. We exchanged ideas and materials.

We may also have joined one or more professional training organizations, such as The American Society for Training and Development (ASTD) or The National Society for Sales Training Executives (NSSTE).

We also learned a lot from our suppliers of training materials and equipment. Programmed instruction, a method of self-instruction through reading and the use of a workbook, began to be used more and more as a sales-training tool. Many of us learned how to write a programmed text, which was another new and difficult skill.

Of course we don't want to forget that old stand-by, "trial and error." It's not very efficient, but it does have a great impact on the memory, particularly our failures. I'll never forget the first case study I wrote. It involved a fictitious salesman and his fictitious territory, complete with several hundred pages of information about the "demographic characteristics" of the area, along with more than you could ever remember about his customers, graphs, charts, and assorted collateral material. The assignment was to study the territory and make recommendations about how it could be improved, how the salesman was performing, along with 10 or more unrelated questions. And the case had to be solved in one short two-hour period. As you might have guessed, it was a disaster! The participants couldn't even review the material in two hours. I do not recommend the trial-and-error system . . . but it will always be with us.

TRAINER SELF-DEVELOPMENT TODAY

Today's sales-training manager does a lot more than train sales-representatives. He or she is usually responsible for the development of the entire sales force from the sales manager on down. This means that we get involved in programs of individual development for supervisory and managerial personnel, as well as for specific salespersons.

If we do a good job with sales training, we will probably be asked to assist in management-development programs for marketing personnel, if not for people in areas completely outside of sales and marketing. When this happens, our need for additional knowledge and skills increases.

Since we probably run an entire training department, it is necessary for us to have the *management* skills that we teach to others. We are directly responsible for the results of others, which implies the need for good supervisory skills, along with all the other skills required of a line manager.

I will not discuss here the development needs relative to being a manager; this is covered well in many other texts. I will, however, mention several needs relative to being a manager of a *training department*.

When it comes to *developing yourself* to handle these many and varied tasks, you should first look at the *critical* skill areas necessary to manage the headquarter training function. They are:

1. Good rapport with top management, including marketing and sales managers.
2. Good analytical skills, determining real needs.
3. Developing specific goals for the department.
4. Planning and scheduling.
5. Measuring the effectiveness of the department.
6. Publicizing the activities and accomplishments of the department.
7. Selecting only the best people for your department.
8. Good consulting skills.
9. Program design.
10. Helping your subordinates develop.
11. Preparing department budgets and costing out programs.

WHERE TO START?

After reviewing all these knowledge and skill areas, you may ask yourself, "Where do I start?" You may feel there is so much to learn that you will never have the time to learn it all. The truth is that you will never know *everything* about all these subjects. But don't worry, you really only need to know enough to do your work in a satisfactory manner. Also, you will feel better about it when you consider all of the things you *already* know about each topic.

Most of these skills are not *exclusive* to the sales-training manager's position. Many are skills you've used in previous jobs, or even in school or at home. For example, a good parent has certainly developed counseling skills in talking with his or her own children. You most likely are better at some of these skills than you realize.

SET PRIORITIES

Start by picking those areas where you feel a need *now—today;* select a development area where you can put your newly acquired knowledge or skill to the test immediately. Let's say that the sales manager has asked you to help with a problem salesperson, a long-term employee who used to be a top performer, but recently has fallen behind for no apparent reason. You have been asked to work with the salesperson to try to uncover the problem(s) and see if you can be helpful.

This assignment may require a number of skills, but most certainly counseling is a key one. *Now* is when you need counseling skills, so *now* is the time to try to acquire them, or at least to refresh your memory. You must ask yourself, "How can I learn this quickly? Is there something I can read? Who do I know that is particularly strong in this area? Perhaps I can talk with that person, find out what's most important."

One approach that I've found helpful when I'm not sure what I *need* to know about a particular subject or skill area is to write out on paper what I *think* is important, basing my ideas on past experience and what appears to me to be good common sense. I then relate my ideas and thoughts to other people and ask for their reactions. I find this approach more productive than simply asking others for their ideas. I get a better reaction, and the other person is better able to understand "where I'm at" with the particular subject.

HELP FROM THE OUTSIDE

Unless your organization is most unusual, you will probably not find within its walls the people or programs to help you acquire the specific skills needed to be a professional sales-training manager. You will need to look *outside* for assistance.

If you're just getting started and you don't know what you need to know, you should enroll in a basic course for sales-training managers. Such a program is the five-day Sales Trainer's Clinic, conducted twice annually by the National Society of Sales Training Executives. This program covers the basics of the position and provides practical help that you can put to work as soon as you return to the job. Similar courses are conducted by the American Management Association, the American Society for Training and Development, as well as consultant organizations that conduct such workshops for profit. Once you've completed the basic course and have acquired some work experience, you will be in a good position to know what additional help you will need.

There are many specific courses, seminars, and workshops available around the country. They usually zero in on a specific topic, and are generally two to three days in length. Examples of some that are available:

- How to Prepare and Conduct a Meeting
- How to Use Role Playing Effectively
- Audiovisual Techniques/Equipment
- Transactional Analysis
- Analyzing Performance Problems

The important thing is first to determine what you want to know and then to begin to look at what's available. Don't sign up for the first workshop you hear about. Ask questions about who's running the program. Who are the speakers or instructors? What is their background and experience? Study the course outline; see if it fits your needs. Ask for a complete list of participants in a recent program. Then call several at random to see what they learned and whether they recommend it.

PUBLICATIONS

If you're a reader, and chances are that you fit this description since you're reading this handbook, then there's a whole new world out there for you to enjoy. Much has been written about training and development. Not quite as much has been written about sales training specifically, and it's a bit more difficult to locate. But still, there's a lot available.

You're not likely to find much in your local library, but they may be able to borrow books for you, if you know the title, author, and publisher. A good source of help is the American Management Association library in New York City. If your company is a member, they will loan and mail a book to you at no charge. This library also has a large selection of unpublished works, such as doctoral dissertations, research reports, and magazine articles. Other sources are:

The Conference Board
845 Third Avenue
New York, New York   10022
            and
333 River Road
Ottawa, Ontario K1L 8B9 Canada

The Research Institute of America, Inc.
589 Fifth Avenue
New York, New York   10017

If you are qualified and selected to be a member of the National Society of Sales Training Executives, you will have available to you a large number of member Editorials on sales-training topics. Each member of this organization is required to write a paper annually and distribute copies to all other members. Much practical and useful information and ideas are thereby exchanged.

GET TO KNOW TRAINING PEOPLE

Wherever you live or work, there are always a number of men and women in companies nearby who have responsibilities similar to yours. Search them out and get acquainted. Join the local chapters of ASTD and NSSTE. Don't be afraid to ask for help. Most training people are always willing to take the time to talk with you. If they don't have the answer, they probably will suggest other trainers you can call. Of course, your willingness to reciprocate is important in keeping up such contacts.

CONCLUSION

The professional training field is changing rapidly. It's changing because people at work are changing, and their attitudes toward their employer and their work are different. The mass approach to training is *OUT*. Individual development is *IN*.

In sales training, product-knowledge training, though still essential, is not the complete training need. Selling-skills training is receiving maximum attention. The interface between buyer and seller on a *person-to-person* basis is where training really pays off. Consultative selling, problem solving, and negotiation selling are being talked about more and more. Naturally, sales psychology and the findings of the entire behavioral-science field are becoming more significant to our work today.

What does this imply in terms of your own development? It means that you should devote considerable study to the behavioral-science area, particularly as it relates to the kinds of work and the kinds of problems faced by your trainees.

There are so many areas for study and so many new things happening every day, it's impossible to devote even a little attention to everyone. What you must do is take a look at where your needs are "on the job today," and design a program to learn these things first. Once you've done this, then turn your attention to where you feel your needs will be in the future, both in terms of your current position and where you see your next job.